WINNERS WITHOUT LOSERS

Winners without Losers

Why Americans Should Care More about Global Economic Policy

A COUNCIL ON FOREIGN RELATIONS BOOK

Edward J. Lincoln

Cornell University Press

Ithaca and London

Founded in 1921, the Council on Foreign Relations is an independent, national membership organization and a nonpartisan center for scholars dedicated to producing and disseminating ideas so that individual and corporate members, as well as policymakers, journalists, students, and interested citizens in the United States and other countries, can better understand the world and the foreign policy choices facing the United States and other governments. The Council does this by convening meetings; conducting a wide-ranging Studies Program; publishing *Foreign Affairs*, the preeminent journal covering international affairs and U.S. foreign policy; maintaining a diverse membership; sponsoring Independent Task Forces; and providing up-to-date information about the world and U.S. foreign policy on the Council's website, CFR.org.

First published 2007 by Cornell University Press

Printed in the United States of America

Library of Congress Cataloging-in-Publication Data

Lincoln, Edward J.
   Winners without losers : why Americans should care more about global economic policy / Edward J. Lincoln.
      p. cm.
   Includes bibliographical references and index.
   ISBN 978-0-8014-4622-1 (cloth : alk. paper)
   1. International relations—Economic aspects.   2. International economic relations.
3. Economic history—1945–   4. Economic policy.   5. Globalization—Economic aspects.
6. United States—Foreign relations—1945–1989.   7. United States—Foreign relations—1989–   I. Title.
   JZ1252.L56   2007
   337—dc22
2007021944

CONTENTS

PREFACE

This book was inspired by my experience, over the past quarter-century, of being a lonely economist surrounded by political scientists and Washington policy makers. In my own field, Japan and East Asia, I was often the token economist at meetings to discuss U.S.-Japanese or U.S.-Asian relations. I would present comments on how economic issues fit into the particular topic. Everyone would politely thank me and then suggest that we turn to "broader issues." By this, they usually meant security issues. I found this puzzling because I feel that economic issues are important and that they have a significant bearing on other diplomatic and security issues.

Meanwhile, I was watching the Japanese economy and, to a lesser extent, the rest of East Asia. The more I saw, the more amazing the story became. Arriving in Japan for the first time in 1971, it felt as though I was in a country that was exciting but still considerably behind the United States—much of the housing was poorly constructed, the air was dirty, the trains and subways were unbelievably crowded, and my nose was often assaulted by the odors from nonflush toilets, but Japan was clearly a society rushing forward. Today, visitors to Tokyo often wonder if it is the United States that has slipped behind.

The first time I wandered through Southeast Asia, in 1972, I went armed with Joseph Conrad and sought the remnants of the past. Southeast Asian countries were far behind Japan, and I saw many places of abject poverty. Going back to Singapore in 1990, I had difficulty locating the area of the city where I had stayed in a cheap hotel, finally discovering a familiar, fenced-off block where bulldozers were destroying two-story colonial-era buildings, making way for a new batch of gleaming high-rise apartments.

And when I first went to China, in 1985, our group was driven around in Soviet-style limousines (the Red Flag car) down streets that during rush hour were seas of pedestrians and bicyclists. Cars were sufficiently infrequent that the driver had to beep the horn constantly to get people to move aside. We proceeded like a ship, parting the waters and having them close in again behind us. Today, Beijing's streets are choked with cars, buses, and trucks, but the pedestrians and bicyclists are hard to find. The same is true of Shanghai. When I first visited there, in 1987, I walked along the riverside promenade in the Bund, the old center of the city that was dominated by buildings that predated the outbreak of war with Japan in 1937. On the far side of the Huangpu River, there was virtually nothing—just a few rusty warehouses and some farms. Today, that side of the river is Pudong, a city in its own right with several million residents, a futuristic observation tower and many gleaming high-rise office buildings and apartments, and spreading suburbs of manufacturing plants heavily populated by foreign-owned firms.

Surely, I thought, these huge changes in Asia must have a bearing on questions of war and peace. But I did not want to write a book that was only about Asia. I may be a Japan/Asia specialist, but the time had come to write about the overall connection of economics and international relations. Doing so provided a wonderful opportunity to explore in greater depth what has happened to other parts of the world.

This book focuses on developments since the end of the Second World War. To some readers, this time span may seem long. Indeed, when I recently wrote an op-ed that mentioned the end of the Cold War, the editor commented that most of her readers would view such a reference as "ancient history." But the older one gets, the shorter these time spans seem. I was born not many years after the end of the Second World War, and this project has been an opportunity to reflect on the sweeping economic changes that have occurred during my lifetime.

The first chapter of this book adopts a metaphor for the place of economics in international relations: a three-legged stool. This image had its origin in U.S.-Japanese relations in the mid-1990s and was reflected in the speeches of Walter Mondale, the ambassador to Japan (for whom I worked as a special economic adviser in the American Embassy in Tokyo in 1994–1996). Our relationship with Japan was like a stool, the legs being economics, security, and politics. At that time, the security and political legs were sturdy—the bilateral security treaty and the bilateral military relationship were proceeding well, and politically the Japanese and U.S. governments were usually on the same side of global issues. But the economic leg was weak, burdened by the dissatisfaction of U.S. businesses over myriad hindrances to market access. So Ambassador Mondale, and others in the administration, explained that it was important to focus on strengthening the economic leg. I see our current relationship with the world in somewhat the same terms. Indeed, if anything, our military leg has been pumped up while the economic leg has atrophied.

My intention is to look at the impact of economic developments on international relations and the implications for U.S. foreign policy. This book does not take up the usual diplomatic and security issues. Indeed, I have specifically avoided providing an overall analysis of international relations. Rather, I focus on the underappreciated and understudied importance of economic development.

Readers will see that this book is heavy on statistical detail. It is difficult to grasp what is happening around the world without looking at numbers. Journalists can write colorfully about call centers and other information technology (IT) operations in Bangalore, India, but economists find more value in the numbers. Believing that a picture is worth a thousand words, I have put much of this information in graphs. Readers will not, however, find much obscure economic jargon or theory. My intent has been to avoid the technical approach of economics, other than to point out from time to time that economic research supports certain conclusions.

As with all Council on Foreign Relations projects, this book benefited from a series of study group meetings. I presented draft chapters to this group and benefited enormously from the comments of its members. Harry Harding, former dean of the Elliot School of International Affairs at George Washington University, generously agreed to chair the five sessions of this group in 2005 and 2006. The members who attended one or more of these sessions were Erika Barks-Ruggles, Steve Clemons, Mac Destler, John Judis, Yoshihiko Kojo, Toshiyuki Kosugi, Michael McDevitt, Thomas McNaugher, Henry Nau, Kevin Nealer, Chris Nelson, Diana H. M. Newton, David Andrew Olson, Nilmini Rubin, Robert Samuelson, Robert Solomon, Bruce Stokes, Tsuneo Watanabe, Charles Wolf, and Linda Yang. I am also grateful to two anonymous readers who provided useful comments. Along the way, my two research assistants at the Council on Foreign Relations contributed greatly—first Angela Stavropolous and then Ashle Baxter. Additional assistance came from Chad Waryas and Divya Reddy at the Council, and Albert Lee at NYU. I thank Roger Haydon at Cornell University Press for taking on this project and for his helpful suggestions concerning the manuscript, along with the others at the Press who shepherded this project through from rough manuscript to finished book, including Candace Akins, Susan Barnett, Sara Ferguson, and George Whipple. David Prout compiled the index. This project was supported by a generous grant from the Center for Global Partnership.

EDWARD J. LINCOLN

New York City

WINNERS WITHOUT LOSERS

INTRODUCTION

On January 20, 2005, in his inauguration speech, George W. Bush outlined the broad themes and goals for his second term in office. A week later, he did the same in more detail in his State of the Union address to Congress. As might be expected given the dramatic events since 2001, foreign policy figured heavily in both speeches. The president indicated a stern determination to stay the course in Iraq and made the spread of democracy an overarching goal for U.S. policy. Whatever one thinks about these aspects of the Bush administration's foreign policy, both speeches lacked any reference to foreign economic policy. The president did not make a call for the completion of the then-stalled Doha Round of multilateral trade negotiations in the World Trade Organization (WTO), he said nothing about how to cope with the anxieties caused by increasing globalization, he failed to mention foreign aid, and he was silent on the need to deal with international financial crises.

Perhaps his administration's exclusive focus on security issues and an ideological goal such as democracy seems unsurprising. The continuing war against terrorism and the aftermath of the Iraq war required a military response in his second term. Promotion of democracy is a recurring theme in U.S. foreign policy that resonates with our self-image as a well-run democratic society and our tendency to tell the rest of the world to follow our example. In contrast, economic issues generally look like technical issues that have some bearing for our economic performance but are best left to specialists.

Wrong. We are currently in danger of making our world less safe by ignoring or downplaying economic issues. What happens to the global economy is deeply intertwined with our broad foreign policy goals of peace, security, and prosperity—more deeply than commonly recognized.

Think of foreign policy as a three-legged stool—with military security, diplomacy, and economic policy as the legs. At the present time, the stool is tilted because the economic leg is shorter and weaker than the other two. This book addresses why the stool is crooked and how the economic leg needs to be strengthened. In a nutshell, the argument is:

- The economic world in which Americans live has been dramatically transformed in the sixty-plus years since the end of the Second World War, with explosive economic growth, broad adoption of market mechanisms (as opposed to state ownership and control over economic transactions), new institutions for global economic governance, and rapidly rising international economic interdependence.
- Those changes have had critically important effects. The rationale for armed conflict among sovereign states has dropped dramatically, but other countries struggle with poverty or mismanage their economies in ways that can affect our peace and security.
- This transformed world requires constant effort to maintain and improve both the rules of the economic system and its performance. Doing so requires that foreign policy focus relatively less on traditional military and diplomatic policies and more on economic policies.
- Current U.S. foreign policy fails to address these needs by putting far too much emphasis on military security approaches and far too little emphasis on economic policy.

If George Bush wanted a better theme for his inaugural speech, he should have outlined a vision for a world of winners without losers. At home, this would involve a stronger focus on keeping the engine of economic growth running smoothly while ameliorating the losses to those in society who lose income or jobs due to exposure to global competition. Abroad, this would involve pulling more countries onto the escalator of rapid economic growth so that the disparity in income levels among nations diminishes. A world of affluent countries would be very much in the U.S. national interest—in terms of both economic benefit and security. An affluent world would buy more of the kinds of goods and services that the U.S. economy excels at producing. Equally important, an affluent world would be free of the tensions producing mortal conflict that emanate from those around the globe who are angry over the unequal distribution of affluence. Is this goal pie-in-the-sky wishy-washy liberal romanticizing? Well, accomplishment of such a goal will certainly not happen in my lifetime. Realistically, neither the U.S. nor the global economy will be free of variations in income and wealth. Nonetheless, the current gap between winners and losers need not be so wide, and it is not in the U.S. national interest for it to persist. Think of a world of winners without losers as a lofty long-term goal, toward which U.S. domestic and foreign policies should strive. What a shame that the U.S. political leadership in recent years has been unable to articulate such a vision.

The world in which Americans live has changed fundamentally in critically important ways. The United States is more connected to the rest of the world through flows of goods, services, and investment than ever before. The economy is heavily (and irreversibly) reliant on overseas sources for a wide variety of raw materials. Americans are much more affluent. Technological change has enabled us to travel and communicate easily, cheaply, and rapidly throughout the world. These burgeoning economic connections are loosely overseen by a set of imperfect but important multilateral institutions created in the mid-twentieth century. Maintaining peace and increasing prosperity require careful management of our growing international economic relationships and the multilateral institutions that govern them. Using or threatening to use military force has little to do with succeeding at this task.

Among developed nations, deepening economic interconnections have largely eliminated the possibility that one or more will challenge the others militarily—the conditions that fostered two devastating world wars in the twentieth century are gone. Imperialism collapsed, affluence increased, and a new set of rules and multilateral institutions was created for international trade and investment. Furthermore, nations that used to be regarded as enemies—Russia and China—have been drawn into an international economic engagement with the outside world, diminishing the probability that they will return to being military threats in the future.

Almost a century ago, Norman Angell wrote in what turned out to be a famously wrong analysis that rising affluence and economic interdependence had made war irrelevant and foolish—just before the outbreak of World War I.[1] His timing was wrong, but his basic insight was correct; rising affluence and interdependence have reduced the rationality and probability of aggressive military action as governments weigh the economic losses they would suffer through military adventurism *versus* the gains they could achieve without military action. Since the time Angell wrote, the major powers have become much more affluent. In addition, the collapse of imperialism and the mid-century creation of new multilateral institutions and rules fostered a more stable environment for international economic interaction. And after a slump in the decades from World War I to the 1960s, global economic interdependence has been rising again and is now as high as or higher than in 1914. As a result, Angell's description of the world, or at least of the great powers, is more apt today than when he wrote in the early twentieth century.

As the probability of armed conflict among the great powers has diminished, the main threat has shifted to conflict involving less-developed states, internally (as in the prolonged civil war in Mozambique in the 1980s), among themselves (as in the case of Iraq's invasion of Kuwait), or with major powers (as in the tense stand-off with North Korea and Iran over nuclear weapons development)—and now with nonstate terrorists spawned by perceived injustices in the global system and inflamed by religious extremism.

These threats are substantial, even though they hardly compare in magnitude to the prospect of Armageddon that dogged our lives during the Cold War. Where do these threats fit in the message of this book? The U.S. government, mesmerized by being the world's sole superpower, currently looks to military options and underplays the importance of economic policies in dealing with these threats. Sometimes a military response may be the only viable option; the president had broad public support for the invasion of Afghanistan as part of the war on terror, on the grounds that removing the Taliban regime was the only way to get at the immediate and dangerous threat of the Al Qaeda terrorists it harbored. But often military options do little or nothing to solve the fundamental problems facing this nation around the world. Military force can combat terrorists, but it does not necessarily change the human conditions that produce terrorism. The U.S. invasion of Iraq, for example, encouraged terrorist recruitment by enhancing the U.S. image as an evil, imperialist, infidel enemy invading the Middle East, an enemy that needed to be driven away and punished at any cost. Policies to promote economic growth and development, on the other hand, are an important part of altering the social, political, and economic conditions that have fostered deep discontent and terrorism. To be sure, some argue that the invasion of Iraq was a necessary precursor to building a more prosperous, stable, and democratic state. Aside from the fact that this favorable outcome was difficult to discern as of 2007, we must ask whether forcibly creating a more favorable environment for Iraq's economic and political development was worth the cost in American, coalition, and Iraqi lives. Certainly other despotic, unjust states that have affronted human rights have yielded to nonmilitary pressures over the years, including South Korea, Taiwan, South Africa, and some (but not all) of the former Soviet Union and Eastern Europe.

The Story Writ Large

This is a book about economic change and its implications for foreign policy. It does not attempt to be a comprehensive study of international relations. Many have written about the other two legs of the foreign policy stool and about what is right or wrong with our military and diplomatic policies of recent years. More, however, needs to be said about the economic leg of the stool. So, this book is, for example, a story of the creation of institutions such as the International Monetary Fund (IMF) and the World Bank, but it does not deal very much with the United Nations (an organization that is important but predominantly about diplomacy). Likewise, the development of nuclear weapons at the end of the Second World War was critically important in discouraging the major powers from initiating another major war—although this conclusion was not at all evident to me as I raced home on my bicycle from junior high school on a warm October afternoon in 1962 in the midst of the Cuban missile crisis, desperate to know if nuclear Armageddon was upon us. Economics certainly does not provide the drama of potential nuclear confrontation, but it is just as important to understanding how our contemporary world works.

Our story actually begins two and a half centuries ago. Many of the post–World War Two developments that are my main focus are actually continuations of a process that began over two centuries ago with an acceleration of technological change and economic growth. The first Industrial Revolution, beginning in the late eighteenth century, in turn, had strong roots in developments in the preceding several centuries, but it remains a convenient demarcation point in global history. Since that time, the pace of technological change and economic growth has accelerated, bringing the world to levels of affluence and interdependence unimaginable two centuries ago.

But, mostly, this book is about what has happened since the end of the Second World War in 1945. Just within that short period of time, major changes in technology, economic institutions, and ideas have reshaped the world. Continued rapid technological change has enabled an enormous growth in income levels in many parts of the world, and changes in telecommunications and transportation technology have underwritten increasing economic interdependence. In the realm of ideology, the basic conflict between the ideas of markets (capitalism) and state allocation (communism) largely ended with the market-based reforms in China and the collapse of the Soviet Union. Among the key institutional changes have been the demise of imperialism as an organizing basis for international trade and investment and the creation of a new set of rules and institutions to replace it—principally the so-called Bretton Woods institutions, which consist of the IMF, the World Bank, and a multilateral trade organization that began as the General Agreement on Tariffs and Trade (GATT) and was transformed in 1995 into the WTO.

Fundamentally, technical change is the reason economies become more affluent over time; it enables workers and the capital equipment with which they work to produce more. The process of productivity improvement unleashed by the Industrial Revolution has continued, indeed accelerated, in the past half century. Americans are now almost unimaginably better off in material terms than they were two centuries ago, and even in the past half century, the level of per capita output in the United States has tripled.

Of all the technical changes that have occurred, two are particularly important to increasing global interdependence: transportation and telecommunications. The ability to do business abroad depends on transporting a product long distances and still selling it at a competitive price. Falling transportation costs have made this much easier. In the nineteenth century, for example, the iron and steel industry was located close to deposits of iron ore and coal, and nations endowed with these natural resources benefited from the ability to build these productive industries. But by the 1960s, new developments in bulk ore carriers enabled resource-poor Japan to build a globally competitive steel industry by importing iron ore from Australia and coking coal from the United States. In general, the cost of transportation today—even for manufactured goods moving halfway around the world—is only a small fraction of the final retail price of these goods.

Furthermore, the ability to manage investments or even sales operations abroad depends critically on the cost of communication. The dramatic change in telecommunications technologies, dropping telecommunications costs and enabling a massive explosion in volume, has enabled expanded trade, management of direct investments, and global financial flows. In recent years, the drop in telecommunications costs has even enabled trade in service industries once thought to be outside the scope of international trade. Call centers, back-office paperwork, and software development can now be spread around the world with workers and managers linked by instantaneous and cheap communications links. Whereas the hype or scaremongering about the rapid rise of outsourcing in the service sector is overdone, the spread of possibilities for expanded trade from manufactured goods to services is an important development that will cause international economic interdependence to deepen.[2]

On the institutional front, the move away from imperialism has been epochal. Embodied in the concept and practice of imperialism was the notion that states needed political control over their foreign sources of supply and captive markets for their exports in order to ensure that they had the dominant (if not exclusive) access to those resources and markets. That system was inherently conflictual. In a world with a small number of major imperial powers, grabbing territory denied its benefits to others, locking the major powers into a zero-sum game. The collapse of that system and its replacement with the IMF, World Bank, and GATT/WTO created a framework that is open to all on an equal basis. Armed conflict by the major powers to acquire and hold territory is no longer a major fear.

Equally important has been the shift in ideas about how economies should be organized. Goods, services, labor, and capital can be allocated by either markets or governments. The concept of capitalism (or market-based economies, as economists generally call it today), developed in the late eighteenth century by writers such as Adam Smith, emphasized the benefits of allowing markets and profit-seeking individuals to operate freely. But the social and economic turmoil associated with capitalism in the nineteenth century quickly spawned an alternative view espoused by Karl Marx and others, who argued that the evils of capitalism—exploitation of the masses of society by a handful of wealthy individuals—could be avoided through state allocation of economic resources. The epic struggle between capitalism and communism lasted from the mid-nineteenth century until the recent past. Beginning with the market reforms in China in the early 1980s and then the dramatic collapse of the Soviet Union, the ideology of communism has largely dissipated.

The fall of the Soviet Union also marked the end of the Cold War, a struggle that had locked much of the world into opposing blocs that had little trade and investment contact with each other. The members of the Bretton Woods institutions, for example, had mainly included countries in the Western bloc. But the end of the Cold War transformed these multilateral institutions into truly global organizations, for the first time providing the world with a set of institutions to loosely govern trade and investment relations among most nations. The expansion in membership also made these institutions more unwieldy. Nevertheless, the collapse of communist ideology and reform of former communist states has been an enormously positive event for both the evolution of the ideas governing economic organization and international economic interaction.

Although the ideology of markets has prevailed, this is not a time for Americans to feel smug about the triumph of a pure free-market ideology. In important ways, Karl Marx and other critics of capitalism also succeeded—not by creating a socialist world but by stimulating modifications to the concept of *laissez faire* capitalist economics. A very long continuum exists between the polar cases of markets and government allocation. All so-called market economies have governments that regulate or otherwise interfere in markets out of a desire to make the system work better—fixing market failures or moderating extremes in the distribution of wealth and income. Even in the United States, the boundary between freely operating markets and government control is constantly shifting. And among market economies the variation in the market-government boundary is wide. Particularly after the trauma of the Great Depression and the Second World War, many economies moved far in the direction of socialism, with government ownership of key industries and extensive social safety nets. The past three decades has brought considerable reform, moving many of these economies back toward greater reliance on markets, but a wide variety of market-based economic systems remains.[3] What is important is that the ideological, political, and armed clash between the polar extremes is largely over. Americans may disparage the overly generous social safety nets in some European countries or the recent turn toward socialism in Venezuela and Bolivia, but the sense of a life-and-death struggle over economic systems is gone, with a chastened, modified, and variable market-based systems as the outcome.

Over time, a wider swath of the world's population has been swept up by growth and rising affluence. Two hundred years ago, the new affluence from industrialization was largely confined to one nation—Great Britain. Even in the 1950s, advanced industrial nations were few in number, mainly the United States and the recovering nations of Western Europe. Today, affluence characterizes most of Western Europe, North America, Oceania, and Japan. Substantial parts of the rest of East Asia— South Korea, Taiwan, Hong Kong, and Singapore—are well on the way to advanced nation status. Other parts of developing Asia are less affluent but have grown at unusually high rates for the past quarter century, lifting hundreds of millions out of poverty. This transformation of a substantial part of the world and its continuing spread represents an amazing triumph in a very short period of time in human history.

Asia provides a principal example in this study of how economic change affects international relations. Japan's experience since 1945, the spread of rapid growth to other market economies in Asia, and China's recent and dramatic economic reengagement with the world provide important examples of how the process of economic growth and interdependence is spreading and impacting international relations. The Japanese government learned that the nation could live with a high dependence on imported raw materials and food without having recourse to military means to resolve international disputes. China now benefits from inward direct investment and deep trade ties with the rest of the world that would be jeopardized if the government chose to use military force (e.g., against Taiwan). Southeast Asian nations have learned to accept large inflows of foreign direct investment without fear of political domination despite their very bitter experiences with Western (and Japanese) imperialism that ended only in the mid-twentieth century. The positive transformation of most of East Asia in the past half century is truly stunning.

Good News or Bad News?

The preceding discussion paints global economic developments in a very positive light. This involves fundamental assumptions or convictions. Greater affluence is good; trade enhances prosperity so its expansion is good; rising affluence and trade nudge the world away from mortal conflict. Simplistic? Perhaps. But the belief in the value of rising incomes lies at the core of economics. These propositions are not universally accepted, to say the least. Should we extol rising affluence or condemn modern materialism? Should we glorify the efficiencies of Wal-Mart or lament the decline of small mom-and-pop shops? Should we applaud the low cost of food in modern society or descry the disappearance of the small family farm? Should we support continued growth or be horrified at environmental degradation and global warming? This philosophical and moral debate has been going on a long time. I come down firmly in favor of the positive value of technical change and rising affluence—and that judgment pervades the analysis of the rest of this book. Most of human society, after all, has embraced the choice for greater affluence when given the chance. To be sure, growth and development have had a dark underside in the form of environmental problems—and over the next century dealing with global warming may prove to be the most important foreign policy challenge faced by the United States. These are not problems to be taken lightly, although this book does not focus on these issues. Nevertheless, the solution to concerns over the environment and climate change (or even the family farm and mom-and-pop shops) does not lie in stopping economic growth but in finding solutions as the economy continues to grow. In fact, rising affluence affords the advanced economies of the world an opportunity to tackle environmental issues to an extent that was not possible when incomes were lower.

I am equally positive about the value of open trade and investment. Economists have argued for two centuries that open international trade makes societies more productive. Furthermore, greater openness to trade may also enhance economic growth, in the view of some economists. Therefore, if we accept the proposition that rising affluence is desirable, then rising international trade and investment (or at least what economists call direct investment) should be accepted as positive developments as well. Economists have had difficulty selling this fundamental insight about international trade to governments and the public, but it remains one of the few concepts in economics on which economists universally agree. That difficulty was illustrated powerfully in the highly visible antiglobalization movement that gained visibility in the late 1990s and in the occasional protectionist rumblings in Washington. But the arguments against international trade simply do not hold up to scrutiny.

The linkage between rising affluence and the expansion of trade and investment to military conflict is the subject of chapter 2. If we accept the logical argument made in this chapter, then rising affluence and economic interdependence have a positive value far beyond just making human lives more comfortable in a material sense. Some readers will have trouble with this argument, but keep an open mind and remember that the conclusion is that these economic developments *reduce* the incentive and probability of interstate armed conflict, not that they have *eliminated* the possibility of war.

This positive view of the role of economic development and interdependence motivates most of the discussion in the rest of this book. However, this story has a number of caveats. After all, although East Asia offers a powerful, positive lesson, it also harbors two of the most dangerous security problems in the world—North Korea, with its determination to develop nuclear weapons, and the Taiwan Straits, with the possibility of Chinese invasion to reunite Taiwan with China. Some of these problems stem from the incomplete nature of the ongoing global economic revolution—particularly in the case of those parts of the world still mired in poverty (the subject of chapter 6). Some others simply lie outside the scope of economic factors, including nationalism and religion. The following chapters explore some of these continuing problems—of which there are four principal types.

First, some parts of the world, unable or unwilling to embrace domestic growth, trade, and investment, lag worrisomely behind, suffering from poverty and creating a source of tension or danger in global affairs. Not every government has figured out how to establish and operate a market-based economy successfully. Some are mired in a difficult transition away from failed socialist experiments, whereas others lack internal political cohesion or have outright civil war. North Korean paranoia (and the resultant determination to develop nuclear weapons), for example, is driven by its being an isolated, impoverished, despotic state with a dysfunctional state-run economy surrounded by large successful nations.

Second, even some nations that have prospered moderately, and especially those that have grown through raw material exports, have performed badly. When a dominant ethnic group, religious sect, or existing upper class grabs the bulk of economic gains for itself while the rest of society remains in poverty, the result is conflict. Saudi Arabia, the birthplace of

Osama bin Laden and many other members of Al Qaeda, is an outstanding example of a nation that appears on the surface to have done relatively well due to its huge oil reserves but that has badly bungled the process of economic development with disastrous results.

Third, although many of the points made in this book may seem self-evident, there is always the danger of unlearning them. National control over the territory where natural resources exist is irrelevant to national prosperity, yet Japan and China are currently embroiled in a nasty dispute over who controls the seabed in the East China Sea where there may be substantial oil and gas deposits. Similarly, many discussions among foreign policy specialists in Washington about U.S. policy in the Middle East include comments about the "obvious" need to project military power there because (wink-wink, nod-nod) of the oil. More broadly, Americans often seem incapable of recognizing that they live in a world of economic interdependence, in which they must compromise rather than simply unilaterally asserting or imposing their desired outcomes.

Fourth, the pillars of the international economic system—the Bretton Woods institutions—are imperfect and could be vulnerable to adverse economic developments. A severe global recession, a widespread international financial crisis, or anger over the perceived unfair distribution of the gains from trade agreements could lead to an unraveling of these institutions and the rules of the game. That certainly happened in the 1930s, and although the current system is much better defined and more robust that anything that preceded it, crisis and institutional failure are conceivable. Without these rules, national paranoia over the security of energy supplies or other contentious economic issues are more likely to spin out of control.

Because of the importance of these problems, the message of this book is nuanced. For a major power such as that United States, both the rationality and probability of major conflict has been reduced by the global economic developments of the past half century. But that fact does not prevent the U.S. government from making the wrong policy choices—using military power when it is neither necessary nor desirable. Furthermore, inattention to the economic leg of the foreign policy stool could cause the current favorable global system to unravel, returning the world to a situation in which states see their options in zero-sum conflictual terms. Even if that world does not involve war among the great powers (after all, the deterrent of mutually assured destruction through nuclear war is still with us), it would be a world of greater tension, increased numbers of armed conflicts, and weakened economic performance. Even without a major war, this outcome is something that U.S. foreign policy should actively seek to avoid.

The Existing Debate

Academics, Washington policy wonks, politicians, and journalists have long debated theories of international relations and their foreign policy implications. The debate has revolved around three camps: liberals, realists, and neo-conservatives. The uninitiated reader should be wary of the first two labels, which give the misleading impression that the realists must be inherently correct because their view is "real" and, therefore, that the liberals must be unrealistic and wrong.[4]

This book falls into the liberal tradition, which emphasizes the role of cooperation and the importance of international institutions that reinforce cooperative behavior. The classic exposition of the contemporary liberal view was written by academics Robert Keohane and Joseph Nye in 1977, in which they coined the phrase "complex interdependence" to describe how the world had changed economically and the impact that this was having on foreign policy.[5] But the liberal school of international relations has flaws. For one thing, the political scientists who dominate the field rarely look carefully at the actual economic data. Richard Rosecrance, another academic, has produced two books that tout how much the world has changed economically with the increase in international trade and investment. Amazingly enough, however, neither of his books presents very much data to substantiate his claims. As a result, the analysis is frequently subject to embarrassing exaggerations that make it vulnerable to attack from skeptical realists.[6]

In similar fashion, Thomas Friedman's *The Lexus and the Olive Tree* paints a wide-eyed look at the benefits of capitalism, trade, and investment. As he puts it, governments around the world face a decision about putting on the "golden straightjacket" of international economic cooperation, a choice that brings them enormous prosperity if they accept the constraints on their international behavior. Although his basic insight is largely correct, the distinction is exaggerated, and the anecdotal and enthusiastic view that he presents is jarring to anyone who cares about statistical evidence.[7] The same can be said of Friedman's more recent book, *The World Is Flat*, an interesting but much exaggerated view of the outsourcing of service-sector jobs. One of this author's objectives is to offer a more careful analysis of the extent to which the United States and the world are becoming more interdependent.[8] My apologies to the reader if my book turns out to be less entertaining than Friedman's, but I believe that the reality is actually quite exciting even without the hype.

Nonetheless, this book shares with Friedman and others in the liberal camp of international relations an emphasis on the importance of rising interdependence, multilateral institutions, and spreading affluence as factors that have fundamentally altered the world of international relations. The book also shares the concerns of some cautious liberals that this altered world is in danger of being undermined through either neglect or bad policy. Robert Gilpin wrote in 2000:

> A number of books proclaim that, whether we like it or not, global capitalism and economic globalization are here to stay. Unfettered Markets, they argue, now drive the world and all must adjust, however painful this may be. Yet, as I argue, despite the huge benefits of free trade and other aspects of the global economy, an open and integrated global economy is neither as extensive nor as irreversible as many assume. Global capitalism and economic globalization have rested and must continue to rest on a secure political foundation. However, the underpinnings of the post–World War II global economy have steadily eroded since the end of the Soviet threat.[9]

I thoroughly agree with Gilpin that some have exaggerated the extent of globalization and underestimated the need to work at maintaining or fixing the foundations of the current global economic system.

In stark contrast to the liberal approach, realist theories posit that nation-states are in perpetual conflict as they attempt to gain and exercise power internationally, with *power* defined predominantly in military terms. Think of the world consisting of nations that behave like testosterone-laden teenage boys on the school playground. Peace in this world comes only if one boy is so physically dominant that no one else dares to mess with him or (depending on which realist theory we subscribe to) if a balance of power exists between a couple groups of boys so that the players are mutually deterred from starting a fight that they are unsure of winning.

Economic developments tend to get short shrift in realist writings. Henry Kissinger even managed to write an entire lengthy book on the theory and practice of diplomacy, covering the sweep of Western history from the eighteenth century to the end of the Cold War, without any discussion of the key economic ideas, developments, or institutions that were so integral to global affairs! In Kissinger's world, there is no need to talk about such major developments as the collapse of imperialism, the creation of the Bretton Woods system, or the economic engagement of China with the outside world.[10]

Other realists have been contemptuous of the liberal view, arguing that it overestimates the extent to which economic interdependence has thickened or the extent to which these changes have had an impact on international relations. Kenneth Waltz, one of the leading academic figures in the realist camp since the 1950s, was (and remains) dismissive of the liberal school, arguing that economic interdependence is far less significant than commonly supposed (and less than on the eve of World War I in 1914) and that interdependence does not prevent war (just as it did not in 1914). The contempt for liberals such as Keohane, Nye, and Friedman fairly drips from his pen.[11] Back when Keohane and Nye coined the phrase complex interdependence, Waltz had a point—interdependence was on the rise in the 1970s but was not so significant. Much has changed in the succeeding thirty years, however, as the following chapters show. Thus, when Niall Ferguson wrote essentially the same criticisms in 2005—that interdependence was no thicker today than in 1914 and has little impact on international relations—his dismissal rings rather hollow.[12] These realists seem to be stuck in the past, stubbornly refusing to seriously consider what has happened to the world around them. The realists, to put it simply, have an increasingly unrealistic view of the world. And yet, the realists do have an important point—there is no guarantee that interdependence will *necessarily* create a more peaceful world.

To the extent that realists incorporate economics, they often see economic growth and rising affluence as simply one part of the array of factors creating national power, with agricultural capability, raw material endowment, industrial capacity, and technology providing the means to build and use military power. Although the realists are entirely correct that economic factors enhance the possibility of creating and projecting military power, this very narrow view of the economic world seems heavily rooted in the imperialist system that still prevailed at the end of the Second World War, when contemporary realist theories had their start. This is certainly the approach of Hans Morgenthau, the grandfather of the modern realist school of thought, who wrote an enormously influential book on the subject of realism in international relations in 1948, a book read by generations of college students for decades thereafter.[13] The realist view does not consider the possibility that economic growth and interdependence themselves might reshape international relations in ways unrelated to the zero-sum calculations of relative power that lie at the core of their theory. Mutual gain through cooperation is a powerful force in economics, and the data explored in this book show that cooperation in the form of global trade and investment has been rising dramatically in the past several decades.

Yet the notion of a world consisting of a collection of narrowly self-interested states jockeying for power and influence continues to have a strong following in the United States. Indeed, there is even a school of neo-realists that places more emphasis on military power (to the exclusion of other dimensions of power) and the inherent desire of states to exercise that power internationally than do traditional realists. One of the leaders of that school, John Mearsheimer, argues that the U.S. government should slow or prevent the growth of China because the Chinese government will gain military capability through economic growth and will inevitably seek to use it to gain hegemony over Asia.[14] This is an absurd idea. China is not an inevitable enemy, and in practical terms it would be very difficult for the United States to slow the growth of China because no other nation would join such a misguided crusade. Containing China in this fashion would actually turn the Chinese government into exactly the sort of aggressive power that Mearsheimer worries about. We would like to laugh off such conclusions as the musings of an ivory-tower academic trapped in the implications of the logic of his flawed worldview, but his ideas have a distressing popularity in parts of the U.S. government.

More recently, a new school of thought has arisen that resembles realism in some respects but deviates in important ways—the neo-conservatives. Their starting point is the current hegemonic dominance of the United States, much as the realists see the world. But instead of accepting this global system as a stable and sufficient outcome (as long as the United States actively prevents the rise of rivals), the neo-conservatives want to use this era as a time to spread "American" values. In their view, the United States has mission to spread the gospel of democracy and capitalism. Thus, whereas Mearsheimer worries that China will simply seek to project power in Asia, the neo-conservatives fret that China is not a democracy and has a repressive government that tramples on human rights and religious freedom. If the U.S. government can only spread human rights and democracy to China (and other parts of the world), the Chinese government will not challenge U.S. hegemonic power and will live with the outside world in peace. This belief in the contribution of democracy and human rights to global peace was adopted by the Bush administration in its second term. There may be a connection between democracy and a reduced incidence of war, but the causal connection is by no means tight, and it is not clear how effective U.S. foreign policy can be in pushing other nations to move toward democracy. The neo-conservative agenda was struck a powerful blow by the ongoing mess in Iraq, where the attempt to topple a vicious dictator, impose democracy, and even reshape the political landscape of the broader Middle East fared poorly. Nevertheless, the basic neo-conservative concept of using U.S. superpower status to remake the world in the American image remains very much alive.

As part of this new approach, consider Thomas Barnett, a consultant on strategic policy who wrote a book in 2003 that was reputedly popular at the Pentagon at the time. Barnett actually begins by endorsing the liberal notion that growth, trade, and investment bind nations together in a more peaceful manner. He also agrees with this book, arguing that the main security problems in the world involve poor states. However, he then goes on to argue in rather chilling fashion that the United States bears a responsibility to forcibly remove dysfunctional political regimes in poor countries, replacing them with democracy and capitalism so that they can join the rest of the world in pursuing successful economic development. He even argues that other developed nations desire us to carry out such policies (as in the case of the invasion and occupation of Iraq) even if they fail to join us in direct participation in attacking such regimes![15] The East Asian policy elites with whom I am most familiar would find this a nonsensical notion.

A major goal of this book is to combat both the realist/neo-realist and neo-conservative views of the world, which are out of touch with the reality of rising economic interdependence and its implications for foreign policy. Democracy is certainly a laudable and lofty goal for U.S. foreign policy. But the issue is one of priority—and the primary need is for a world of peace and prosperity. Having a world that also shares our own institutions and beliefs would be nice, but this pales in comparison to having peace and prosperity. Furthermore, institutions such as capitalism and democracy are far more likely to be robust if they emerge internally rather than being imposed from abroad. Rising affluence from economic growth may not necessarily cause democracy, but it certainly creates conditions that push in that direction (with newly affluent groups in society demanding a political voice). U.S. foreign policy can nudge these trends along, but they do not deserve to be at the forefront of policy. Cuba, for example, is run by a dysfunctional, aging revolutionary dictator with a failed vision of economic development. The decision to reform should come from inside Cuban society itself, which will probably not happen until Castro is gone (a leadership transition that was underway as Castro's health failed in 2006 and government control passed to his brother Raoul). But the probability of success in such changes would have been far less if the U.S. government had forcibly removed Castro from power at any point during his long reign. The Cubans need to work out for themselves what they want in terms of both a political system and an economic structure, driven by their own desire to join the collection of more economically successful nations in their neighborhood.

This book, therefore, sits squarely in the liberal camp of international relations. Affluence, interdependence, and economic institutions matter a great deal for peace and security. But these factors are not the sole determinants of international relations; nor are their current implications for international relations fixed in stone. These caveats lead us back to the analogy of the three-legged stool. Realists need to understand that human affluence and the desire to maintain it, or to become even more affluent, are a powerful motivator for cooperative behavior and avoidance of military conflict. Neo-conservatives need to understand that using military power and heavy-handed diplomacy to press an idealistic goal such as democracy can undercut our ability to maintain and improve the economic aspects of our policy. But liberals need to understand that economic interests do not always prevent government from acting on the basis of neo-realist power calculations or neo-conservative enthusiasm for reshaping other countries or regions—as our decision to invade Iraq so amply demonstrates.

Outline of the Book

My goal is to explore the economic changes that have transformed the world since 1945—looking at growth and affluence, trade, and investment. Along the way, individual chapters emphasize the positive economic developments and also explore some of the problems discussed earlier, although, on balance, most of the story is a very positive one. Then this book explores what this global transformation implies for U.S. foreign policy. The focus on economic change, however, does not mean a repudiation of the importance of military power or diplomacy—only that these two legs of the stool are better understood and generally get most of the attention in books about foreign policy. If Americans do not address the imbalance in our own foreign policy, U.S. international relations could be in danger of sliding off the crooked stool.

This book is not intended to be a geographically inclusive study. Instead, the focus is on particularly distinctive and important developments. The U.S. experience, the evolution of the European Union, the East Asia experience, and the plight of poor countries dominate the following chapters. The Middle East gets some coverage in the chapter on poor countries, but it is not the major focus of this book. In my opinion, the Middle East has become a black hole for Americans studying foreign policy since 2001—sucking in all the attention and research at the expense of the rest of the world. It is time to refocus and realize that there is much going on outside the Middle East that is important to U.S. security and well-being. Nor is there much discussion of Latin America, a region of the world important to the United States because of its geographical proximity. The purpose here has been to pick regions, countries, and issues that illustrate the core points of this study, not to provide a comprehensive overview of the world.

Chapter 1 begins the discussion with the story of the key economic changes in the world, with an emphasis on the years since the end of the Second World War. This is an oft-told tale familiar to anyone with a high school education, but it is a tale worth retelling, focusing on those economic developments that have a bearing on international relations. Familiarity may also breed contempt; people tend to take this story for granted, so it is a useful to be reminded of just how dramatic the change in the world has been.

Although the emphasis in this book is on the story of the sixty-plus years since the end of the Second World War, some of the economic changes date back to the beginning of the Industrial Revolution in the late eighteenth century. The past two and a half centuries obviously brought enormous growth in affluence in many countries, driven by a number of important changes including new technology, the creation of modern capitalism, and the separation of economic affluence from the ownership of land. But in the last half century, there were several particularly important changes on which this study focuses: the collapse of imperialism, the creation of the Bretton Woods system, the continuation of high levels of economic growth, and technological changes that both increased productivity (and affluence) and dramatically reduced the cost of moving goods and services around the globe. Both the level of economic affluence of the successful industrial nations and the extent of international economic interaction were literally inconceivable to individuals two centuries ago; the transformation of the world has been truly amazing. And even in the last half century (the span of this baby-boomer author's life) the transformation of the United States and the world has been dramatic.

Chapter 2 explains how the economic developments presented in chapter 1 transformed international relations. In general, this chapter points out how the world has become enmeshed in a system that has substantially reduced the probability of conflict among the major powers because nations and the individuals or corporations in them can engage in economic interaction in a mutually beneficial manner. However, chapter 2 also considers the problems the current system faces. These include continued poverty in parts of the world, poor management of apparently successful economies with raw materials, failure to understand the lessons of interdependence, and failure to maintain the key institutions of global prosperity.

Chapter 3 looks more closely at the experience of the United States. Since the end of the Second World War, the United States has become far more connected to the outside world. The nation has experienced a rising reliance on imported oil and other raw materials. Overall, imports and exports have grown substantially as a share of the economy. Foreign firms invest heavily in the United States, and American firms have large investments around the world. Large numbers of foreign students now study in the United States, and an increasing number of Americans study or travel abroad. These changes add up to an America that is much more interdependent with the rest of the world than it was a half century ago.

Chapter 4 delves into a dramatic change for another set of industrialized nations—the evolution of the European Union. At the end of World War Two, who would have imagined that the mortal enemies France, Germany, and Britain would voluntarily lock themselves into a close formal economic embrace? In the early years, the Soviet military menace provided an additional reason for these countries to band together, but both the depth and breadth of the embrace has expanded since the end of the Cold War, with a single currency for a subset of these countries and expanded membership.

Chapter 5 takes a more detailed look at the peaceful transformation of East Asia, another dramatic story of the past half century. This part of the world has been wracked by violence over much of the past century—including the Chinese revolution, the Japanese imperial advance and collapse, the Korean War, and the Vietnam War. But remarkable changes have been occurring. Japan's enormous growth despite losing its empire and its peaceful management of its dependency on imported raw materials since the end of the Second World War provide powerful examples of the irrelevance of military force to achieving and maintaining affluence and economic security. China's decision to open its economy to trade and investment and its willingness to join the WTO are also immensely important. China is now deeply intertwined with the rest of the world through trade and investment, much to the nation's economic benefit. Finally, Southeast Asian nations have also embraced inward direct investment in the past two decades without fearing a loss of sovereignty—a remarkable shift in policy given their mid-twentieth-century struggle to escape imperialism. This chapter also acknowledges and tackles the problems in the region, especially the stand-off with North Korea and the tensions between China and Taiwan.

Chapter 6 takes up the problems faced by poor countries. A number of states have failed to climb on to the economic escalator (or have fallen off). Stuck in poverty and political instability, these states are the primary source of security threats today. Political instability plagues many of these states and complicates the task of setting them on the path to industrialization and international economic engagement, but attempting to do so is in both the U.S. national economic and security interests. A special issue considered in chapter 6 is the problem of states that happen to possess large quantities of natural resources (such as oil), states that often fail to make sensible use of their good fortune. The experience of these economies is a sobering cautionary caveat to the overall positive benefits that flow from trade and development, although even in the developing world there is good news as well.

The concluding chapter of this book takes up the policy implications of the analysis. The U.S. government has largely kept economic and security policy separate, with economic policy often relegated to secondary status. Negotiating a broad reduction in global trade and investment barriers is a complex technical process that fails to create the aura of adrenaline-pumping excitement and vital importance that the life-and-death implications of military policy do. But economic policy matters tremendously for the overall U.S. foreign policy goals of peace and stability. A breakdown in the Bretton Woods institutions, for example, could lead to international chaos, returning the world to the days of the tense rivalry among major powers that characterized the first half of the twentieth century. Meanwhile, failure to focus on the problems of poor states allows the gap between rich and poor to widen further. Being the world's only super power does not remove the need for U.S. compromise and cooperation in making the global economic system work better. This chapter, therefore, offers specific recommendations on policy choices, including policies to foster healthy growth at home, cope with the anxieties of global competition, lower trade and investment barriers, maintain and reinforce the multilateral economic institutions, and draw poor countries on to a path toward successful economic development. More broadly, this chapter—and indeed this entire book—is a plea to incorporate these issues more fully into broader U.S. foreign policy. Establishing a vision of a world of winners without losers would provide the rhetorical umbrella for this new direction in policy.

1. THE WORLD TRANSFORMED

Enormously important economic changes have occurred around the world since the beginning of the Industrial Revolution in England in the late eighteenth century—changes that have fundamentally altered the landscape of international relations. This chapter looks briefly at these long-term developments and then concentrates on the dramatic shifts since the end of the Second World War. In just the last sixty-plus years, old ideas and the economic systems they spawned have collapsed while other ideas and systems have triumphed. In this brave new world, technological change and economic growth have roared ahead.

The story of economic growth and development since the beginning of the Industrial Revolution is a familiar one and one that many people simply take for granted. People also take for granted the world around them as it exists at the moment, paying scant attention to the small changes that occur each year. But even over relatively short periods of time, however, the accumulation of economic changes produces dramatic results. Just in the lifetime of this baby-boomer author, the affluence and quality of life in America have undergone substantial improvements. This story of global economic growth and development is worth revisiting to demonstrate how profoundly the world we live in has been transformed. Of course, the subject is a large one and this short chapter can hardly do it justice, but even the basics add up to a stunning picture.

Two Centuries of Revolutionary Change

The Industrial Revolution unleashed a process of accelerated economic change that continues today. Many aspects of life today—what people choose to do on a daily basis and what matters in their personal lives—would be unimaginable to someone living as recently as two hundred years ago. The most obvious changes have been technical, and there is some tendency to think of economic progress in technical terms. After all, in the long run, the reason societies become more affluent has to do entirely with the application of new, more productive technologies. At the time of the American Revolution, for example, travel across the Atlantic was on wooden sailing vessels that took weeks to make the journey, whereas today travel is on jet planes that make the crossing in less than eight hours. Early changes included the creation of new mechanical methods for mass production (especially textile machinery) and the industrial application of steam power. The early twentieth century brought the use of electric power and the internal combustion engine. The second half of the twentieth century brought the computer and other aspects of the information technology (IT) revolution. However, beyond the obvious importance of improvements in technology per se, there are three important features of the continuing revolution begun over two centuries ago that are particularly relevant to international relations: new economic institutions, rising affluence and quality of life, and separation of affluence from land.

New Economic Institutions

As important as the technical changes that unleashed the Industrial Revolution were the emerging economic institutions that enabled society to harness the power of new technologies. These institutions constitute the foundations of capitalism: private property, limited liability corporations, and financial markets. Capitalism, of course, was controversial for a long time (a subject explored later in this chapter). But these new revolutionary institutions created the foundation on which most of the economies of the contemporary world are based.

The first innovation was the development of the concept of private property and especially ownership of land and other assets. Until at least the seventeenth century, the concept of private ownership of land was often vague. To be sure, ownership of goods occurred much earlier; vigorous markets for buying and selling agricultural products and simple manufactured goods existed for thousands of years. However, in many societies, including medieval Europe, land was controlled by the state and given by the political leader to his followers. At the bottom, the farmers who actually worked the land often had no ownership rights at all. Once allocated by an incoming political regime, land tenure could be quite stable—amounting to a form of de facto ownership. But the key element of private property is the right to buy and sell. If landholdings were handed out by the king, then the lords owning the tracts of land were not in a position to undo the king's will by independently selling their land or buying other land. Creating a world in which individuals own assets that they can buy or sell freely and legally was a major transformation in how economies work.

At least one contemporary economist—Hernando de Soto—has argued that the failure to create clear, simple, workable rules for owning, financing, buying, and selling real assets lies at the core of the failure of poor countries to develop economically. De Soto, a Peruvian economist who played a leading role in economic reforms there in the 1990s, makes something of a fetish out of property rights. But even granting that he exaggerates the picture somewhat, property rights are a key building block of modern economies. Among other benefits, he notes that the ability to borrow against the collateral of real assets is a powerful tool enabling all levels of society–from farmers and shopkeepers to large corporations—to raise the finances necessary for expanding their output.[1]

The second important development was the creation of the limited liability corporation. Until the advent of proto-corporations in the sixteenth century, only the state or the church (in Europe) had the ability to mobilize the labor of large numbers of people. Why? The state and the church had the scale of operation to both collect the financial resources from large numbers of people (through taxes and tithes) and command their subjects' labor to carry out large projects such as building bridges, castles, or cathedrals. Private business was largely family run, and the scale of these enterprises was limited by the financial resources available to individual families or raised from relatives and close personal friends. Therefore, manufacturing remained small-scale and rudimentary—for example, individuals hand-weaving cloth in their homes on looms that they constructed themselves. Some operations might be larger, financed by local lords rather than peasants, but even these were generally limited in scale—for example, gristmills, wineries, small-scale mines, and the like.

The desire of merchants in Europe to finance long-distance trade by sea in the sixteenth and seventeenth centuries is what initially led to the formation of early corporations, empowered by governments to raise the private financing necessary for flotillas of vessels and tradable goods to send across the oceans. These organizations invited wealthy individuals to become partial owners. In Britain, however, a disastrous speculative bubble involving the South Sea Company (a trading venture) led to restrictions on the formation of corporations for a time, requiring permission from Parliament to establish a corporation from 1720 until the law's repeal in 1825. In France, a legal framework for corporations was included in the Napoleonic Commercial Code of 1807.[2] Thus, by the early 1800s, this new form of economic organization was becoming increasingly accepted and popular.

Corporations created a means to mobilize money and labor on a scale previously possible only for governments, breaking the state's monopoly over the large-scale mobilization of capital and labor. With the advent of the Industrial Revolution, this form of organization took on a greatly expanded importance as the means to create business enterprises of sufficient scale to build factories, canals, and especially railroads. The canals built in China a thousand years ago were financed by government, but in England the canals created in the late eighteenth and early nineteenth centuries were built by corporations. In the United States, the first canals built in New York, Pennsylvania, and Maryland were financed by state governments, but the railroads that began very soon thereafter were purely private-sector enterprises built by newly created corporations.[3]

The third innovation was the creation of modern financial markets and institutions. Human society has had lenders and borrowers for a long time, but generally in the form of individuals or families (e.g., the Medici in Italy) or certain ethnic groups (e.g., the Jews) and not in the form of sizable institutions with both depositors and borrowers. To be sure, economic historians tell us that deposit-taking banks began to develop in thirteenth-century Europe (and even earlier in the Roman Empire, until its collapse), but they were certainly not widespread.[4] A well-developed market for housing mortgages, for example, did not develop until the twentieth century. Imagine, for example, that the first commercial bank in the state of New York was not created until 1784, just after the American Revolution. Suspicion about banks fueled early debates in the U.S. government, with Thomas Jefferson and others who held a bucolic image of America angrily opposed to the efforts of Alexander Hamilton to push policies favoring the establishment of private institutions for banking and credit formation.[5] For most people, until banks became widespread, credit was a matter of borrowing from friends and relatives and often frowned on by religious and social mores. Even Shakespeare has his character Polonius advise his son Laertes to "neither a borrower nor lender be."[6]

Along with banking, modern finance needed the same kind of property-right recognition afforded to real assets. Markets for buying and selling the equity shares in the newly emerging corporations were developing from the fifteenth century, but the stock market in its modern form is a creature of the nineteenth century. So, too, was the bond market. One of the seminal developments in the United States necessary for bonds came when the bankrupt Continental Congress paid soldiers at the end of the American Revolution with IOUs—think of U.S. soldiers being paid today with U.S. government bonds. Needing cash, and doubtful that their IOUs would ever be redeemed, many veterans sold them to financial specula- tors, generally at deep discounts. Alexander Hamilton, the first Secretary of the Treasury in the new U.S. government, advocated redeeming these IOUs at face value by paying the cash to the current holders. This proposal created a huge debate, with his opponents (Thomas Jefferson and others) arguing that it was immoral to pay "speculators" rather than the original holders. Hamilton, narrowly victorious on this issue in Congress, firmly established the basis for U.S. bond markets, making financial instruments a form of private property that could be bought and sold the same as other private possessions.[7]

These institutional changes were vitally important for how the world evolved. When the state controls land, then individuals in the elite are dependent on personal relationships with the state to prosper and those at the bottom are stuck on the land with few opportunities for change. Even without state control, societies with ill-defined property rights create problems for individuals because they cannot use property as collateral for loans. In a world of private property, individuals from the top to the bot- tom of society can buy and sell land or other assets (including bonds and equity shares in corporations), putting them to the best economic use. But property rights alone are insufficient—it took the rise of financial markets (in which real property could be purchased, sold, or put to use as col- lateral for loans) and corporations to complete the transformation. Then, ambitious individuals could raise money for investments in new economic enterprises with the hope of profiting from the outcome. Polonius (as well as the medieval church) may have decried "usury," but debt is critical to the growth of our economies. Transferring money (at a price) from those in society who save (that is, consume less than they earn) to those who want to build homes, offices, and factories is what enables economies to grow.

Corporations, meanwhile, opened the way for expanded international trade by private groups, separate from the power of the state. Trade has existed since antiquity, but the scale of investment required to create trade circling the globe came only with the rise of the new corporation and the financial markets to fund them, first in Europe and later in other parts of the world. The evolution of today's corporate organizations, engaging in extensive global operations and responsible for what is loosely called globalization, had their origin, therefore, in these important institutional changes occurring only a few hundred years ago.

Rising Affluence

The industrial revolution touched off a sustained increase in economic growth and affluence. Figure 1.1 shows one estimate of global economic affluence. Of course, any economic data earlier than the 1940s should be taken with a grain of salt because many governments simply did not collect or compile much economic data (the very concept of gross domestic product, GDP, as a statistical construct did not exist until the 1930s). However, Angus Maddison, a leading scholar of historical economic statistics, has bravely attempted an estimate of population, GDP, and GDP per capita for individual countries and the world over a prolonged period of time. Figure 1.1 indexes global GDP per capita, setting 1820 at 100. From 1500 to 1820, the increase was very modest—18 percent in three centuries. But in just the 130 years from 1820 to 1950, per capita GDP tripled. This was indeed a revolutionary change in the world.

The gains of the past two centuries are not simply a matter of the level of affluence but also of the transformation in the quality of life resulting from the enormous technical changes that have raised productivity. The relative cost of manufactured goods plummeted, enabling lower-income people to own products that only the very wealthy could aspire to in the past. Consider something as humble as the nail—an important manufactured product for buildings and furniture. In 1800, 50 pounds of nails in the United States cost at wholesale $10.67; almost a century

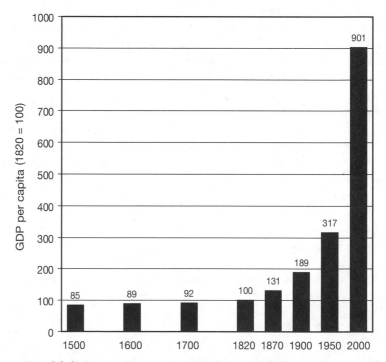

Figure 1.1 Global GDP per capita, 1500–2000 (1820 = 100). *Source:* Angus Maddison, *The World Economy: Historical Statistics* (Paris: OECD, 2003).

and a half later in 1945, the price was only $2.85—a huge drop when we consider that these numbers are not adjusted for overall inflation in the economy over this period of time. Similarly, the wholesale price of a square yard of cotton cloth, $17.38 in 1800, had fallen to only 15 cents by 1945.[8] In 1800, cotton cloth and nails were luxury items; today, they are simply common staples. Not all manufactured goods have dropped so dramatically as these two products, but even products that have increased in price have risen less rapidly than incomes.

A parallel technological revolution in medicine has had a dramatic effect on human life—reducing infant mortality to trivial levels, dramatically increasing life spans, and reducing the amount of time people spend being sick or disabled during their lives. When William Swain (a young man who left a detailed diary and set of letters published in a popular book in the 1980s) traveled overland from Buffalo, New York, to California in 1849 to participate in the Gold Rush, he frequently wrote about health—reassuring those at home that he was well or worrying to himself whenever he was not. He worried for good reason because cholera and other diseases struck down many who attempted what was then an arduous overland journey.[9] At that time, the life expectancy of white males in America was only 38 years, and even those who survived the often-fatal childhood diseases could expect at age 20 to live only to age 60. By 2001, white male life expectancy was 75 years.[10] A similar shift has occurred globally, with average life expectancies rising from about 30 years in 1800 to 67 by 2000.[11]

Independence from Land

Throughout human history, life depended on the fruits of the land—animals to hunt and plants to gather. Since the time humans learned to cultivate crops and domesticate animals, human economic activity has involved the occupation of plots of land in a more permanent fashion. Possessing land, and acquiring more of it, was the route to affluence and power. Without our modern property rights, it was the political elite that controlled the land and became wealthy through taxing the farmers. However, the Industrial Revolution broke the close relationship between affluence and land rather dramatically.

The shift away from the dependence on land to generate jobs and output has been stunning. Figure 1.2 shows the share of employment in agriculture for a small group of industrial economies. As befits the first nation to experience the Industrial Revolution, the share of employment in the United Kingdom was already fairly low by 1870 (23 percent), whereas the United States still had 60 percent of its employment in agriculture, not much lower than later-comer Japan (67 percent). But a hundred years later, all these countries had less than 10 percent of their employment in agriculture, and today the level is below 5 percent. As dramatic as this shift is, it is important to recognize how recent the change has been. In 1870, the United States was madly building railroads, steel mills, and other visible pieces of modern industry, but the economy as a whole was still predominantly agricultural.

This dramatic shift had as much to do with technical change in agriculture as it did with the rise of new industries. A dramatic rise in productivity in agriculture led to rising food production per acre and per worker. Able to feed growing populations with fewer workers and no increase in cultivated land, economies were able to shift people and land into other uses. This process continues today.

Only a few opportunities existed for affluence unconnected to land prior to the Industrial Revolution. Seaborne commerce and some urban trades offered a route to wealth but not for a very wide swath of society.

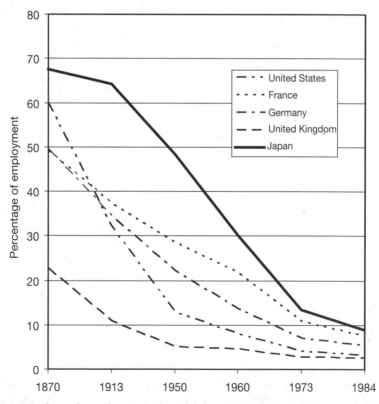

Figure 1.2 Share of agriculture in total employment, 1870–1984. *Source:* Angus Maddison, "Growth and Slowdown in Advanced Capitalist Economies: Techniques of Quantitative Assessment," *Journal of Economic Literature* 25, no. 2 (1987): 689.

Cities were centers of population not tied to the land and produced pockets of wealth, learning, and art over the past several thousand years. Venice, and its wealthy families, was built on trade, but its history was something of an exception. The vitality of these urban pockets of population independent of the land should not obscure the fact that they were small. And the affluence of cities had much to do with the ability of the political elite to tax the farmers. The Industrial Revolution, however, opened up a means to gain wealth through owning a factory or other business. The new opportunities to become wealthy went far beyond the small-scale manufacturing and artisanship in previous centuries. The use of steam power, followed by internal combustion engines and electric motors, removed even the necessity of limiting the location of factories to areas with streams of water that could be used to turn waterwheels. No longer was wealth confined largely to those who controlled land and taxed the farmers living on it.

A Revolutionary Half Century

The changes just described have been underway since the late eighteenth century. Even by the early twentieth century, the impact of the continuing Industrial Revolution had been very substantial. A new class of wealthy business people had risen in Europe, North America, Japan, and some other parts of the world. In the early industrializing countries, even the incomes of the working class had risen substantially. By the 1920s, for example, automobile ownership was spreading rapidly among the middle class in the United States. But the subsequent severe economic depression of the 1930s and the horrific experience of the Second World War were profoundly discouraging events. In 1945, it was easy to be very pessimistic about the human condition. Was capitalism a failure? Could Europe and Japan be rebuilt? Was the United States condemned to sink back into a 1930s-style depression? Was the advance in technology a blessing or simply a curse, bringing more efficient methods for mass slaughter? Many of the cities of Europe and Japan were nothing but piles of rubble, and millions of unemployed, homeless refugees struggled to feed themselves.

Out of the devastation of 1945, however, a new era of prosperity emerged—one almost beyond imagination. This story is not just one of renewed economic growth and affluence; it is also a story of huge changes in ideas, institutions, and interdependence. A century-long battle between the competing ideologies of capitalism and communism came to an end; the age of imperialism collapsed; a new set of multilateral institutions arose to govern international trade and investment; and technical change continued to spread its magic. The consequence of these changes has been dramatic growth, the spread of affluence to a broader swath of the world's population, and a dramatic increase in trade and investment. Together these changes represent a fundamental paradigm shift in how the world operates.

The Collapse of Communism

Almost as soon as the Industrial Revolution got underway, it spawned a bitter critique. The dark underside of capitalism included a widening divide between rich and poor. Arguably, the quality of life for blue-collar workers in the new factory system worsened in the first half of the nineteenth century as wages remained low and workers toiled in very unsafe working conditions and lived in crowded, unsanitary, and unhealthy urban slums. The lot of most people throughout human existence has been to live in poverty while supporting a very small affluent ruling class, but it must have been particularly galling to see the owners and managers of the new factories building fabulous new wealth on the backs of poorly paid workers. And let us face it, the newly rich capitalists were an easy lot to hate—they were arrogant bullies who flaunted their wealth through conspicuous consumption and treated their workers with considerable contempt. Just over a century ago in 1892, Andrew Carnegie and Henry Frick hired hundreds of Pinkerton thugs to break a strike at their steel mill in 1892, resulting in an armed battle that took a dozen lives.[12] Even today, U.S. society spawns unscrupulous business leaders; Kenneth Lay and others who destroyed Enron while lying to their workers and shareholders are only the latest in a long line of fabulously wealthy captains of industry who thought they could walk away with billions while their workers were left with worthless pensions. I return to the problem caused by the recent explosion in wealth for a tiny fraction of U.S. society in the conclusion of this book.

Anger over the inequities of capitalism led to both a critique and an alternative model of economic organization, initially conceptualized by Karl Marx, one of the great intellectuals of the nineteenth century. Rather than being based on private property, greed, and a wealthy ruling class, Marx believed private property should be abolished and income distributed (relatively) equally. The state, rather than individuals, should own the land, factories, and other real assets—managing them for the benefit of all. Thus, communal (hence, communism) well-being rather than individual gain should be the overriding principle of social and economic organization. Knowing that the ruling class in capitalist societies would not willingly give up its economic and political power, Marx and Friedrich Engels called for revolution, ending their famous 1848 Communist Manifesto with the ringing phrase, "Working men of all countries, unite!"[13]

In Western Europe and the United States, the communist challenge failed. Revolutions across Europe in 1848 collapsed, and the brief Paris Commune of 1870 was suppressed. Eventually, however, the revolutionary communist movement took hold in Russia, a repressive monarchy struggling badly with the early phases of industrialization in the early twentieth century. The Russian Revolution of 1917, unleashed against the backdrop of an unpopular bloody fight against Germany in World War I, finally toppled the imperial government. The new Soviet Union radically transformed the organization of the economy. True to its communist ideals, the new government seized control of land and the means of production. Instead of Adam Smith's invisible hand, the government ran the economy with intricate economic plans that allocated investment resources, industrial supplies, production targets, and workers using a bureaucratic process.

The success of the Russian Revolution in overthrowing the imperial regime and the radical transformation of the economy was a terrifying shock to the capitalist countries. In addition to providing a psychological boost to local communist movements, the new Soviet government actively fomented revolution around the world. The Great Depression of the 1930s raised the level of anxiety about the communist challenge in capitalist countries. The Depression deeply shook people's faith in the capitalist model while the Soviet Union underwent rapid industrialization.

This confrontation between capitalism and communism was temporarily interrupted by the Second World War. Hitler's sudden and unexpected invasion of the Soviet Union in summer 1941 automatically allied the Soviet Union with Britain and then the United States. Nevertheless, the alliance was an uneasy one, with some wondering if the war would simply continue when British and U.S. forces finally met Soviet forces in Germany in May 1945. Although that did not happen, the Soviet government used its occupation of East Germany and Eastern Europe to install communist governments. Soon the de facto alliance crumbled and Western opposition to these aggressive actions of the Soviet Union spawned the Cold War. Beginning with the abortive Soviet attempt to push the Allies out of West Berlin, the Cold War became a global confrontation. The success of the Communists in the prolonged, bloody Chinese Civil War in 1949 increased fears in the Western bloc. This struggle was further fueled by the collapse of imperialism (considered next in this chapter), a collapse that provided fertile ground for communist revolutions in the newly independent colonies.

The history of the Cold War is a complex story, and armed confrontation—both cold and hot—is a major part of it. But an equally important part of the story was the failure of Soviet-style socialism to deliver the economic benefits promised. State allocation of productive resources proved to be highly inefficient. Collective farms with quotas had no incentive to be efficient, factory managers with no profit motive had little incentive to run their factories efficiently, workers and managers facing no market discipline had no incentive to provide quality products, and the ideal of communism hardly eliminated the issue of an overbearing ruling class—who were now the party cadres in control of a bureaucratic system.

Cracks in the communist world began in China with reforms in the early 1980s under Deng Xiaoping. The economic reform process began slowly and cautiously in China, but over time moved the economy decisively away from the socialist model. In the Soviet Union, reform began under Mikhail Gorbachev in 1985. When the Berlin Wall fell in 1989 and Gorbachev allowed the satellite states in Eastern Europe to break away, most of these nations moved quickly away from Soviet-style socialism. Finally, the Soviet Union itself collapsed, unleashing further economic reforms in Russia and the newly independent former republics.

Where does this leave the world today? The process of reform, especially in Russia, has been difficult and painful. But the concept of communism and the system of complete state control over the economy has clearly collapsed. Some tout the triumph of capitalism as a result. But the critique made by Karl Marx and others was rooted in the ugly realities of early capitalism. In the long struggle to combat communism, capitalism itself was greatly transformed, smoothing its rough edges. Partly because of these modifications, economists prefer to use the term market-based economies, rather than capitalist, to describe the contemporary model. Unemployment insurance, social security systems, competition law, corporate accounting disclosure rules, progressive income taxes, welfare programs, and even government ownership of some industries were among the modifications. As a crude indicator of how extensive government involvement in the economy is, consider figure 1.3, showing the share of government spending as a percentage of GDP in the Organisation for Economic Cooperation and Development (OECD) countries. Although it varies widely, government spending is a sizable share of the economy, bolstered by transfer payments through unemployment, social security, health care, and other mechanisms. For the OECD countries as a whole, this ratio has been around 40 percent, with the United States somewhat lower at approximately 35 percent and the European members of the OECD higher at 48 percent in 2004.

Even in the market-based countries, however, the trend of the past two decades has been to roll back some aspects of direct government involvement in the economy because of perceived failures. Just as the

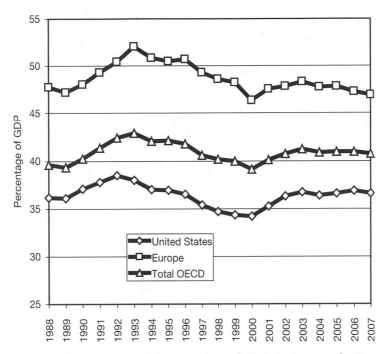

Figure 1.3 Total government spending as a share of GDP, Organisation for Economic Cooperation and Development countries, 1988–2007. *Source:* Organisation for Economic Cooperation and Development, Economic Outlook, December 2005, available at http://www.oecd.org/dataoecd/5/51/2483816.xls (February 2, 2006).

communist countries recognized that state control was an inefficient way to run an economy, so too did the Western governments that had nationalized some basic industries. In addition, overly generous unemployment benefits and statutory difficulty in dismissing workers led to high unemployment rates in countries such as France and Germany. The U.S. social welfare programs of the 1960s were widely perceived to be failures by the 1990s. Although the overall role of government spending in the economy has not changed much for the United States, figure 1.3 does show that the European countries, on average, have reduced the role government, from 52 percent in 1993 to 47 percent by 2005.[14]

Nonetheless, the organization and operation of market-based economies today is a far cry from nineteenth-century capitalism, and the formerly downtrodden workers have experienced huge increases in income over time as these economies grew and harnessed new technologies. The fact that capitalism could be modified and adapted without breaking the magic power of private property, profits, and markets helped to push the Soviet model into oblivion. Property rights and the other elements of capitalism have proven to be enormously powerful mechanisms. The lesson of the collapse of communism is that bad ideas eventually fail, much like the Ptolemaic solar system, when reality fails to live up to the theory. Meanwhile, the advanced economies have accumulated both a better theoretical understanding and more policy experience in running market-based economies. But lest we become smug, it is important to remember that the collapse of the communist/socialist alternative was dependent in part on controlling the dark underside of capitalism. Socially unacceptable levels of income and wealth inequality, suppression of poor workers, and other evils continue to dog some market-based societies. Even in the United States, we wonder how far the current conservative swing can go without unleashing a political backlash from voters tired of an increasingly unequal society. By 2005, even Federal Reserve Chairman Alan Greenspan was expressing concern over the widening income gap in the United States.[15] Furthermore, the fact that governments better understand how to run market-based economies does not mean that the understanding is perfect. The 1997 Asian financial crisis and the initial bad policy advice given to the crisis-affected countries by the IMF serves as a sober lesson in how imperfect our understanding is of the mechanics of the increasingly global capital markets.

Imperialism and Its Collapse

The system of imperialism practiced by the leading industrial powers since the sixteenth century collapsed in the first two decades after the Second World War. In recent years, it has become fashionable to refer to U.S. relations with the post–Cold War world as a new kind of American empire.[16] Nonsense. There is nothing in U.S. relations with the world today that remotely resembles the old system of imperialism, which involved direct political control of colonies (despite the unfortunate reality of the occupation of Iraq, a temporary affair not aimed at permanent control). What the authors writing about the new American empire have in mind is that the United States has (or should have) the dominant voice in global policy formation due to its military and economic might (and, in some cases, direct maintenance of military bases in other countries). Although the nature of U.S. influence in the world is a vitally important topic (and the subject of the conclusion of this book), a country's having influence is far different from its exercising direct political control over its colonies. The danger in the inflated rhetoric of those touting an American empire is that it feeds the delusions of the neo-conservatives that they can and should shape the world as they see fit.

The seizure of territory and the people living there is undoubtedly as old as human history, but the modern form of imperialism began in the sixteenth century, as the expanding European powers sought exclusive political control over territory outside Europe. The reasons for this expansion are complex, but among them was a desire to gain the economic benefits of these territories on an exclusive basis. Consider, for example, the long competition between the Dutch and British over exclusive control of the highly lucrative nutmeg trade with Indonesia, which included a number of rounds of armed conflict. Eventually, the British gave up (trading their possessions in Indonesia for New York), and Indonesia became a Dutch colony. This desire to have exclusive rights was simply an extension of the premodern pattern; leaders believed that they needed exclusive control over economic assets in order to benefit from them. This approach proceeded somewhat cyclically and had its last major expansionary phase in the second half of the nineteenth and the early twentieth century, involving not only the principal European powers but the United States and Japan as well.

The story of the two decades following the Second World War, however, was one of the virtual elimination of this system. By the mid-1960s, most colonies had emerged as independent nations. Looking back from the early twenty-first century, it is shocking to recall how recently imperialism was dismantled. When I was in elementary school in the 1950s, our somewhat out-of-date world maps hanging on the classroom walls still had large swaths of the Earth shaded in different colors for the British, French, and Dutch empires—and as children we accepted this as the natural order of things.

The history of imperialism is a long and complex one, but what matters for the story of this book is its existence as a mechanism or paradigm for organizing trade and investment. Imperialist powers engaged in extensive trade with and investment in their colonies, whereas trade and investment between empires was more restricted. To be sure, British or American merchant ships could visit Indonesia and engage in trade, but not as freely as the Dutch, and direct investment in Indonesia was a Dutch prerogative.

Table 1.1 provides a glimpse into how this system worked, showing the trade of five former British colonies. Their experiences varied, but for most Britain was their key trading partner, even though it was thousands of miles away. India, the jewel in the crown of the British Empire, sourced 72 percent of its imports and sent 33 percent of its exports to Britain in the 1892–1896 period. Keep in mind that these data do not include the trade with other colonies within the British empire; the fairly low share of trade with Britain for Sri Lanka, for example, is probably due to an overwhelming share of trade with nearby India. Australia was even more tightly tied to Britain through both exports and imports—with both imports from and

Table 1.1 Trade with Britain as a percentage of total trade, 1867–1996

	Imports			Exports		
	1867–1871	1892–1896	1992–1996	1867–1871	1892–1896	1992–1996
India	69.2	71.9	5.8	52.6	33.2	6.3
Australia	64.4	71.0	6.0	70.4	68.7	3.8
New Zealand	50.0	64.1	5.9	48.7	81.1	6.2
Canada	49.9	33.0	5.9	31.4	54.9	1.5
Sri Lanka	29.6	24.9	5.1	71.7	70.8	8.2

Sources: International Monetary Fund, Direction of Trade Statistics (CD-ROM) (Washington, D.C.: IMF, July 2001); A. W. Flux, "The Flag and Trade: A Summary Review of the Trade of the Chief Colonial Empires," *Journal of the Royal Statistical Society* 62, no. 3 (1899): 495 (chart).

exports to Britain running around 70 percent of total imports and exports in the 1890s. But a century later, and a half century after independence, these percentages were all reduced to a single-digit level. What a difference independence made! The dramatic drop in the share of trade with Britain shows the extent to which empire skewed patterns of trade.

The corresponding story of investment is mixed. From the standpoint of the major investing countries, flows to their own colonies were not necessarily dominant. For the British, the world's largest international investors prior to the First World War, an estimated 46 percent of all investment was in the empire and dominion states (Canada and Australia) in 1914. For France, however, the bulk of foreign investment was in the rest of Europe, not in its colonies (which absorbed only about 10 percent of investment). Germany was much like France. Altogether, perhaps as much as 25 percent of the foreign direct investments of the major investing nations was in their colonies in 1914.[17] Unfortunately, there is little data on how important these capital flows were from the perspective of the colonies. Nevertheless, given the fact that these colonies (such as Indonesia or the colonies in Africa) had very poor populations and essentially no domestic financial markets until colonization occurred, it is likely that the inflow of investment from their colonial masters was a large share of the total domestic investment.

Thus, for both trade and investment, the existence of colonies had a considerable impact. The collapse of the system liberated trade and investment flows from the artificial preferences created by colonial empires. Former colonies suddenly had control over their own trade and investment policies, and they could deal with the outside world on a sovereign basis. Many of these new nations were understandably wary of foreign economic interaction—in an earlier age foreign soldiers and the loss of independence had followed close in the wake of trade and investment. For some, the initial response was to pursue import substitution, using high import barriers and restrictions on inward investment to enable domestically owned corporations to dominate the market. These policies were generally a failure—another example of a bad idea that held sway for a time. Only in the past two decades have most of the formally colonized nations begun to dismantle these barriers, bringing the initial phase of the postimperial era to an end. Nonetheless, the important issue here is the collapse of imperialism as an organizing system for international trade and investment.

New Multilateral Institutions

Since the end of the Second World War, a number of new multilateral institutions have emerged to deal with global or regional issues of trade and investment. The list is a long one: the IMF, the World Bank, the WTO, the annual G-7 Summit Meeting (now the G-8) and more frequent G-7 finance ministers meetings, the OECD, the International Energy Agency (IEA), the Asia Pacific Economic Cooperation (APEC) forum, and others. Of course, there are also new noneconomic organizations, such as the United Nations (UN), the World Health Organization (WHO), and the International Atomic Energy Agency (IAEA). These are vital organizations as well, but my purpose here is to look at the primary economic organizations that have provided an alternative framework to imperialism for the loose governance of the global economy.

In the waning days of the Second World War, the allied powers met at Bretton Woods, a fading resort hotel in the mountains of northern New Hampshire, to thrash out a new economic architecture for the postwar world. Their remarkable product was called the Bretton Woods System, comprising the IMF, GATT (now transformed into the WTO), and the International Bank for Reconstruction and Development (more commonly known as the World Bank). The Bretton Woods participants intended to create a strong International Trade Organization (ITO) to parallel the IMF, but the U.S. government had objections, so the ITO was not part of the 1944 Bretton Woods agreements. Instead, the U.S. government agreed to a somewhat watered-down proposal for the GATT at renewed negotiations in 1947. These institutions provided a new framework in which governments could interact on a much more equal basis than under the imperial system to establish rules for trade and investment. The organization, scope, and rules of this system have changed a great deal since the 1940s, and there are angry arguments over the need for further reforms or even establishment of new institutions, a subject considered in the conclusion to this book. Nevertheless, these institutions provided a new and novel mechanism to enable trade and investment.

The WTO and its predecessor the GATT provided a mechanism for organizing global trade. Members were committed to offering what is known as most favored nation (MFN) status to other signatories, meaning that a reduction in an import tariff offered to one trading partner must be offered to all other members of the organization. The system allows for exceptions—customs unions or free trade areas—where a pair or small group of members agree to eliminate all (or virtually all) barriers among themselves, but the dominant paradigm is the commitments made by all members to extend trade concessions to all the other members. The new system also established a formal procedure for protesting the actions of a trading partner alleged to violate commitments made as a GATT/WTO member.

At its inception at the end of 1947, the GATT comprised only nine members. Even if we include those joining by 1952 (mainly the former axis powers and some of the countries they had conquered that were just reemerging from occupation and reconstruction), the number was only thirty-two countries. From this modest beginning, the system gained a steady stream of new adherents, so that by 2006 the WTO had 149 members. Today there are only a few important countries not yet inside the system, principally Russia, and by the end of 2006 the negotiations for its accession were largely completed.[18]

The end of the Cold War provided a boost to WTO membership. At its inception, the GATT had been an organization for the Western bloc in the Cold War. In some respects, it could be considered part of the glue intended to hold allies and friends together, although the original architects of the system were motivated by a desire to prevent the ruinous protectionism of the 1930s and to enable the benefits from expanded trade, not by a desire to play a role in the geopolitics of the Cold War. Nevertheless, the end of the Cold War did open the way for the WTO to become a truly global institution, symbolized best by the accession of China in 2001. That said, the end of the Cold War should not be overemphasized; some Soviet-bloc members had obtained membership well before the 1990s, including Poland (1967), Hungary (1973), and the former Yugoslavia (1966). And many of the nations joining the WTO since the end of the Cold War were not part of the former Soviet bloc. Overall, however, membership in the GATT/WTO expanded from one hundred in 1990 to its 2006 level of 149—almost a 50 percent increase.

The evolution of the GATT in its first several decades included the initiation of large multilateral rounds to lower tariff barriers broadly among member countries. In the 1990s, the framework was further strengthened by creating a more formal organization, the WTO, with stronger dispute resolution procedures and broader coverage of issues involving trade in services as well as rules and regulations (other than tariffs) impeding trade. In the years since this trading system was created, quotas have been largely phased out and average tariff levels have fallen substantially. In just the dozen years from 1989 to 2001, for example, the average tariff level of developed countries fell from 8.2 to 3.9 percent. When the averages are weighted by the amount of actual trade affected by each individual tariff, the drop has been from 5.8 to 3.0 percent.[19] Thus, the tariff protection imposed by developed countries is relatively low on average and still falling. The story for developing countries is somewhat more dramatic, as shown in figure 1.4. Unweighted average tariffs have fallen from 35 percent at the beginning of the 1980s to 12 percent by 2000, whereas the weighted average has dropped from 20 to 10 percent. Although tariff levels remain higher on average in developing countries than in the industrialized ones, the decline since 1980 has been substantial—with the bulk of the drop coming since the late 1980s.

In similar fashion to the GATT/WTO, the IMF has provided an international framework for financial relations. The initial purpose of the IMF was to provide an umbrella organization for the operation of the quasi-fixed exchange rates among the major economies established as

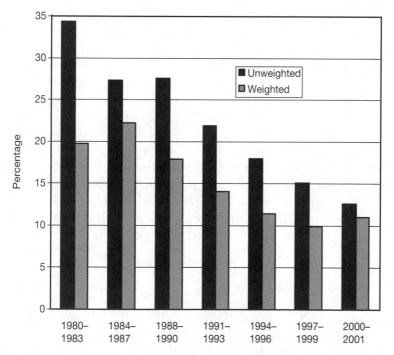

Figure 1.4 Average tariff level in developing countries, 1980–2001. *Source:* United Nations Conference on Trade and Development, *Development and Globalization: Facts and Figures* (New York: United Nations, 2004), 71.

part of the Bretton Woods agreement. That system was born out of a belief that beggar-thy-neighbor currency devaluations in the 1930s had been a factor in spreading the Great Depression and was anchored by the U.S. dollar's convertibility into gold at a fixed rate ($35 per ounce of gold), with other currencies then tied at a fixed rate to the dollar. Although fixed rates have some obvious advantages—such as removing all uncertainty of future exchange rates when engaging in international trade and investment (although the system permitted occasional revaluations), the system proved unworkable. The basic problem came from the need for countries to alter their exchange rates if they experienced different rates of productivity growth and inflation than their trading partners. Productivity rose rapidly in Japan during the 1950s and 1960s with only moderate price inflation, for example, so that its exports became increasingly price competitive on global markets, and by the late 1960s the country was running a sizable current-account surplus. The Bretton Woods system put the adjustment burden on countries running trade or current-account deficits (thereby facing a need to devalue) rather than the surplus countries. This asymmetry occurs because deficit countries face an absolute constraint of running out of foreign exchange reserves to maintain their exchange rate, whereas surplus countries face no such constraint. Eventually the system broke down. The United States, which was experiencing current-account deficits by the beginning of the 1970s, rather dramatically announced a decision to end convertibility of the dollar into gold in August 1971, putting the dollar on a de facto float against other currencies. An attempt to salvage the system with a new set of fixed rates emerged in the Smithsonian Agreement that December, but the system broke down again by early 1973 and generalized floating among all the major currencies has been in place since then.

After exchange rates moved to a floating basis in the early 1970s, the role of the IMF shifted, it having lost its initial role in managing the fixed rates among its principal members. Today, the IMF provides several functions: an attempt to prevent international financial crises by monitoring macroeconomic developments in its member countries, provision of policy advice to members, provision of emergency loans to members facing balance-of-payments problems, provision of loans to assist with structural adjustment and reform policies, and even technical assistance to members. Because the large industrial nations have floating rates (meaning that they simply do not face balance-of-payments crises), most of this activity by the IMF is directed at its developing country members. Many developing countries continue to maintain some form of fixed exchange rate regimes and need outside expertise in revamping their financial sectors to cope with international capital flows.[20]

As a policy matter, the IMF has been nudging its developing country members toward both floating exchange rates and a reduction in controls over international capital flows. This policy direction has been controversial, especially at the time of the Asian financial crisis of 1997, when critics argued that the enthusiasm for open financial markets had led the IMF to press developing countries into removing restrictions on capital flows before their immature domestic financial sectors were capable of handling the change and before they had moved to floating exchange rates. Discussion of these problems is relegated to the conclusion; for the purposes of this chapter, it is sufficient to note that, despite the criticism, the IMF carries out an important role as a global financial monitor and lender of last resort when developing countries get into international financial problems.

The other Bretton Woods institution is the World Bank. Initially, the Bank was intended to provide loans for the reconstruction of war-devastated Europe and serve as a substitute for commercial European banks, many of which were bankrupt in 1945. Only after the 1950s, through pressure from the developing world, did the Bank evolve into its current role as a provider of low-cost loans to developing countries. During the 1960s, the World Bank system grew to include several regional development banks as well—the Inter-American Development Bank, the African Development Bank, the Asian Development Bank, and in the 1990s the European Bank for Reconstruction and Development (providing development assistance to Russia and Eastern Europe).[21]

The effectiveness of the World Bank system has been challenged heavily in the past two decades, and a number of reforms have already occurred. I revisit the problems and proposed solutions in the conclusion to this book. For the moment, the important point is that the existence of the World Bank system opened the way for developing countries to obtain preferential financing for projects related to economic development outside the old imperial system. Although the flows of finance to build infrastructure during the colonial period may have been substantial and may have contributed to economic development, they were tied to imperial political domination. Once colonies around the world achieved independence, however, often the newly independent governments had difficulty obtaining both the financing (domestic or international commercial lending) and technical expertise to provide necessary infrastructure, a void that the World Bank was intended to fill from the 1960s to the present.

Continuing Technical Change

The story of accelerated technical change stretches back to the beginning of the Industrial Revolution, but several changes in the past half century have had a particularly important impact on the evolution of the global economy. These critical changes are the revolution in transportation, dramatic changes in telecommunications, and the IT revolution. These three changes have had a major impact on international trade and investment.

In transportation, important changes have occurred on two fronts: ocean and air transportation. These have driven down the cost of moving goods across oceans, the cost of loading and unloading freight, and the price of international passenger travel. The drop in the cost of transportation has allowed a much wider range of goods to be transported long distances. The Japanese, for example, burst into the American automobile market with automobiles produced in Japan and shipped across the ocean, a transaction rare prior to World War II because transportation costs would have been too high. At that time, automobiles moved on general cargo freighters—loaded by crane and carefully embedded with other cargo using wooden frames. By the 1960s, however, automobiles were moving on dedicated roll-on/roll-off ships, built like giant ferry boats so that autos could be driven on and off, and clamped in place quickly and easily. Larger vessels, especially very large bulk carriers for raw materials, and the invention of containerized freight have also made a dramatic difference.

These changes have led to low ocean-shipping costs. Ocean freight rates vary with supply and demand, but the spot-market cost of transporting a barrel of oil all the way from the Persian Gulf to Japan, for example, averaged around $1 from 1980 to 2000, adding little to the price of the oil.[22] From their debut in international shipping in 1966, containers now move virtually all nonbulk freight internationally. Prior to containerization, international shipping costs were typically 5–10 percent of the retail value of products carried. The average has now dropped to about 1 percent.[23] In the case of containers, the efficiency gains have come from the dramatic reduction in the time and effort needed to load and unload vessels—from as much as several weeks prior to containerization to as little as twenty-four hours today.[24] Of course, economic change has played a role as well because the value of manufactured goods per unit of weight has gone up. A ton of computers is worth a lot more than a ton of steel—a fact that has reduced transport costs as a share of the final of the product over time as high-value added products have become more significant in international trade.[25]

What containers and bulk carriers did for ocean transportation, jet aircraft, wide-body aircraft, and airline deregulation did for passenger travel and air freight. Older readers may remember the term "jet set"—a reference to members of high society who could afford the price of the newly introduced, fast jet aircraft and flew to vacations in exotic distant places. Early jets increased the speed of travel, but did not lower the price (although labor costs were reduced a bit because of shorter trip times). The big cost and price drops came with wide-body jets, beginning with the Boeing 747, introduced to commercial service in 1970, and then with airline deregulation. The larger aircraft lowered per-passenger costs dramatically. Airline deregulation, beginning in the United States in 1977, brought increased competition and squeezed excess profits and unusually high wages from an industry that had been officially cartelized through government regulation since the 1930s.

These changes in aircraft and regulation have had a dramatic impact on the price of travel. Air travel is now transportation for the masses (not to mention becoming crowded and uncomfortable). Pan-Am's first trans-Pacific flight flew from San Francisco to Manila on November 22, 1935. There were twenty-two passengers, each paying $675.[26] In today's dollars, that roughly equals $9,600. The slightly longer flight to Hong Kong on Pan-Am's Boeing Clipper required nearly a week, including sixty hours of flight time at a cost of $760, or well over $10,000 in current dollars.[27] Today, this same San Francisco to Hong Kong trip is a nonstop flight taking fourteen and a half hours and costs around $500 per ticket, a minuscule one-twentieth of the 1935 price in real terms.[28]

In telecommunications, there has been continuous progress, lowering the cost of existing forms of communication (the telegraph and telephone) and creating new ones (facsimile machines and the Internet). Just thirty-seven years ago, when I called Tokyo for the first time from Washington, D.C., the process required calling a local operator (who called an international operator, who contacted a counterpart international operator in Tokyo to make the local connection at that end), hanging up, and waiting for the U.S. international operator to call back some ten minutes later. The price was $10 for the first three minutes and $3 per minute beyond that. That fifteen-minute call for $46 took a noticeable chunk out of my meager summer intern pay. Today, of course, I can dial directly, and I have a long-distance package that charges 10 cents per minute to call Japan. Of course, those contacting Japan through e-mail or chat software (rather than a telephone) have a zero marginal cost for their messages.

Finally, the IT revolution, increasingly interrelated to the telecommunications revolution, has also been stunning in its speed and scope. The IT story of the past sixty years since commercial electronic computers first came into existence, has been one of ever-dropping prices and rising capabilities for storing, manipulating, and transmitting information. One commonly cited yardstick for measuring the development of information-processing technology is Moore's Law. In a 1965 article, Intel co-founder

Gordon Moore predicted that the number of transistors that could fit on a single chip would double approximately every year, later revising the estimate to every two years in 1975. In practice, his observation has proven amazingly accurate. This exponential advance in processing technology has been paralleled by a similar decline in the cost of the technology. In 1965, a single transistor cost more than $1, but today chips can be manufactured with transistors that cost less than a ten-thousandth of a cent.[29] Storage, once done on bulky magnetic tapes, has also been revolutionized, cutting costs, expanding capabilities, and improving ease of access. Overall, the cost of computer power has been falling by 30 percent a year in real terms since at least the beginning of the 1970s.[30] In the 1990s, the creation and global expansion of the Internet has paved the way for the very low-cost transmittal of data around the world.

As these costs fell, new opportunities for international trade arose. As recently as the 1980s, it was not conceivable that many companies would find cost savings in moving back-office clerical work abroad, that software engineers scattered across different countries could work together on a project in real time, or that a doctor could read x-rays instantaneously from halfway around the world.

The impact of the telecommunications and IT changes on international trade should not be exaggerated, as is often the case in the media; Thomas Friedman's best-selling *The World Is Flat* is typical of the exaggerated view of the extent to which these changes have opened up the outsourcing of nonmanufacturing jobs.[31] But just as with transportation, the scope of economic activity that can be outsourced is continuing to expand, enabling trade in services that was previously impossible. This broadening of the scope of international trade can be painful, as groups of workers in society suddenly find that their jobs have been relocated somewhere else in the world. But as painful as this transition may be, economists still firmly believe in the long-term benefits of international trade in making the world more efficient and affluent. How to handle the anxieties caused by this change is an important question, addressed in the conclusion to this book.

Growth and Interconnectedness

The post–World War II changes I have discussed have resulted in enormous changes in the global economy. Look again at figure 1.1. Global GDP per capita tripled in just the fifty years from 1950 to 2000. This explosion in affluence is a sobering reminder that until recently human society was poor and that the availability of even basic food and shelter was often questionable. When Harvard economist John Kenneth Galbraith wrote his famous book *The Affluent Society* in 1958, he was motivated by the insight that for the first time in human history people, at least in the United States and Europe, could count on having food and shelter, and much more besides.[32] A basic problem of human existence had been solved because of the economic forces unleashed by the Industrial Revolution. Even half a century ago, this was a significant statement. Today it hardly enters the consciousness of Americans. There are certainly homeless and malnourished Americans even today but not because the economy is incapable of producing sufficient food and shelter—ours is a problem of policy, not lack of abundance. Indeed, Galbraith's book was an attack on government policies that permitted some members of U.S. society to remain mired in poverty and ignorance despite the overall affluence of society.

Of course, what is true for affluent U.S. society is not necessarily true for the rest of the world. However, the circle of success in economic development has been expanding quite rapidly. Table 1.2 shows what happened in the half century from 1950 to 2000. The percentage of the world's population in countries with at least 50 percent the level of U.S. per capita GDP expanded from 6 to 15 percent, and if the threshold is lowered to 25 percent of the U.S. level, then the expansion is from 16 to 20 percent. Even this shift still leaves much of the world's population poor, and their plight is the subject of chapter 6.

Meanwhile, the combination of falling import barriers resulting from the GATT/WTO mechanisms and falling transportation, telecommunications, and IT costs, as well as the continuation of the long-term increase in economies of scale, has led to an explosion of global trade in goods and services in the past half century. Economists see the expansion of global trade as a very positive development. Students in introductory economics courses learn about the static benefits of trade; the theory of comparative advantage states that an economy benefits from opening up to trade by reallocating its domestic productive resources (capital and

Table 1.2 Change in relative level of GDP per capita, 1950–2000

	1950	2000
Number of countries with at least 50% U.S. GDP per capita	6	27
Percentage of world population in these countries	6	15
Number of countries with at least 25% U.S. GDP per capita	20	49
Percentage of world population in these countries	16	20

Source: Angus Maddison, *The World Economy: Historical Statistics* (Paris: OECD, 2004).

labor) to those activities at which the nation is the most efficient relative to the rest of the world. Those gains are important, but some economists now also argue that trade is good for economic growth as well. Countries that are open to trade tend to grow faster than those with high import barriers and little trade.[33] This is a very important point because the anti-globalization movement that became popular in the late 1990s assumes that trade is bad. The antiglobalizers focus on the losses of the industries that shrink as an economy opens up. Our sympathy for those who lose jobs due to trade liberalization, however, should not obscure the critical economic conclusions: trade forces economies toward greater efficiency and enhances economic growth, both of which are good for society as a whole. Therefore, the rise of the global ratio of trade to GDP in the past half century has been a beneficial development for the global economy.

Figure 1.5 shows what has happened to the ratio of global exports (goods plus services) to global GDP since 1960. From 12 percent, this ratio has risen steadily to around 25 percent (temporarily dropping a bit from

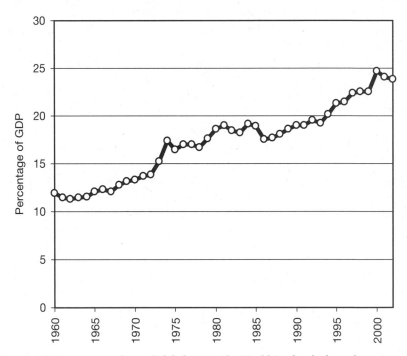

Figure 1.5 Exports as a share of global GDP. The World Bank calculates the ratio separately for exports and imports. In theory, the series should be identical (what the world exports, it imports); in reality, they are slightly different but not sufficiently so to show both. *Source:* World Bank, *World Development Indicators 2005* (CD-ROM) (Washington, D.C.: World Bank, 2005).

25 percent to 24 percent from 2000 to 2003). Thus, the ratio of exports (or imports) to GDP has doubled in the forty-plus years since 1960.

These data include both merchandise and services trade. Services deserve a special word. Unfortunately, the World Bank started publishing data on services trade only in 1975. Nevertheless, these data show that services trade has expanded slightly faster than merchandise trade, especially in the years from 1980 to the mid-1990s. By 2003, the ratio of global services exports to global merchandise exports was 24 percent. That is, services trade is much smaller than trade in goods, but the size is significant and the ratio is rising.[34] Given the fact that merchandise trade has expanded rapidly—rising as a share of global GDP—the obvious conclusion is that the services trade has expanded rapidly as well and, in some periods, faster than even the merchandise trade. Both reductions in barriers (such as deregulation of foreign participation in local telecommunications businesses in a number of countries) and the drop in travel, telecommunications, and IT costs have played a role in the rapid growth of services trade, as previously discussed.

For merchandise trade, the structure of trade has changed dramatically. Until the twentieth century, a large portion of global trade was governed by what economists call absolute advantage or very broad comparative advantage—imports were often products that simply did not grow or lie buried in the ground at home, including Indonesian nutmeg, Chinese tea, and tropical sugar. Early industrializing countries, such as England, exported manufactured goods in exchange for raw materials, agricultural products, and some low-value-added manufactured goods from developing countries. Others exported raw materials physically located within their borders. The American colonies of the European powers shipped silver, lumber, tobacco, sugar, rum, and other raw materials or agriculture-based products to Europe in exchange for manufactured goods. George Washington, for example, exported tobacco in exchange for manufactured goods such as fancy printed wallpaper to decorate his home at Mt. Vernon. Indeed, the British were so intent on maintaining this exchange of manufactured goods for raw materials and agricultural products that they actively discouraged the American colonies from establishing manufacturing operations—a prohibition that was one among many grievances that led to the American Revolution.

But as industrialization spread, and as economies of scale grew, a new form of trade arose in which countries both exported and imported manufactured goods. The trading of manufactured goods for manufactured goods has connected large parts of the world in a new and very different manner than was the case a century ago. In just the four decades from 1962 to 2001, the share of manufactured goods has risen from 58 to

78 percent of global trade, whereas raw materials and agricultural products have fallen from 42 to only 22 percent.[35] Some of this shift is due to relative price movements—prices for raw materials and agricultural products have fallen relative to manufactured goods (despite the temporary burst of oil and other raw-material price inflation in the 1970s). Cynics might also argue that the fall is due in part to the barriers that developed countries maintain against agricultural imports from the developing world. However, agriculture was less than 2 percent of global trade in 2001; even if we believe that the removal of barriers might triple the volume of agricultural trade, this would increase agriculture to only 6 percent of global trade, hardly enough to erase the overall picture of a rising dominance of manufactured goods in global trade. To a greater and greater extent, nations are exporting manufactured goods for other manufactured goods.

Parallel to the rapid expansion in international trade, there has been a recent explosion in foreign direct investment. The term *direct investment* implies a situation in which the purchaser has operating control over the purchased asset. A firm can engage in such investment by buying a controlling interest in an existing company; establishing its own new, wholly owned subsidiary; or creating a new joint venture (sharing control with a local partner). Direct investment is a particularly important part of international economic engagement. We might think that such investments are a substitute for international trade; a firm can either export to a foreign market or invest there to produce the product locally. But it turns out that direct investment is more often complementary to trade. The investment may involve setting up a local sales and after-sales service operation for exports. Even if it does produce locally, the subsidiary might provide a means of acquiring local marketing expertise, which then enables the parent firm to export other products to be sold in the market. Or the investment might be a means of jumping over import barriers, in which the parent firm exports parts or subcomponents to be assembled locally. Finally, for many service industries, local investment is the only means for engaging in the market. Citibank, for example, exports banking services to Japan by operating a subsidiary in Japan with retail banking offices in Tokyo.

Figure 1.6 shows what has happened to global direct investment flows since 1970. The most meaningful way to measure investment data is the ratio of the flow of direct investment to total fixed capital formation (i.e., an economy's total annual investment in factories, equipment, office buildings, housing, roads, and other transportation facilities). What figure 1.6 shows is that this level was quite low until recently—running at about 2 percent from 1970 to the mid-1980s. Thereafter, the level rose sharply, reaching 12 percent in 2002. Of course, one element in these

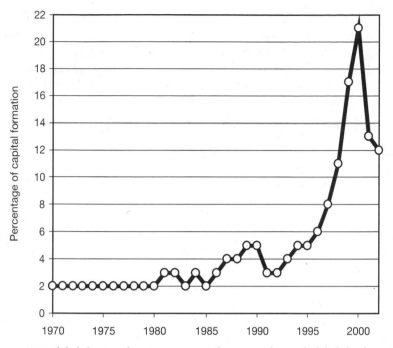

Figure 1.6 Global foreign direct investment flow as a share of global fixed capital formation, 1970–2002. *Source:* United Nations Conference on Trade and Development, Foreign Direct Investment Database, available at http://www.unctad.org/Templates/Page. asp?intItemID=1923&lang=1 (September 24, 2004).

changes was the unusual bubble in the late 1990s as firms rushed to participate in the IT boom in the United States and Europe. Like all bubbles, this one collapsed after 2000, but it still left the level of global direct investment flows much higher than before.

Other forms of international financial investment have also expanded explosively—even faster than direct investment. These investments include portfolio equity investments, commercial bank loans, and purchases of corporate and government bonds. As nations have liberalized their restrictions on international capital transactions, and as telecommunications and IT have made international investments easier, all forms of these transactions have expanded. Consider, for example, international assets held by investors in the EU countries. Holdings of international assets other than direct investment grew from only $876 billion in 1980 to $17.4 trillion by 2003. Direct investments grew over the same time period from $162 billion to $4.9 trillion.[36] Thus, the holdings of portfolio investments dwarf the size of direct investment; for the EU portfolio investments abroad were 3.5 times the size of direct investments.

In the nineteenth century, in a global setting in which countries did not have controls on the outflow or inflow of capital, foreign direct investment and other forms of investment also expanded. As with trade, the decades after World War I brought a proliferation of capital controls in many countries, which were dismantled only slowly after World War II, even in the advanced industrial nations. As noted earlier, many former colonies discouraged direct investment as part of their import substitution policies. A comparison to capital formation prior to World War I is not possible because the statistical data on investment in that era are spotty. However, Angus Maddison, an economic historian, tells us that the British engaged in a massive amount of investment abroad from the 1870s to World War I, with as much as one-half of domestic savings flowing abroad (rather than being invested at home). Investments by France and Germany are also supposed to have been large. Was this flow as large as the flow in the past two decades? Crude estimates suggest that the earlier capital flows may have been even larger (in a relative sense) than they are now. Nevertheless, the flows have grown once again to a significant level.

The expansion of international investment flows to, or close to, the unusually large flows of the early twentieth century is quite an accomplishment given the collapse of imperialism (which had facilitated smooth investment flows to colonies), several decades of capital controls in the industrialized countries (put in place to protect their fixed exchange rates in the Bretton Woods system), and the wariness of newly liberated colonies toward foreign investors. With management of direct investments made easier by the transportation and telecommunications revolutions (making it easier for managers to travel to and communicate with operations abroad), the upward trend should continue.

Other investments are also enhanced by falling controls on international transactions and better information flows. Nevertheless, developing countries have discovered that reducing barriers to sometimes volatile short-term capital investments can be dangerous if they have poorly developed financial sectors and if they try to maintain a fixed exchange rate. Controversy over whether or how to regulate short-term portfolio investments has blossomed since the Asian financial crisis in 1997. Some form of continuing controls appear to be justified—small countries with rudimentary financial sectors can be overwhelmed by these kinds of investments (as opposed to direct investment), which can be quite volatile. However, clearly the trend over the next several decades will be for the renewed loosening of such controls and the continued expansion of international portfolio investments.

The controversy surrounding short-term portfolio investment also should not obscure the importance of the rise of direct investment. These investments enhance the global spread of technology in the form of equipment used in factories or even corporate managerial skills and thereby enhance economic growth. Much of this flow is among the advanced industrial economies, but flows to developing countries are significant as well (as chapter 5 shows for East Asia). That many developing countries have embraced inward direct investment is an important positive shift in global affairs in the past two decades.

REVOLUTIONARY economic change dates back to the late eighteenth century. But, as this chapter demonstrates, just in the sixty-plus years since the end of the Second World War, the change in ideas, global institutions, and technology have altered the world in profound ways. First, the world has become almost inconceivably more affluent, and that affluence has expanded to a broader swath of the world's population—although many parts of the world remain very poor. Second, the world has become much more interconnected through both trade and investment. Even if the skeptics are partially correct in saying that the world was just as interconnected in 1914 (on the eve of World War I) as it is today, the interconnections today exist in a fundamentally different institutional setting and the return to 1914 levels is a remarkable achievement.

The economic miracle unleashed by the Industrial Revolution is a continuing story. There is no doubt that in the next several decades global growth should continue at a high level while trade and investment should expand rapidly as the technological factors propelling the world in this direction continue to operate. This outcome depends, however, on the willingness of governments to support open policies on trade and investment and to support or improve the multilateral institutions that loosely govern the current system—a topic addressed in the conclusion of this book.

2. ECONOMIC CHANGE AND INTERNATIONAL RELATIONS

What are international relations and foreign policy all about? What should the U.S. government want to achieve? The answer is peace and prosperity. We Americans want to protect ourselves from armed attack and enjoy international conditions that enable our economy to grow. Lofty ideological goals, such as the promotion of democracy, enunciated by various U.S. presidents over the years, are certainly self-satisfying but should be a secondary objective. Democracy is not a magic bullet that will produce a peaceful world, and as a policy objective it can even be contradictory to keeping the peace. That is, if the United States engages in forcible regime changes with the establishment of democracy as a declared goal (as was the administration's claim in the case of the invasion of Iraq), the pursuit of this goal creates conflict and drives undemocratic regimes into a more antagonistic posture toward the United States. Therefore, in this book I stick to the position that the main objective of foreign policy should be the promotion of conditions conducive to peace and prosperity. Prosperity and democracy are not entirely unrelated; rising prosperity may not necessarily cause societies to move in a democratic direction, but it certainly helps.

The fundamental proposition of this book is that peace and prosperity ought to be easier to achieve today because the rationale for war has diminished and the architecture of international economic engagement has improved. There is, in fact, some statistical evidence to support this proposition; there has been a steady decrease in the incidence of war since the beginning of the 1990s.[1] Because peace has become easier to achieve, at least among the great powers, U.S. foreign policy should rely less on military security and more on the management of a complex and overlapping set of international negotiations and dialogs related to economic issues. These often involve contentious negotiations—there is nothing warm and fuzzy about the nature of international economic negotiations, but the outcomes involve elements of policy flexibility and cooperation. Traditional notions of power do not work well in this environment. Thus, the goals of peace and prosperity rely less on the maintenance of military power and more on negotiations in which the U.S. government may be the first among equals but is hardly a sole superpower. Future problems facing the world—such as global warming or pandemic diseases—also require negotiated, cooperative outcomes.

To say that military power matters less than in the past to achieve peace and prosperity may sound strange at a time when the United States has launched two wars in three years and now presides over the armed occupations of both Afghanistan and Iraq while it continues a military effort to pursue terrorists abroad. Yet these immediate military operations obscure larger trends in how the world is evolving (and, at least in the case of Iraq, military invasion represented a highly dubious use of military force). The alternatives to military power in achieving U.S. foreign policy objectives are the subject of the conclusion. Before getting to the policy choices, it is important to delineate how the economic transformation described in the previous chapter has affected international relations.

The Positive Impact of Economic Change

Overall, modern economic growth and institutional change has produced a world in which the probability of conflict among the major powers has diminished significantly. As discussed in the introduction, British writer Norman Angell argued just before the outbreak of World War I that the vast increase in affluence coming from industrialization and interdependence should deter governments from aggressive war because they risked economic loss from armed conflict and stood to gain nothing of value from armed victory.[2] Poor Angell has been the butt of unkind comments by realists since that time because he appears to have been so dreadfully wrong. However, he never said that war would *not* occur; he simply said that it would be increasingly stupid because nations had much to lose and nothing to gain from aggressive war. A century later, we can say with more confidence that the economic development of the world since the end of the last great conflict has proceeded in a way that makes Angell's conclusions more valid.

This argument is not new. Political scientists espousing the liberal view of international relations have argued for decades that rising economic interdependence was producing a world in which conflict would be less likely. As explained in the introduction, Joseph Nye and Robert Keohane coined the term complex interdependence back in the 1970s to describe what was happening to the world.[3] Their position was dismissed by the realists—at that time interdependence appeared to be at a considerably lower level than it had been in Angell's day.[4] But in the three decades since Nye and Keohane resurrected the notion that economic interdependence could have an impact on international relations, the interconnections in the world have become much closer, as shown in the data presented in chapter 1. This concept, therefore, deserves careful thought.

So what are the changes that have diminished the probability of major conflict? One useful way to think about what has changed is in terms of the choices and incentives facing individuals and states. Kenneth Waltz, one of the intellectual leaders of the neo-realist school on international relations, examined the causes of war in his classic 1954 study *Man, the State, and War* at three levels: the individual, the internal politics of the state, and the system of interaction among states.[5] These three levels of analysis are still a useful way to look at how the economic transformation of the world affects questions of international relations—even though Waltz himself has remained steadfastly dismissive of the role of economic change or interdependence as a factor in international relations.

Individuals

At this level, Waltz tells us, "wars result from selfishness, from mis-directed aggressive impulses, from stupidity."[6] Think of conflict as the natural consequence of living in nations run by testosterone-laden male competitors. Individuals desire power over others and some of them will attract supporters and attack competitors—in their own societies or across national boundaries. From Genghis Khan to Adolph Hitler and Osama bin Laden, human history has been afflicted by charismatic indi-vidual leaders who have wrought destruction on parts of the world. If this represents an inherent human trait, then mortal conflict will remain a constant in human existence.

Let us look, however, at the incentives facing individuals. Ever since human beings began farming, a major means of achieving affluence was through the control of land. Real affluence in poor agrarian societies came not from farming itself but from exercising control over farmers, from whom rents or taxes could be extracted. Because the technology of agri-cultural production improved only slowly, the dominant way to gain afflu-ence and power lay not in getting greater output from the land one owned but from gaining control over more land. Furthermore, the technology of agricultural production was sufficiently simple that aggressive individu-als could seize land from others and tax the output of the farmers—the supervision of the farmers' work was not a complicated managerial issue.

Thus, if we subscribe to the view that conflict is due to the inherently aggressive nature of human beings, then the pre-industrial organization of the world was designed for endless armed conflict as individuals sought to gain affluence and power through grabbing control of land from others. Those motives might be enhanced by the vagaries of climate, with some groups desperately seeking land elsewhere when their own crops failed or using the added affluence and population growth resulting from good harvests to finance and staff military adventures abroad.

Think about the career possibilities for second sons in a pre-industrial age. If only the eldest son inherited the family property, what was the younger son to do? The major alternative to inheriting the property was to join the military. Consider, for example, William the Conqueror, who offered land grants in England as an inducement for Norman knights to participate in the invasion of 1066.[7] For young members of the elite who happened not to possess land in Normandy, this was a very enticing offer and a chance for personal affluence—and one that worked. They became the new landed aristocracy of England—with both political power and personal wealth. Indeed, political power and personal affluence were not clearly separated until recently in human society. Even as late as the Napoleonic Wars, military careers carried the possibility for personal gain even if the acquisition of landed estates was no longer as much of an issue. The British Navy, for example, let its officers and sailors profit from the sale of captured enemy vessels and their cargoes until the end of the Napoleonic era.

The Industrial Revolution, however, opened up new avenues for aggressive individuals to pursue their goals. The profits from running an industrial enterprise suddenly provided a means to prosper that was divorced from controlling land. Even if one's aggressive tendencies revolved more around commanding other people than amassing wealth, new industrial organizations offered the satisfaction of commanding the labor of large numbers of people. Competition in the marketplace even offered some of the emotional attributes of war. Just think about the tendency of the media to describe corporate behavior in military terms. A hostile takeover may not be mortal combat, but the terms in which it is described suggest that it provides some of the same personal adrenaline-pumping satisfaction. Younger sons no longer needed to seek a military career to satisfy their ambitions; they could start or join a company and, if successful in the competition against their peers, gain a level of personal affluence and power over the labor of others well beyond that of the landed aristocracy.

With this shift in economic opportunities, wealth moved decisively from a landed aristocracy to the modern business sector. Ambitious young

Americans join investment banks, not the farm sector or the military. So for those individuals with dominant personalities, a burning desire to gain wealth and prestige, or a desire to exercise influence over others, the corporate route offers an alternative to a political or military career. Furthermore, a military career no longer carries the opportunities for plunder and personal financial gain that it did in 1066 or through the time of the Napoleonic wars.

A second issue for individuals is what economists call opportunity cost. When life was short and living standards were low, going to war—with the risk of death but also the prospect of large personal gain—might be an attractive choice for many. But when life is long and affluent—and personal gain from warfare small—who wants to go? Appeals to patriotism can work but not always. Recall the Vietnam War protests, driven by affluent college students who were not amused by the contrast between the opportunities of civilian careers at home versus the dubious honor of participating in a controversial war. Today's volunteer army has found sufficient numbers of recruits—mainly from the lower economic tiers of Americans, for whom a secure paycheck in the military is enticing—but recruitment suffered and enlistment rates sagged in the wake of the Iraq war and continuing occupation (necessitating both lower standards and greater monetary rewards for joining to keep the numbers up). With global per capita GDP tripling in the half century from 1950 to 2000, people have much more to lose today.

Even if the incentives facing individuals have changed decisively over time, we cannot entirely rule out the possibility of warped individuals who still desire to use force to achieve their ends. The current global security challenge, after all, concerns international terrorists—misguided individuals operating outside state authority. Obviously they have not been swept up by the lure of participation in the business world. Therefore, we cannot say that the economic changes of the past fifty years have categorically led individuals away from organized violence. For some individuals, religious or other ideologies provide an overpowering motive for violent action (as discussed later in this chapter). Nevertheless, the size of the terrorist movement needs to be kept in perspective—Al Qaeda involves only a few thousand individuals at most. Other groups that have their roots in radical Islam swell these numbers somewhat, but the numbers are not large. Small numbers of individuals can certainly wreck havoc, as happened on 9/11, and they could do even more if they were able to obtain and detonate a nuclear weapon. But the fact remains that relatively few individuals in human society today become international terrorists. Dealing with them is primarily a matter for intelligence and police work plus prudent protective actions, not the use of military might.

The following chapters of this book do not often return specifically to this change in individual incentives. But keep this factor in mind when we look at the dramatic rise in affluence in the advanced industrial countries and the shift of economic structure (and international trade) away from agriculture. I am convinced that the change in individual incentives unleashed by the emergence of capitalism and the Industrial Revolution has had a profound effect on individual incentives and behavior. In the United States, Europe, Japan, and other affluent parts of the world, military careers are no longer sought by many. More important, individuals in these societies no longer think of personal gain as a potential benefit of going to war.

If there is a part of the world where the individual incentive for conflict remains alive, it is predominantly in parts of Africa and the Middle East, where ethnic and religious strife has often been fundamentally about control over the incoming financial flows from the export of national assets—mainly oil. In these cases, grabbing control of the levers of government is akin to the Norman land grab in England a thousand years ago.

States

What applies to individuals, according to Waltz, also applies to states—with governments using foreign threats (or opportunities) as a rallying cry to build political support at home. Beyond that political motive, pre-industrial states were largely income-generating mechanisms for political leaders. Relative to the complex governing functions of states today, premodern states were rudimentary, and the creation of sufficient tax revenue to sustain an affluent lifestyle for the leaders was a leading objective.[8] Historians applaud the sophisticated political structure of ancient Greece and Rome, but in reality the role of government was simple and the correlation between political power and personal wealth was high in these societies. As with individuals, the political leadership of any state pursuing greater wealth and power needed to acquire more land. But the Industrial Revolution opened up a means for the state to prosper without territorial conquest. Any government adept at creating an institutional framework conducive to growth and industrialization could prosper just as much, or more, than it could by gaining new territory. The financial benefits spewing forth from modern economic activity simply overwhelm the old opportunities based on ownership, taxation of land, or seizing additional land.

The rapidly growing states in East Asia in the past half century epitomize this reality—Japan, South Korea, China, and others have produced rapid economic growth without territorial conquest. Indeed, Japan is probably the preeminent example of a nation that has learned this lesson—growing quickly and rising to the ranks of the affluent, industrialized nations after losing all of its overseas empire in World War II (a story considered in chapter 5). The governments of these East Asian states came to recognize that producing domestic growth through industrialization was critical to their continued political legitimacy. Several of these states, including Japan and South Korea, are heavily dependent on imports of critical raw materials, including oil, iron ore, and coal. However, they have discovered that political control over the sources of supply or the use of military power to ensure access to those supplies is unnecessary for stable access to raw materials—a point explored later in this chapter with respect to oil.

We could argue that China illustrates Waltz's concern over internal state politics, that governments pursue aggression to rally the public behind the government. The Communist Party, fearful of losing its political control, uses threats against Taiwan as a means to rally the public behind its leadership. But, in this case, the interesting feature is not the periodic sword-rattling but the failure to follow through. The reason why China has not invaded Taiwan lies partly in its leadership's recognition that invasion would jeopardize the rapid domestic economic growth that is even more vital to maintaining political stability (a subject explored in greater detail in chapter 5).

The Interstate System

As Waltz puts it in his book, a world of sovereign states "with no system of law enforceable among them, with each state judging its grievances and ambitions according to the dictates of its own reason or desire—conflict, sometimes leading to war is bound to occur."[9] But this is not true today. Since 1945, global institutions have undergone profound transformation in a direction that diminishes the probability of conflict. The UN is an obvious example; but let us focus here on economic institutions.

Prior to the Second World War, imperialism was the dominant paradigm. In one sense, imperialism was a response to both the lack of enforceable international contracts (with imperial powers imposing their own contract systems within their empires) and the lack of trust among widely divergent cultures as the industrially advanced Europeans began to deal with a variety of primitive, or at least very different, cultures. Imperialism provided for the stability of the supply of raw materials—from Indonesian nutmeg to North American timber for shipbuilding. But this system built state conflict into the economic paradigm in the form of the conquest of colonies and struggles among the great powers, locked into a zero-sum contest to gain control over a finite quantity of global territory. This approach to international trade and investment almost inevitably led to conflict among major powers, including the Seven Years' War (and its North American component, the French and Indian War), the Spanish-American War, the Russo-Japanese War, and the European tensions that eventually led to World War I.

Even Americans were caught up in this conceptualization of the world order and the trade and economic benefits flowing from it. In his excellent study of U.S. thinking about imperialism, John Judis notes that U.S. business leaders saw the capture of the Philippines from the Spanish as a stepping stone to the Chinese market. He quotes Whitelaw Reid (a turn-of-the-twentieth-century editor of the *New York Tribune*) as saying that the extension of U.S. authority over the Philippines would enable the United States to secure a "commanding position on the other side of the Pacific—doubling our control of it and of the fabulous trade the Twentieth Century will see it bear."[10] That kind of thinking was essentially no different than that of the British and Dutch three hundred years earlier.

Why should governments in the twentieth century have believed that military force and political control were necessary for successful trade? One reason was simply "old think" extending the previous agricultural-based reality; affluence depended on owning or commanding the land that was the source of economic output at home. Another reason was a lack of any widespread rule of international law. Among European powers, a long history of contract law existed. But what about the Indonesians when the British and Dutch first arrived? When the Dutch left behind a small outpost with a few dozen traders and a large stock of goods to exchange for local spices, with the next Dutch flotilla to relieve the garrison not expected for a couple of years, why not just kill the Dutch and seize the goods?[11] Local trading customs existed, but from the standpoint of the Indonesians the Dutch and British were from outside the existing world of economic relations and the effort by both the Dutch and British to establish trade was fraught with periodic violence with the local population.

But, as described in chapter 1, the imperialist system collapsed over the first two decades after the Second World War. By the time this collapse was over, many states (including former colonies) had a relatively well-developed domestic rule of law. To be sure, U.S. business rails against the lack of rule of law in places such as China, where courts are weak and bribery is extensive. But in China and most other countries, the concept of contract law is sufficiently well developed that brute military force is no longer a conceivable recourse in forcing compliance with contracts.

Meanwhile, the web of international organizations described in chapter 1 has provided international rules and guidelines that affect government behavior. Global trade and investment now have oversight provided by the WTO and IMF. With these accepted international rules (and authorized *economic* retaliation when one party fails to abide by them), corporations no longer expect their governments to support their commercial interests with military force. States no longer see the need (or assume the right) to gain political control over territory in order to enable trade and investment. And, finally, the contemporary global economic system is on a more equal basis, free of the threat of military power to enforce economic gain. The morally repugnant carving up of the coast of China a hundred years ago into different enclaves controlled by foreign powers and policed by their own soldiers is inconceivable today.

Consider, for example, what a difference the existence of the IMF has made for the management of international debt issues. When the Japanese embarked on industrialization in the late nineteenth century, the government worried about borrowing from abroad for fear that any difficulty in repaying international debt would provide an excuse for the European powers to use military power to enforce repayment. The government was right to be apprehensive. In 1902, Germany blockaded Venezuela and even landed troops when the Venezuelan government was unable to repay a loan to Germany (and withdrew only when pressured by the U.S. government). In similar fashion, Theodore Roosevelt had U.S. troops seize control of the Dominican Republic's customs house to remove money to pay U.S. and European creditors.[12]

Today the world is very different. It is inconceivable that any of the major nations of the world would even consider use of military force to enforce the repayment of debts. For all its flaws, the IMF provides an institutional setting for working out the problems of countries unable to meet their international debt obligations. The IMF made some initial missteps in the Asian financial crisis of 1997 and created resentment around the region for some of the conditions it demanded in exchange for loans, but none of the crisis countries—Thailand, Indonesia, and South Korea—needed to worry that Western firms would use the crisis to call on their governments to seize control of territory. Despite complaints in the region about the IMF forcing economic reforms on them as a condition for help, those demands were not designed to make the crisis countries more Western but to make their economies and financial markets more robust so that a repeat crisis in the future would be less likely.

Many governments have also learned that in their quest to grow and industrialize, economic benefits do not depend on the local ownership of the corporations creating the new wealth. Governments in less-developed countries have discovered that they can improve their level of affluence by attracting investments from companies owned by foreigners. Thus, the government does not need to have political control over the owners of the parent companies. What matters is the employment and productive technology that the corporation brings into the country. Local managers learn new skills (and earn higher incomes), workers have expanded employment opportunities, and eventually the technology diffuses to locally owned firms (legally or otherwise). Even if the owners of the firms are abroad, local individuals find ample opportunity to benefit, and, of course, the host governments gain tax revenues. That developing countries now feel comfortable allowing foreign-owned companies to operate inside their borders is a tribute to other changes of the twentieth century (discussed a bit later in this chapter).

To be sure, host governments could choose to extract a very large portion of the profits of production (or even nationalize foreign investments), but if pushed too far, the owners will simply relocate elsewhere. The world has a new kind of national competition—a competition to create sufficiently favorable rules and incentives for inward direct investment to entice foreign firms to invest. This is a remarkable change for the governments of developing countries and especially for those that experienced the humiliation of colonization only a few decades earlier.

As a result, the years since the end of the Second World War have enmeshed governments in the new international economic system. Historians point out that the middle decades of the twentieth century—from the end of World War I through the 1970s—were a time of slumping international investment. The Great Depression, the Second World War, the collapse of imperialism, and the suspicions of liberated colonies concerning foreign firms, as well as a belief in the inherent appropriateness of industrial policies to grow domestically owned manufacturing firms, all contributed to this decline. But as the data in chapter 1 indicate, there has been a rapid rebound in investment since the beginning of the 1980s. Even if the cynics are correct that trade and investment linkages today are no denser than in 1914, it is still a considerable achievement to get back to that point without imperialism. Chapters 5–6 examine the rise of foreign direct investment flows into developing countries in more detail.

What does this systemic shift imply for conflict? A lot. Unlike imperialism, the current global economic system is not inherently conflictual. States need not grab territory to ensure raw material supplies or to sell their exports because they can trust the global market system. If states get into international debt problems, the IMF and not the military forces of the creditors will intervene to work out a solution. Governments can, and do, engage in bitter trade disputes—just look at U.S.-Japanese trade relations from the 1970s to the 1990s—but they do so without seriously considering withdrawal from the overarching rules of the WTO (explored further in the conclusion to this book). Cynics might argue that countries such as Japan have gotten away with many violations of the spirit of the WTO in the past half century, but the point is that overall commitment to the system has prevented the U.S. government from drifting in a more protectionist direction (and even Japanese markets have become more open over time).

Of course, in this new global economic system, governments can still choose to exercise military power or take unilateral actions against other nations, but they do so at the risk of damaging their economic relations and, thereby, prosperity. Why should Germany and France, for example, fight another war? With open borders, German and French firms can prosper by trading with each other and with the rest of the world, as well as investing in one another's country. Individuals in both societies have prospered to an unbelievable degree since the end of the war. Why should they risk their prosperity in a war that would bring destruction at home for a questionable gain? French farmers may occasionally protest the importing of food and wine from other European countries, but the fundamental reality is that these societies have accepted the increased competition that comes with the lowering of trade and investment barriers and recognize that they have gained economically as a result of these changes. As discussed in chapter 4, the region continues to become more open internally despite occasional protests and backsliding.

ECONOMIC change since the end of the Second World War has had a powerful impact on reducing the rationale for conflict. Some aspects of these changes predate the mid-twentieth century, such as the end of the causal link between affluence and the control of territory. But even that effect has become more pronounced with the tripling of per capita GDP since 1950. The opportunities for wealth through business are now so large that achieving wealth through armed aggression is irrelevant for individuals in affluent societies. Governments have discovered that they can cause their societies to grow economically without territorial conquest and that producing growth lends political legitimacy to the ruling government. The collapse of imperialism and its replacement by the Bretton Woods institutions, as well as other multilateral economic organizations, has enabled states to interact in a less conflictual setting. The advanced nations no longer see themselves as locked in a zero-sum conflict with their industrial competitors. Former colonies no longer need to fear political or military domination as the price for trade and investment. And the deepening trade and investment ties over the past several decades have substantially raised the opportunity costs for governments that contemplate armed aggression. As a result, the rationale for war and the probability of major conflict has diminished.

Continuing Problems

To say that the probability of war has diminished does not mean that it is gone. Some important causes of war have diminished or disappeared, but other issues remain or have increased in importance. What are these sources of concern?

• Possible shocks that undermine the trust or commitment to the existing international economic system.
• An unraveling of the global economic system due to governance problems stemming from the lack of common goals as the system became truly global in the wake of the Cold War.
• An unraveling of the global economic system due to inattention or bad policy choices.
• Conflict from noneconomic sources: nationalism, ethnicity, ideology, and religion.
• Continuing poverty or domestic economic mismanagement in parts of the world.

These are all serious issues, but, as I argue in the conclusion to this book, they are all surmountable. Let us consider each of them separately.

Systemic Shocks

Political commitment to the current system and its deepening economic interdependence could be seriously undermined by a large-scale shock, some more probable than others. Possible shocks include a 1930s-style global depression, an international financial crisis, another oil crisis, or perhaps a major medical pandemic. Governments faced with a large unexpected crisis often react poorly; fear and haste produce bad policies, such as the rampant protectionism of the early 1930s.

The occurrence of an economic depression reminiscent of the 1930s, however, has a very low probability. Economics remains an imperfect science, but economists and policy makers understand macroeconomics much better today than they did in the 1920s, and governments have better institutions and policy tools to cope with negative shocks. Japan, for example, experienced a huge drop in the stock market and real estate market in the early 1990s, drops akin to those in the United States in 1929, but it went through the 1990s with relative stagnation (1 percent average annual real GDP growth) rather than a depression.

An international financial crisis leading to global depression is also conceivable, with cascading international debt crises and currency devaluations or depreciations. The world had such a crisis in 1997–1998 involving Thailand, Indonesia, Korea, Argentina, and Russia (and other states to a lesser degree). As painful as that crisis was (especially in Indonesia), it did not lead to the unraveling of the global system. The IMF made mistakes early on, and its policies were resented in Asia, but the system itself survived. The IMF corrected its mistakes, and the affected countries recovered. A worse crisis is conceivable, but it is not likely. U.S. current-account deficits and mounting international debt are a matter of concern for many, but even in this case any future shakeout is not likely to cause a collapse of the IMF or flows of international investment and trade. Nevertheless, even a remote possibility implies a need to consider both the further reform of the IMF and corrective policies for U.S. current-account deficits (considered in the conclusion to this book).

A severe resource supply crisis could also potentially cause fearful governments to react badly. Something akin to the 1973 crisis in oil is conceivable. In a time of tight supply conditions caused by economic growth, another cartel effort to restrict supply, a natural disaster knocking out some supply capacity (think of Hurricane Katrina in 2005), or regional armed conflict eliminating some supply capacity is conceivable. Governments could react to a crisis of this sort by abandoning faith in the efficacy of global markets and returning to more nationalistic approaches to supply security. As I point out later in this chapter when considering the oil market, markets *do* work, so competitive, zero-sum policy games played by governments in the face of a supply disruption would be very unfortunate and misguided.

A major medical crisis could conceivably cause similar fearful reactions. Imagine a deadly flu pandemic originating in one part of the world and causing massive loss of life across the globe. Governments might respond by shutting down trade and travel with the affected countries or by hoarding vaccines and other medicines for their own citizens. Such actions might create deep resentment and foster a more conflictual global environment. But, although a devastating global pandemic is conceivable (the 1918–1919 influenza pandemic is a recent precedent), the possibility that such a crisis could cause global conflict seems remote. First, the conditions that turned the Bubonic Plague into a devastating pandemic in late-medieval Europe simply do not exist in the advanced nations today. Second, the mechanisms for cooperation in response to epidemics are much stronger than in the past, including the existence of a multilateral institution, the World Health Organization (WHO). Therefore, although a devastating global viral pandemic is conceivable, it is difficult to imagine one driving major governments toward an antagonistic confrontation as they react to protect their own populations.

The more serious possibility for medical pandemics lies in developing countries, in which (as discussed in chapter 6) medical care remains limited and malnutrition and unsanitary living conditions provide an ideal breeding ground for new diseases. HIV/AIDS originated in Africa, and the concerns over bird flu in 2005–2006 involved a strain of the disease originating in Asia. Should a virulent new disease occur, it is possible that it could spread with massive results before the advanced nations could bring in sufficient medical assistance. Large losses of life in poor countries would cause economic contraction and potentially inflame political turmoil.

The three possible crisis scenarios sketched out here are conceivable, but they are not very probable. Nevertheless, as remote as they may be, they do represent dangers that deserve attention to further diminish their probability and international agreements to minimize the danger of misguided, uncooperative actions by fearful governments. I return to the question of how U.S. policy should respond in the conclusion to this book.

Governance Difficulties

In a sense, the international economic system that has emerged since the end of the Second World War has been the victim of its own success. What began as rules among a small collection of market-based economies in the Western bloc has expanded to cover most of the world. As discussed in chapter 1, the end of the Cold War opened the way for the system to become truly global. The problem is that with increasing numbers of governments participating, agreement on policy is more difficult to obtain. Although these governance problems are real, they should not be exaggerated. As chapter 1 points out, the GATT already had one hundred members prior to the end of the Cold War and expanded to 149 by 2006. Even so, the WTO is far more unwieldy now than it was when the membership consisted of the small group of only nine countries that founded the GATT in 1947.

More important than the expansion in numbers, the end of the Cold War brought an end to a convenient convergence of political and economic interests. That is, the members of the Bretton Woods institutions had at least some common desire to fend off communism. Governments saw cooperation through the IMF as a means of maintaining collective prosperity (in competition with the Soviet bloc) and avoiding economic crises that might provide a wedge for communist agitation or insurgencies. The World Bank provided a means for jointly bolstering developing countries that might be targets of Soviet- or Chinese-financed insurgencies. And the GATT lowered trade barriers in a manner that members felt was beneficial to their national interests—a lowering not available to trading partners in the Soviet bloc (countries that were mostly not members of the GATT). The political glue that helped to buttress these multilateral institutions came to an end with the collapse of the Soviet Union. Now, participating governments must rely solely on common economic interests to maintain these institutions and their policies.

The question is whether economic interests across the broad sweep of the globe are pulling governments together or driving them apart in the absence of the Cold War glue. In some respects, the divisions seem prominent, with national economic interests diverging between big countries and small ones, affluent nations and poor ones, and market-based economies and those that still have some form of socialism. These divisions create divergent national interests and greater difficulty in reaching decisions. This is especially a problem in the WTO, which is a very democratic organization in which individual countries make their own decisions on what concessions to make in multilateral trade negotiations.

The IMF is less democratic, and this, too, has led to problems. There is a tendency at the IMF (and World Bank) to regard developing countries as clients, not members, as having failed in some way to pursue good economic policies, so they must be cajoled, threatened, and pushed toward better policy. If these countries were given more of a voice in these organizations, the organizations feel that their ability to push the developing countries around might be jeopardized. On the other hand, the developing countries feel that the IMF is run by arrogant macroeconomists from advanced countries who really do not understand the problems and conditions in the developing world. Indeed, I have a close friend who worked in 2005–2006 as an advisor (funded by U.S. Agency for International Development, USAID, money) to the Kosovo Ministry of Finance; during his year he was appalled at the arrogance, pettiness, and lack of real understanding evinced by visiting IMF officials.

The workability of the Bretton Woods institutions, as a result, is now a matter of concern. Should they be more democratic? Should they be more transparent? Would such changes improve or diminish their ability to serve their purpose? These are difficult questions (and I address them again in the conclusion to this book). Despite the problems, I remain convinced that even without the political glue of the Cold War, sufficient common economic ground exists to enable these institutions to survive and fulfill their function in undergirding global economic interdependence.

Inattention and Bad Policy

The fact that the U.S. government and many others have made decisions since 1945 to lower trade and investment barriers, pursue domestic economic growth, and create and strengthen the Bretton Woods institutions does not mean that domestic politics will necessarily continue to produce such positive outcomes. Governments can unlearn lessons that appeared to be firmly in place. Economists, for example, have pushed the idea that free trade is beneficial ever since the time of David Ricardo, the famous British economist of the early nineteenth century. Since 1945, many governments have endorsed this idea by lowering trade barriers. Yet there is a long-standing political problem associated with this process—the pain that comes from opening markets at home is concentrated in and visible to the companies and workers in the industries that lose out because of the lowered protection, whereas the gain to the economy from increased exports in areas where the other countries have lowered barriers tends to be spread across many industries and is so diffuse as to be largely invisible. There is always the danger, therefore, that industries and unions negatively affected by the lowering of trade barriers will expand their political clout and bring an end to trade liberalization. Many in Washington worry that such a shift in U.S. politics is underway. This danger should not be overestimated—a long-time observer of Washington trade politics, Mac Destler, of the University of Maryland, argues that the globalization of the U.S. economy has now proceeded so far that the ability and desire of U.S. businesses to obtain protection from the federal government has weakened substantially in the past two decades.[13] Nevertheless, it would be wise to reinforce this process; even as U.S. business becomes more global, U.S. workers become more dissatisfied. I return to this problem in the conclusion to this book and endorse the expansion of programs to ease the pain and costs of adjustments to expanding trade.

There is also the question of pushing misguided policies at multilateral organizations. U.S. policy has drifted toward a more ideological commitment to free markets, and the U.S. government has pressed for more emphasis on such policies at the World Bank and the IMF since the 1980s. Although markets are critically important to successful economies, there is a danger of seeing them as the universal solution. The history of U.S. and European capitalism (discussed in chapter 1) included important modifications to contain the undesirable social and economic results of unfettered markets. It would be a shame if the U.S. government unlearned these lessons and foisted a flawed vision of unfettered markets on the developing world.

The danger here is in undermining the global economic system with bad choices—even in the absence of a major unexpected shock, as considered earlier. If the U.S. government or others pursue bad policies at the IMF, World Bank, or the WTO, the commitment of other governments to these institutions could be jeopardized.

Noneconomic Issues

Human beings are complex animals, motivated by emotion as well as rational economic self-interest. Economists have often been criticized as viewing people as human calculating machines, constantly weighing the economic benefits and costs. Although this book intentionally focuses exclusively on economic issues, it is important to acknowledge that conflict in the world has important roots in nationalism, ethnicity, ideology, and religion.

Nationalism is based in part on the propensity to define the outside world as foreign, alien, different, repugnant, weird, or inhuman. During the Second World War, U.S. propaganda portrayed the Japanese as monkeys—denying them their humanity—while Japanese propaganda depicted Americans as devils. In each case, the propaganda campaigns had some resonance with the public because of the extreme ignorance of each society about the other.[14] Even today, U.S. understanding of other societies and cultures is imperfect, although it is far better than in the past, making it more difficult to whip up antiforeign emotions. Chapter 3, for example, looks at the rise in the number of U.S. students studying abroad and of international students studying in the United States—a process that enhances understanding of the outside world. Nevertheless, the past several years in the United States presents a sobering lesson in how an internationally well-connected society can veer in the direction of an antiforeign sentiment—reflected in the over-zealous effort to restrict entry for foreigners and in the almost hysterical effort to paint terrorists in the same inhuman terms that were used to dehumanize the Japanese in the Second World War.

Ethnicity has been another traditional source of conflict. The genocide in Rwanda, for example, provides a terrifying example of ethnic conflict. We do need to ask, however, what triggers these outbursts. Why do different ethnic groups manage to coexist for prolonged periods of time and then resort to violence against one another? One factor is often economics—when times are bad, blame the other group or take solace by improving one's own lot by taking jobs and assets away from the other group. When the violence between Tutsis and Hutus erupted in Rwanda in 1994, the country had experienced several years of recession and falling per capita GDP. In fact, in the year before the genocide, per capita GDP had dropped by 11 percent, a sizable decline in any society.[15] That is not to say that economic prosperity will eliminate ethnic hatred and violence, but it can certainly help reduce the probability of violence. The recent violence in northern Uganda, on the other hand, occurred in a country that has actually experienced considerable growth and development in the past two decades; however, the violent revolutionary group represented individuals who felt deeply aggrieved that the gains from economic growth had accrued mainly to tribal groups in Uganda other than their own. Thus, the issue is both economic growth and the distribution of the economic pie, with conflict fueled by excluding some groups from the benefits.

Ideology is another powerful motivator of violence. The confrontation between capitalism and communism from 1945 to the beginning of the 1990s was discussed in chapter 1. The victory of capitalism eliminated one long struggle over ideology. Reading histories of that struggle, we are struck by the fear and virulent antagonism to socialism and communism in the United States. Today, it is difficult to conceive of the federal government bringing out the U.S. Army, complete with tanks, to confront U.S. citizens. But the government did this in 1932 to drive out the Bonus Army (World War I veterans who had converged on Washington in that Depression year to lobby Congress for the payment of a bonus for their service during the war) on the grounds that the group was infested with "Reds" (who, in fact, were only a tiny presence in the Bonus Army).[16] Today, it is also difficult to imagine a return to an ideological struggle based on competing visions of the nature of the economic/social system. Capitalism will continue to evolve, and it will continue to vary widely across nations. The advanced countries have learned a great deal in the past two and half centuries about how to tame the beast, with economic benefits flowing widely throughout society.

Now that the U.S. fear of communism and the effort of the former Soviet Union to spread its revolutionary message are both gone, it is tempting to say that such ideologically based conflict will not return. Nevertheless, if governments manage their market-based systems badly, then heavy-handed socialism with state control over the economy could reemerge, complete with anticapitalist rhetoric. Bolivia and Venezuela have both lurched in this direction and now have political leaders openly critical of the United States and the other capitalist powers. Meanwhile, antiglobalism has emerged as a new populist ideology. Although antiglobalists managed to mount demonstrations at IMF and World Bank meetings, it is somewhat doubtful that this movement will emerge as a serious cause of conflict. The greater danger is that this movement could prove sufficiently popular to lead governments to alter their trade and investment policies in a more protectionist direction—an example of the problem of bad ideas mentioned earlier.

Other mortal ideological disputes mainly involve religion. The ability of human beings to adopt fanatical beliefs about the correctness of a particular set of teachings concerning the nature of existence and proper behavior is astounding. Certain religions at particular times develop sects imbued with inflexible positions that occasionally justify aggression on the basis of the righteousness of their beliefs. The current international terrorism is associated with extremist Islamic groups, but even the United

States has had a rapid rise of a form of fundamentalist Christianity that is extremely rigid and self-righteous. It is easy to deplore the violent terrorism of Islamic terrorists, but Americans should worry about religious extremism at home as well.

Religious activism has some connection to economic developments, with people turning to religion for solace in times when the economic uncertainty in their lives increases. As with ethnic strife, anger over a shrinking economic pie or perceptions of unfair shares in the economy, rather than matters of incompatible systems of belief, may be at the root of much religious strife. But why religious movements turn in extreme directions or condone the use of violence—whether it is Islamic terrorists or U.S. religious support for the invasion of Iraq—remains outside the pale of economics. We can only hope that the hold of extreme forms of religion is waning in the breadth of its appeal. After all, once upon a time Protestants and Catholics waged long bitter wars across Europe with populations sharply polarized and committed to their beliefs.

Closely tied to religion has been a near-religious belief in the United States concerning the very exceptional nature of U.S. society. Americans seem to believe that they are blessed, whether by divine design or secular accident, to have democracy, affluence, and the best ideas about how the rest of the world should be run. The arrogance that flows from this belief is stunning, and it is a source of endless embarrassment for Americans abroad, who must deal with the puzzlement, dismay, anger, and even pity of foreigners watching the United States from afar. In some respects, the United States is exceptional, but much of the arrogance stems from both an overly simplistic self-image and ignorance of the rest of the world.

Continuing Poverty

To the extent that armed conflict remains a threat in the world, the principal problem lies with internal conflict in poor countries, or international terrorists originating in or harbored by poor states. If religious and ethnic strife is connected partially or indirectly to poverty, then it behooves the U.S. government and the governments of other advanced nations to focus on the problems of poor countries. Chapter 6 provides a detailed look at these countries. Although the immediate crisis-driven response to some of these problems may necessitate military action (such as the invasion of Afghanistan), the long-run solution lies in pulling these nations out of poverty. To be sure, a wide gap between advanced and backward societies has been a feature of human interaction for at least the last 10,000 years, starting with the revolutionary spread of farming.[17] But the stunning growth in productivity in some countries since the beginning of the Industrial Revolution widened that gap immeasurably. This gap was certainly one of the reasons that the imperialist system arose—because rapidly changing European societies had difficulty engaging in economic exchange with much less advanced societies in other parts of the world. That is, killing local populations and taking political control of their territory was a simpler solution to the problem of buying nutmeg than working out a mutually acceptable set of rules and behavior.

Even today, the story of how and why economic change has diminished the prospect of conflict does not apply to all nations around the world. As noted in chapter 1, the circle of successful nations has expanded in the past fifty years, but it is equally true that these nations represent only a portion of the world's population. At the other end are a group of poor nations—Sudan, Afghanistan, Myanmar, Cambodia, and others. Very poor countries are often mired in internal strife (as was the case in Rwanda in the 1990s) or pursue the development of weapons of mass destruction out of fear that their obnoxious despotic regimes are threatened from the outside (North Korea). In between are some countries that appear relatively successful because they are endowed with large oil resources to export but that have badly mismanaged their economies and societies, siphoning off a disproportionate share of economic gains for a small ruling class (Saudi Arabia) or a single ethnic group (Saddam-era Iraq). Chapter 6 analyzes these countries in more detail; here it is important to identify poverty and economic mismanagement as major problems.

Impact: The Market for Oil

The global market for oil provides an excellent opportunity to see how the points made in this chapter work out in a specific case. This case cuts across the regions and countries considered in the next four chapters and provides a convenient introduction to their specific situations. And it is particularly salient given the rise in U.S. anxiety as oil prices rose sharply after 2004. So, let us look at how global change has affected the conflict over oil and other energy sources.

Oil (and energy in general) has a strong hold on people's imaginations. Without oil or other energy resources, we cannot live, which gives the question of supply an understandable emotional prominence. Of course, economists point out that we cannot live without food resources or the silicon that is used for computer chips, or any of a host of other basic inputs about which people do not seem to worry as much. Nevertheless, given the prominence of the issue of oil and energy supply, it deserves some consideration. The good news is that global energy markets work quite well and there is no reason to be fearful about either economic or security crises caused by problems of oil supply. The bad news is that some governments are in danger of unlearning the good news and returning to emotionally driven nationalistic policies.

Markets Work

Despite the emotional anxiety over energy supply, there are several important reasons why we should be confident that oil markets work reasonably well:

- The supply of oil is spread broadly (albeit not evenly) across the world, so that actions by suppliers to cut supply or drive up prices to disrupt the consuming nations for any prolonged period of time fail. Too many producers exist for the producing countries to collude successfully for more than short periods of time.
- Other energy sources can be substituted for oil, and in the longer run technological change enhances this substitution (ultimately moving us away from oil as supplies are used up over the next century). Indeed, given the urgent problem of global warming, this shift away from oil (and other fossil fuels) ought to be welcomed and accelerated.
- Oil is bought and sold in a global market that works the way economists expect; as prices rise, demand falls and supply increases (as new sources of supply come online).
- Since 1974, the major oil-importing nations have had a new multilateral institution that represents a significant step in the direction of cooperation.

Consider how these factors have played out over time. Because oil deposits are distributed unevenly around the globe, international trade grew quickly after the internal combustion engine was invented, and especially as very large deposits were discovered in the Middle East. Trade was disrupted in 1973 when the Arab oil-exporting nations temporarily embargoed exports to the United States and other nations that had supported Israel in the October Yom Kippur War. The embargo was short-lived, but the broader group of exporters known as the Organization of Petroleum Exporting Countries (OPEC) took this opportunity to triple the price of oil exports. The result was a temporary panic, including long lines of cars at often-empty gas pumps in the United States in winter 1974—even though there was no real shortage of gasoline at the time. The tripling of the prices, temporary supply disruption, and panicked policy responses contributed to recession and inflation in the industrialized nations in 1974. OPEC caused a second crisis in 1979 by quadrupling the price of oil at the time of the Iranian Revolution. These two crises in the 1970s seem to show the extent to which a group of suppliers can disrupt markets for political or other purposes. A more careful look at the response to the crises, however, shows six ways in which the markets worked and the OPEC quest for power proved elusive.

First, no single supplier country commands a sufficient percentage of global supplies to play a decisive role. Table 2.1 lists the shares of global production and exports of crude oil. Saudi Arabia stands out as the largest producer (13 percent) and exporter (17 percent), but it hardly dominates. Of course, producers can gang up and try to affect the market collectively, as OPEC did. OPEC is a cartel formed by a group of national producers in 1960 that can collectively increase or decrease production to influence prices to some extent. However, OPEC is a relatively large cartel, with eleven members, not all of which are Arab nations in the Middle East (Indonesia, Nigeria, and Venezuela are outside the region).[18] Since the 1970s, defections have been relatively frequent, casting some doubt on the ability of OPEC to artificially inflate crude oil prices very far above what the market outcome would be. The increase in oil prices in the 2002–2005 period, for example, had nothing to do with a tightening of supplies by OPEC. Rather, prices increased due to an increased growth in demand and unexpected supply disruptions (the Iraq War and the slow recovery of its oil exports after the war, for example).

The fact that it is difficult to use oil as a political lever does not prevent foolish governments from trying. In early 2006, the Russian government temporarily disrupted natural gas supplies to the Ukraine, ostensibly in a dispute over pricing for the 2006 supply contract. In reality, this move

Table 2.1 Global oil producers and exporters, 2004

	Producers			Exporters	
	Amount (million tons)	Share (%)		Amount (million tons)	Share (%)
Saudi Arabia	492	13	Saudi Arabia	333	17
Russia	456	12	Russia	228	11
United States	337	9	Norway	135	7
Iran	203	5	Iran	116	6
Mexico	192	5	Nigeria	112	6
China	174	4	Mexico	105	5
Venezuela	153	4	Venezuela	90	4
Norway	151	4	United Arab Emirates	88	4
Canada	146	4	Canada	83	4
Nigeria	129	3	United Kingdom	75	4
Rest of world	1,455	37	Rest of world	648	32

Source: International Energy Agency, *Key World Energy Statistics 2005* (Paris: IEA, 2005), 11.

appeared to have much to do with Russian displeasure with the Ukrainian government—the Russian-leaning presidential candidate had lost in a bitterly contested and fraud-ridden presidential contest in 2004. Unfortunately, the pipeline from Russia to the Ukraine also extends to Western Europe, so countries there also found their natural gas imports disrupted. Assailed by a storm of protest, the Russian government quickly relented and restored the gas flow. Just two months after the brief interruption of gas supplies, the Russian government had to reassure a meeting of G-8 energy ministers that it was a reliable supplier. The sharp questions from EU Commission president Manuel Barroso and others provided a lesson about the importance of reputation and the limitations to using supply cut-offs for political purposes.[19] Two months after that lambasting, U.S. Vice President Richard Cheney criticized Russian energy "blackmail" in a sharp speech delivered in Lithuania.[20] The lesson to be learned by the Russians is that their position as an exporter of natural gas depends very much on perceptions of their reliability. In the short run, they can possibly score points in their political relations with the Ukraine or other former Soviet states in Eastern Europe—but only at the cost of causing all importers of natural gas to rethink the extent of their reliance on Russian gas, to the detriment of the Russian economy.

Second, the crises of the 1970s spawned cooperation among the governments of the importing nations rather than angry confrontations among governments trying to maintain their own level of imports at the expense of others. Initially, for example, the Japanese were worried that the major international oil companies selling oil to Japan would divert supplies to their home countries at the expense of contracts with Japanese refineries, but that did not happen. More important, the governments of the major importing nations formed their own association, the IEA, in 1974 to promote the sharing of information and other cooperative activities. Although the IEA has only twenty-four members and, therefore, does not represent all the importing countries, all of the major importers belong except China (which has emerged as a major oil importer only in the past few years). Sharing information and discussing policy are one way for governments to allay some of their fears about the behavior of others, and the IEA has played at least a modest role in reducing anxiety among industrialized nations about their reliance on imported oil.

Government-level cooperation evolved in other ways as well, particularly where pipelines to transport oil or gas across national boundaries are involved. In spring 2005, the governments of Bulgaria, Greece, and Russia agreed to build an oil pipeline from the Black Sea to the northern Aegean, providing a means of moving Caspian Sea oil without routing vessels through the narrow and very crowded Bosporus Strait.[21] China and Japan are also competing to cooperate with the Russian government in building pipelines to channel gas to their own countries.

Third, the dramatically higher prices in the 1970s drove consuming countries to follow policies to conserve, stockpile, develop alternative sources of supply, and develop alternative sources of energy (coal, nuclear power, gas, and renewable energy). In the three decades from 1973 to 2002, the share of the total global primary energy supply represented by oil dropped from 45 to 35 percent as nations substituted other forms of energy for oil. Figure 2.1 shows change in the relative shares of the major sources of global energy.

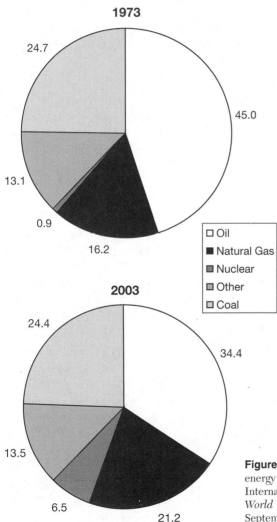

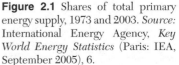

Figure 2.1 Shares of total primary energy supply, 1973 and 2003. *Source:* International Energy Agency, *Key World Energy Statistics* (Paris: IEA, September 2005), 6.

The bulk of the shift in sources has been from to oil to natural gas and nuclear energy. Although natural gas deposits are associated with oil, the large natural gas deposits in the world are distributed differently than oil deposits, so this shift in resources involves a somewhat different set of exporting countries. Renewable energy sources (especially the non-combustible ones in the category labeled "Other") remain a tiny part of global supply, although their role has expanded (from 0.1 to 0.5 percent); this should change in the future as the effort to combat global warming causes an increasing move away from fossil fuels.

Fourth, global oil exports shifted away from the Middle East as importing countries sought to reduce their reliance on a region now regarded as unreliable, and as the higher prices encouraged oil exploration and development in other parts of the world. From 1973 to 2003, the Middle East slipped from supplying 37 percent of the world's oil to 30 percent.[22]

Fifth, higher prices led to greater energy efficiency. On a global basis, efficiency has more than doubled since the 1970s, with kilograms of oil-equivalent energy per dollar of GDP (measured at purchasing power parity exchange rates), dropping from almost 0.5 kg to just over 0.2, as shown in figure 2.2. This shift represents more than a doubling of global energy efficiency in twenty-five years, a huge gain. The improvement for the United States, which had been notably inefficient (in comparison to countries such as France and Japan or even compared to the global average), has been especially large.

Sixth, the OPEC countries learned a powerful lesson about the limits of their ability to manipulate prices. The recession in 1974 and the stagflation of the rest of the decade in the industrialized countries hurt OPEC as well. As recession and slow growth cut oil demand, OPEC revenues suffered. And in the longer run, all the points discussed so far came into play, further limiting global demand for OPEC's oil and hurting their revenues. The OPEC countries could behave like any monopolist, gaining more of the profits from oil extraction for themselves rather than letting those revenues go to foreign firms. But just like an elite athlete (who possesses the resource of athletic prowess much like a country has oil deposits) who is negotiating a contract with a sports team, OPEC found that there are limits to what one can demand without driving the team into bankruptcy or causing the team to hire someone else.

These six aspects of the response to the oil crises provide very important lessons in how well markets have worked. Overall, global oil markets consist of a large number of both government and private-sector participants. Oil and gas deposits in many of the producing countries are

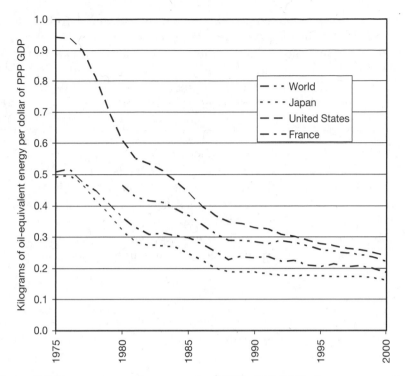

Figure 2.2 Energy consumption per unit of GDP, 1975–2000. Energy consumption is measured in kilograms of oil-equivalent energy, and GDP is measured in terms of purchasing power parity. *Source: World Bank, World Development Indicators 2003* (CD-ROM) (Washington, D.C.: World Bank, 2003).

owned by governments—although the right to explore, drill, and pump is often leased to foreign firms. In some consuming countries as well, governments own all or a portion of the importing and refining business, whereas in others (such as the United States) private-sector firms dominate. The fact that governments participate leads pundits to talk about the "great game" (a reference to British and Russian competition for control of Afghanistan and other parts of central Asia in the late nineteenth century) of global oil markets. But these government and private-sector actors all play their roles in a larger market in which the ownership of oil fields, drilling rights, and ownership of the oil after it leaves the ground are for sale. The oil that is pumped out of the ground moves around the world on the basis of supply and demand, some of it in long-term contracts and some through spot markets. Governments can try to increase dedicated shipments to their own country by buying oil wells abroad and limiting the shipments to their own country. But these actions have no real effect on global outcomes; if one country locks up a portion of its own supply, it demands less on the open market and leaves global supply and demand unchanged. This market may look messy, and it may provide colorful stories of unscrupulous governments and greedy firms, but viewed broadly, it works pretty much the way economists expect.

This point about the functioning of global energy markets matters because the U.S. government has raised the concern, in the official report of the National Security Council (NSC), that Chinese political leaders are "acting as if they can somehow 'lock up' energy supplies around the world."[23] But this fear is simply wrong. The Chinese can "lock up" part of their overseas oil supply (as have the Japanese and some other governments that the U.S. government has not singled out for criticism), but the market is simply too broad and too competitive for the Chinese to corner all the oil supplies they need. Furthermore, once they buy or lease oil and gas fields, they will expand exploration and drilling, increasing global supplies.

Problems

Despite the evidence that energy markets work well and cannot be manipulated very successfully for political purposes, there are some real problems, principally of two types:

• Fossil fuels are finite, and over the next century the world faces a difficult transition away from oil and gas that could be fraught with a breakdown of cooperation.
• Governments, faced with new temporary shortages could unlearn the lessons of the past thirty years and react in nationalistic ways, trying to preserve their access to imported energy at the expense of others.

Over the next century, the world faces an important transition. Given current technologies and consumption patterns, a path of continued global economic growth will cause the demand for oil to outstrip the sources of supply. Demand will rise, and the production of crude oil will probably level off or even decline (with at least some uncertainty on the supply side because no one knows precisely how much oil remains in the ground around the globe). This approaching situation is often described as a problem, threat, or crisis. However, it is really nothing more than a normal economic process.

As demand increases to outstrip supply, prices rise. This should not be regarded as a crisis; this is exactly how economists expect markets to behave. In the short run, the result of higher prices will be more oil supply (because the higher prices justify the added expenses for exploration and enhanced recovery from existing sources) and limitations on demand (from further conservation and diversification to other sources of energy). Governments can, and probably will, assist this process by adopting tax and subsidy programs to discourage the use of oil and encourage the development of alternative energy technologies. Governments may also choose to cooperate internationally, instituting joint research and development plans for new energy technologies or using foreign aid to assist poor countries in increasing energy efficiency. Talking about a crisis may help move the policy process of creating incentives for conservation, diversification, and new technologies along, but the main underlying driver will be the normal economic factor of a rising price. No one knows what sorts of energy sources and technologies will power the world a century from now, but we need not be fearful about the process.

Governments may—and should—adopt policies to accelerate the move away from oil and other fossil fuels given the evidence of global warming. Because this problem is truly global, governments have a strong incentive to cooperate in pursuing solutions. Even though the U.S. government refused to sign the Kyoto Protocol—the first multilateral attempt to deal with greenhouse gasses—we can assume that some other forms of cooperation will emerge over the next decade. These may include international cooperation on the technology of both energy efficiency and alternative energy sources. Given the rising danger posed by global warming, the long-term prospect for high oil prices as supplies fail to keep up with demand should be welcomed as a powerful incentive to promote the shift to nonfossil energy sources. And the need to cooperate reinforces one of the central points of this book—that the solution to the real problems facing the United States in the future requires cooperative behavior.

Governments, however, are capable of unlearning the lessons of past and behaving in less cooperative ways. For example, there was a tendency in the United States during 2004–2005 to view with considerable suspicion the rising oil imports of China and the efforts of the Chinese government to sign contracts or invest in oil fields around the world. The reality is that the Chinese economy is growing rapidly and has outstripped its domestic oil resources. Although China's large share of the increase of global oil demand created breathless comments in the media, we should keep in mind that the increase in global oil trade was only a small fraction of the existing *total* amount of that trade. In 2003, for example, China accounted for only 3.4 percent of global oil imports, compared to 28 percent accounted for by the United States.[24]

Why then was there such a negative reaction to the attempted purchase of Unocal, a relatively small U.S.-owned oil company, by the China National Offshore Oil Corporation (CNOOC) in 2005? The concern was that CNOOC would ship all of Unocal's production to China rather than selling it to the highest bidders in global markets. That may have been a valid concern, especially given that CNOOC was majority owned by the Chinese government. Nevertheless, the amount of oil involved was small—the sale of this company and the redirection of its output to China would not have had a material impact on global supply and demand. Furthermore, the rejection of this attempt by the Chinese to play the normal competitive game of buying and selling corporations only furthered the anxiety in China about the security of the oil supply and helped drive the government toward dealing with unsavory partners—such as Sudan and Iran.

Another troubling issue concerning China has been the dispute with Japan over the boundary between their respective territorial waters in the East China Sea, an area that contains deposits of oil and gas. Japan claims a territorial boundary line closer to China; China claims that the line should be closer to Japan. Unable to reach a bilateral agreement on either the location of the line or on cooperative exploration and production of the oil and gas reserve, the Chinese government began exploration close to the line claimed by Japan (but carefully staying on the Chinese side of the line). The Japanese, in response, threatened to begin exploration on their side of the Japanese-claimed line.

Because the fields involved extend on both sides of the line claimed by the Japanese government, in spring 2005, Japan's trade minister claimed the Chinese were about to "suck out Japan's resources with a straw."[25] This inflamed nationalistic rhetoric was unfortunate—and particularly so for the Japanese who appeared to have absorbed the correct lessons about the reliability of global energy markets since the crises of the 1970s (a subject explored in chapter 5). The reality is that the boundaries of oil and gas deposits rarely match the boundaries of surface property rights. What surface rights provide is the right to own what comes up from a well drilled on one's property. The statement also conveyed a sense that oil and gas resources are a part of national treasure and that their loss would hurt Japan—a dubious proposition. Japan has prospered without domestic oil supplies, and the amount of oil and gas at stake in the current dispute will not make much difference to the overall economy.

The Chinese, with some justification, felt that the Japanese move to drill next to the boundary line claimed by Japan was quite provocative. Whereas the Chinese drilling was to the west of the line claimed by Japan (that is, an area not in dispute), the Japanese drilling would be within the disputed area. The Japanese worried that the Chinese might take military action and considered using naval vessels to protect their operation.[26]

Describing this standoff, one news analysis described it as involving "a feeling, widely held on both sides, that what is at issue may not be just a few barrels of oil, but the whole future power balance in Asia."[27] That assessment is wildly off. Japan did not become a powerful economy by grabbing access to oil resources, nor will it lose power to China should Japan agree to cooperative development of the field or should the Chinese end up with the bulk of whatever lies below the ocean floor. For both nations, what matters is what they do to promote economic growth at home—with oil that can just as easily be purchased on global markets as developed in this particular spot of ocean. Even if the oil field were to yield billions of dollars of crude oil or natural gas each year, the net impact on either the Chinese or Japanese economy would be very small. The main beneficiaries would be the owners of the firms permitted to develop the field—a potentially lucrative gain for a small group of individuals (or perhaps parts of the Chinese government, if the development is run by state-owned enterprises) but a small matter for the economies as a whole.

The East China Sea case is an example of how governments can forget or fail to understand that confrontation is not in their national economic interest. In fact, government-to-government cooperation to settle the boundary would provide an obvious benefit to both. This is what game theory calls a "prisoner's dilemma" issue—cooperation is the best outcome, but with each side attempting to grab the entire benefit for themselves, the reality is no agreement and blocking strategies to prevent the other side from taking everything, so that neither side benefits at all. The two governments could either agree to joint development or reach agreement on where the boundary should be—the details of how much of the possible oil and gas fields end up under the jurisdiction of which government are largely immaterial. Each side (although primarily the Japanese) have allowed irrational nationalist sentiment to prevent what ought to be a relatively simple deal. The escalating dispute over exploratory drilling came, of course, within a broader context of nationalistic provocations on both sides. But the economic benefits from keeping the bilateral relationship intact are so substantial that is difficult to imagine that even this dispute will lead to a real rupture in relations between Japan and China.

Even without a major rupture between China and Japan over the East China Sea dispute, the general tenor of U.S. and Japanese responses to China's oil needs is disturbing. There is no surer way to turn China into a real threat than for the U.S. or Japanese government to adopt a posture of alarm and opposition to Chinese efforts to secure oil supplies around the world. If the U.S. government wants to ameliorate the impact of China's economic rise on global oil markets, then a far better way would be to engage the Chinese government in a dialog about improving energy efficiency and diversifying energy sources away from fossil fuels, because the United States has the technology.

A final oil-related problem where unnecessary conflict is conceivable is the protection of sealanes. Oil from the Middle East moves long distances by sea to consumers in Europe, North America, and Asia. Along the way, vessels pass through some narrow passages, including the Persian Gulf and the Malacca Straits. It is often claimed that U.S. naval power provides the guarantee of safe passage for oil tankers (and, more broadly, for all sea-borne commerce). We should ask, protection from what? There are two possible threats: piracy and war. Piracy is actually a relatively minor irritant. Pirates operate near land, so narrow passages such as the Malacca Straits are a place of some activity. To be sure, piracy has been increasing, with the number of reported attacks worldwide rising from ninety-two in 1994 to 471 in 2000, imposing losses on shippers of roughly $16 billion.[28] Some argue that terrorists (as opposed to run-of-the-mill pirates) are becoming a factor in piracy, but the reality hardly matches the purple prose.[29] Overall, pirates—operating at night in small motorboats—are hardly a threat that should be addressed by the might of the U.S. navy. The last time that piracy was of sufficient scale to require a naval response was the British naval campaign against English pirates in the early eighteenth century, and the U.S. navy's attack on Tripoli in the early nineteenth century. Today, piracy is a police issue, and the major responsibility for control lies with the governments of the nations in which pirates operate. The disruption of sealanes in time of war, on the other hand, does imply a role for naval forces. But that function does not mean that the U.S. navy provides any useful role in keeping sealanes open and safe in times of peace. Even in time of war, it is not clear that naval protection is always necessary.

A common scenario is the closure of the Malacca Straits (either as the result of armed conflict between countries bordering the strait or through some terrorist action to block the channel with sunken vessels). The straits are certainly important because a great deal of shipping passes through them, including all the oil moving from the Middle East to Japan, South Korea, and China. The straits are rated for 72 feet of draft (relatively shallow) and are only 1.5 miles across at the east end.[30] To begin with, blocking the strait would be a rather difficult proposition, even at the narrowest point, involving the precision sinking of many vessels in carefully arranged spots. Armed conflict between Malaysia and Indonesia seems remote—the two are members of the Association of South East Asian Nations (ASEAN), which has proven to be an effective organization in maintaining the peace and promoting cooperation among Southeast Asian nations. A terrorist attempt to close the straits or attack individual ships as they pass through is certainly conceivable, but the ability of any terrorist group to carefully sink a couple dozen vessels in precisely the right spots without interdiction is a remote possibility. The scale of operation and demand for precision is far beyond that required for the 9/11 attacks (and ships do not move as rapidly as planes—making interdiction far easier). Perhaps Indonesia, Singapore, and Malaysia could some day collude to charge a high toll for ships passing through the strait or even collectively close the strait in some policy dispute with northeast Asian countries. All these scenarios are highly unlikely.

Imagine, however, that the Straits of Malacca are closed. The world's oceans are interconnected—meaning that to get from one point to another by sea we can go a number of different ways. If the Straits of Malacca are closed, then ships can go by other routes. Other straits in the Indonesian archipelago exist—the Sunda Strait, the Straits of Lombok and Makassar, the Ombai-Wetar Straits, and the Torres Strait (between Indonesia and Australia). Taking these alternative routes would add distance for a ship traveling from the Middle East to Japan. Traveling through the Sunda Strait would add approximately 10 percent to the shipping distance to Japan, and traveling all the way to the south of Australia and up its east coast would add 70 percent. Adding distance has two impacts: on the demand for ships and on transport costs.

If each ship travels a longer distance for the same shipment, then more ships would be needed in the global shipping stock. At any given time, part of the global freight fleet is not in service—the ships are being repaired or simply are not in use. One estimate in the mid-1990s suggested that closing the Straits Malacca would eliminate much of the available excess shipping capacity—but would not exceed it.[31] Thus, this aspect of closure does not appear to be much of a threat.

The price impact of higher freight rates would also be minimal. Consider the case of transporting oil from the Middle East to Japan. The transportation rate per barrel fluctuated between $1.00 and $2.50 over the twenty years between 1980–2000.[32] Even taking the high end of that range, it represented only 5 percent of the overall price of a barrel of crude oil (at 2000 crude prices—so the percentage would be lower now). Thus, even if the ship had to travel all the way around Australia, this would add only a dollar or two per barrel to the price of crude oil arriving in Japan—hardly enough to have much impact on the prices of refined products such as gasoline.

The point here is that the closure of the Straits of Malacca would have relatively little impact on global trade because detours are readily available and the added cost of using them is not very high. Furthermore, scenarios in which the straits might be deliberately closed have a very low probability. This is an important point because concerns over closure of the straits is a favorite example used by those who believe that the U.S.

navy needs to be strong and ready to prevent anyone from disrupting passage—another case of a mistaken belief that the United States needs, and can use, military power to solve problems. In this case, the problem does not even exist.

To summarize, there are certainly episodes in which governments can or might create conflict either in times of supply disruption or during the longer-term shift away from fossil fuels. These responses, however, are both foolish and unlikely to succeed. Exporters keep relearning that their ability to use their exports as a political weapon is limited. Importers gain nothing through antagonistic government policies—whether they be discouraging Chinese purchases of U.S. oil companies or disputing territorial boundaries. There is no guarantee that governments will behave sensibly, but the lessons ought to be quite clear.

THIS chapter has argued that the fundamental economic changes in the world since 1945 have had a profound impact on international relations. The rationale for war among the industrialized nations has diminished. The world envisioned a century ago by Norman Angell or thirty years ago by Joseph Nye and Robert Keohane is much closer to realization today. Prosperity and rising interconnectedness without the curse of imperialism have altered both the issues and the opportunity costs facing governments.

This positive outcome, however, is not complete. Economic growth in the world has not raised all boats; conditions in some poor countries resemble those the prevailed in the past, with individuals and ethnic groups eager to profit by grabbing limited resources for themselves rather than enlarging the economic pie for all. And just because aggression does not pay, or because global oil markets work quite well, does not mean that governments will always make the best choices. Nationalism, ideology, ethnicity, religion, and just plain stupidity can be powerful forces. Governments, after all, are run by imperfect human beings who are motivated by many ideas, beliefs, and interests. In the conclusion, I take up the question of how to raise the probability of a continued peaceful world. Before we get to that policy discussion, however, the following chapters take a more detailed look at four important parts of the world and how they illustrate the points made in chapters 1–2: the United States, the European Union, East Asia, and the poor countries of the world.

3. THE UNITED STATES

The global developments discussed in chapters 1–2 generally hold true for the United States. The world we Americans live in today is very different from that of the mid-twentieth century—we are much more affluent and much more connected to the outside world. This chapter traces out some of the specific changes affecting the United States and how Americans interact with the rest of the world. Chapter 1 has already dealt with the increase in affluence, a story not repeated in detail here. Americans, too, are three times more affluent than in 1950. The story of this chapter is how this more affluent nation has become much more connected economically to the outside world. The general conclusion is that these developments are very positive—rather than fearing a loss of independence, Americans should welcome and embrace the economic and foreign policy benefits that accompany this thickened web of interconnections.

Nevertheless, being more interconnected with the rest of the world has brought new issues and concerns. Is the United States too dependent on imported raw materials? Is the economy losing jobs to cheap imports to the detriment of the domestic manufacturing sector? Is outsourcing of service-sector jobs draining employment? Is the large reliance on foreign financing a danger economically or politically? These are all questions that have raised doubts in the mind of the public about the nature of economic engagement with the world.

This chapter tackles six important issues:

- Rising exposure to trade in goods and services.
- Rising direct investment flows, into and out of the country.
- Other international financial flows.

- Increasing numbers of international students
- Increasing reliance on imported energy
- Macroeconomic issues: growth, the current-account deficit, and international debt.

Of these issues, the one Americans should worry about is the last—the performance of the U.S. economy and the sustainability of the large current-account deficit (and the resulting build-up of foreign debt), although even on this issue there is much misunderstanding of what really matters and what does not. The other issues discussed in this chapter are largely beneficial—although they often do not come across that way in the media. Understanding the facts, the benefits, and the dangers is important for dealing with the question of appropriate U.S. foreign policy, considered in the conclusion of this book.

International Trade

The United States is a very large continental economy. Historically, such economies were not very exposed to international trade—the large size of the economy enables a broad manufacturing base, and the large geographical size militates against the transportation of imported products to the interior. As a result, the share of exports and imports in the United States is well below the global average. Nevertheless, falling trade barriers and the transportation revolution have brought U.S. exposure to trade to historically high levels.

The data for the United States illustrate the slump in trade that occurred in the 1930s, reducing the relatively high levels that prevailed at the beginning of the twentieth century. Nevertheless, the United States is more exposed to international trade today than it was back in the heyday of trade prior to the disaster of the 1930s, shown in figure 3.1.

At the peak in 1920, the ratio of exports to GDP was 9 percent and imports to GDP was 6 percent, but these shares declined to levels of 3–4 percent from 1930 to 1970—a victim of rising import barriers in the 1930s, the Great Depression, the disruption of the Second World War, and continued high import barriers around the world in the early postwar period. Over the years since 1970, however, trade has risen steadily. By the 1990s, exports were up to 8 percent of GDP (before receding slightly to 7 percent in the past several years) and imports have grown to over 12 percent. Thus, although exports have not risen quite to the level of the early twentieth century, imports are now double their earlier peak.

Services trade has also risen rapidly, even faster than merchandise trade. The amounts are smaller, despite the huge hype about outsourcing

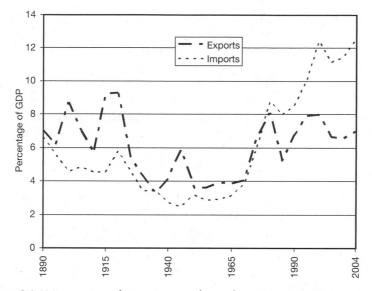

Figure 3.1 U.S. exports and imports as a share of GDP, 1890–2004. *Sources:* U.S. Department of Commerce, *Historical Statistics of the U.S. Colonial Times to 1970* (Washington, D.C.: U.S. Government Printing Office, 1975), 224, 864–65; U.S. Department of Commerce, *Statistical Abstract of the United States 1997* (Washington, D.C.: U.S. Government Printing Office, 1997), 800; U.S. Department of Commerce, *Statistical Abstract of the United States 2003* (Washington, D.C.: U.S. Government Printing Office, 2003), 438, 813.

service-sector jobs, with services 40 percent the size of merchandise exports in 2004 and imports 18 percent.[1] Nevertheless, their importance is rising. In the years since 1986, exports of services rose from 1.7 percent of GDP to 2.6 percent by 2004, whereas imports rose from 1.5 to 2.0 percent.[2]

The rise of services trade has caused much anxiety in the United States. Suddenly people think that their jobs are vulnerable to being moved offshore—an uneasiness inflamed by journalistic books such as Thomas Friedman's *The World Is Flat*.[3] However, more sober analyses indicate that the rise of services trade has had a relatively muted impact on U.S. employment. First, the actual number of jobs that can be identified as moving abroad is relatively small. One estimate is that about 274,000 jobs moved to India during the four-year period 2000–2004 (or roughly 55,000 jobs per year); this was a period of time when the U.S. economy created an average of over 300,000 net new jobs in the domestic service sector each year, despite the slump in the economy in 2001 and the very slow recovery of employment after the recession.[4] Second, many jobs cannot be exported (haircutting, construction, restaurant, and the like).

A McKinsey study of the possibilities for offshoring over the next thirty years came up with only 9 percent of U.S. service-sector jobs that could be theoretically exported and concluded that many of even these jobs will probably remain at home.[5]

Meanwhile, note that the United States has a surplus on services trade—$65 billion in 2004. This means that, despite the hysteria in the media about outsourcing U.S. service-sector jobs, the United States creates more jobs through services exports than it loses through imports. Although U.S. firms may be outsourcing call centers and software engineering, other countries are outsourcing filmmaking to Hollywood, financial services to U.S. financial institutions, and even education to U.S. universities (a particular form of services trade considered later in this chapter).

What do these data mean? Adding services to merchandise trade, exports are now 10 percent of GDP and imports are 14 percent—these are modest but significant levels. Looking at the flip side, 90 percent of domestic output is still produced for the domestic market, and that production accounts for 86 percent of goods and services consumed domestically. Cynics argue that this means that trade is really not very significant in connecting us to the outside world. Nevertheless, international trade is no longer insignificant compared to the levels of the 1960s. These ratios should also continue to grow, especially as opportunities for trade in services widen.

The composition of U.S. merchandise trade has also undergone a fundamental change, away from trade in raw materials and agricultural products toward an overwhelming reliance on trade in manufactured goods. From 1900 to the Second World War, imports of primary goods (that is, raw materials and agricultural products) exceeded manufactured goods. Since 1945, however, the pattern has changed dramatically. By 2000, manufactured goods were an overwhelming 87 percent of total U.S. imports. Despite the oil crises of the 1970s, bringing a dramatic increase in the price of oil, the slide in the share of primary products was only temporarily abated. What is true for imports is also true for exports—in 1900, the United States exported more raw materials and agricultural products than manufactured goods, but by 2000 manufactured goods were 90 percent of total exports.

What do the changes in trade structure imply? The U.S. economy is tied to the world in a much more competitive environment than in the past. Instead of exporting coal to countries without coal, for example, U.S. firms export manufactured goods to markets where they compete against local firms. And the same is true at home. Rather than importing mainly oil and other raw materials, the United States imports manufactured goods that compete against domestic goods. Even firms engaged only in the domestic market often feel the heat of international competition—so the impact of importing 12 percent of GDP is actually much broader than the ratio of 12 percent of GDP suggests. Thus, U.S. manufacturing firms are now in a much more fluid competitive environment. Their success or failure at home and abroad depends to a far greater degree than in the past on competition with foreign firms. This shift has been painful for the workers and shareholders of firms that have not succeeded in a world of increased global competition. Anyone who has ridden Amtrak trains between Washington and New York has seen the old sign on a highway bridge over the Delaware River that reads: "Trenton Makes, the World Takes," with the old, shuttered factories along the track a mute testament to the fact that this is no longer true. Indeed, the shift has been sufficiently painful that the political support in Washington for further liberalization of access to U.S. markets has eroded and been replaced with an undercurrent of support for protectionism. Economists are almost in universal agreement that free trade is beneficial, so this decline in support for open trade policies is worrisome.

Direct Investment

International trade tells only a very partial story of the interconnections between the United States and the rest of the world. An equally critical component is direct investment—corporate investments abroad in which the investor has managerial control over the local entity. These investments are often complementary to trade, providing local marketing, distribution, after-sales service, and other functions.

The United States was, of course, originally founded as a series of colonies with investment from Europe. And in the late nineteenth century, another period of considerable investment occurred, particularly by the British. But with war and depression, the level of foreign inflows of direct investments into the United States declined in the first half of the twentieth century. As recently as 1970, the annual flow of foreign capital into the United States represented less than 1 percent of gross fixed-capital formation, as indicated in figure 3.2. Since that time, however, the inflow of foreign capital has accelerated, beginning in the second half of the 1970s. The pattern has been highly affected by the business cycle; in times of recession (as in the early 1980s and early 1990s), the inflow of foreign capital tends to drop sharply. This drop occurred again during the recession in 2001–2002. Thus, the 15 percent level of 1999 and 2000 was an unusual high. But even discounting this cyclical peak, the trend was clearly upward, and by 2004, the level was back up to 6 percent.

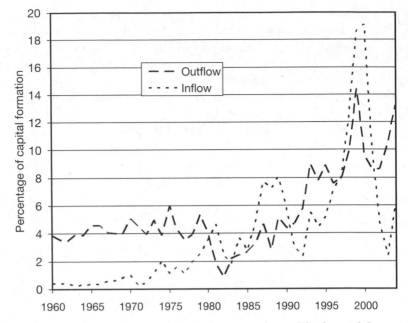

Figure 3.2 U.S. foreign direct investment flows as a share of fixed capital formation, 1960–2005. *Sources:* For balance of payments data, Bureau of Economic Analysis, U.S. Department of Commerce, available at http://www.bea.gov/bea/international/bp_web/ simple.cfm?anon=71&table_id=1&area_id=3 (May 10, 2005); for GDP data, Bureau of Economic Analysis, U.S. Department of Commerce, available at http://www.bea.doc.gov/ bea/dn/nipaweb/TableView.asp#Mid (May 10, 20-05).

A similar story characterizes direct investments by U.S. firms abroad. From 1960 to the beginning of the 1980s, these investments had been running about 4 percent the size of domestic fixed-capital formation. After a drop during the recession of 1981–1982, they surged to the 10–14 percent range. Like inward investment, the flow of outward investment was affected by the brief IT bubble in 1999 and its collapse in 2000–2002, but by 2004 the level was back to 13 percent.

Note that these ratios may seem low but are skewed by the choice of the denominator—gross private-sector fixed investment, which includes residential investment. Some corporations may invest in residential housing in other countries, but most foreign direct investment is in nonresidential activities. Subtracting out residential investment from the denominator in these ratios shows foreign direct investment to be a considerably higher share of investment in the United States, as well as of U.S. investment abroad. By this measure, inward investment in 2004 was 10 percent of U.S. domestic fixed nonresidential capital investment, and outward investment was 20 percent.

As with trade, we can turn these ratios around; 90 percent of fixed non-residential investment in the United States is by Americans and 80 percent of investments by U.S. firms are at home. Skeptics could argue that the economy is still not particularly closely connected to the rest of the world through investment. But keep in mind that much of the investment in any country is by small firms—the local plumber buying a new truck or a local bakery buying a new oven. Foreign investment is carried out by large corporations. In that portion of the economy, therefore, foreign investment has become quite important.

Consider, for example, the transformation of the U.S. auto industry. In the 1950s, foreign cars were a negligible factor in a domestic U.S. market dominated by the Big Three. German Volkswagen and then the Japanese auto manufacturers began to penetrate the market through visible levels of imports in the 1960s. Since the 1980s, foreign auto makers have invested heavily in production in the United States. By 2004, 43 percent of all cars sold in the United States were from foreign-owned firms (without counting Chrysler as a foreign firm, although it is now owned by Daimler).[6] For Japanese brand-name cars, 67 percent of the vehicles are actually assembled in the United States.[7] The factories of the foreign-owned auto manufacturers (excluding Chrysler) employed approximately 60,000 U.S. workers by 2005.[8]

Along with the increase in foreign investment in the United States, attitudes changed. When Arab nations recycled their higher oil earnings in the 1970s in the form of real estate and other direct investments, some Americans were alarmed. And again in the late 1980s, when the Japanese began a brief wave of investment in highly visible properties and corporations, a vague sense of unease arose again—the nation was being sold to foreigners. I was once asked on national network television news whether it was acceptable for a Japanese firm (through its purchase of a Hollywood film studio) to own the Awanhee Hotel in Yosemite National Park—as though the location in a national park made the hotel sacred U.S. property or that somehow the Japanese could take the hotel out of the country or make it available exclusively for Japanese guests. But at least the political system took no action to impede direct investments, and today the inflow is as high as it was in the late 1980s without any public or media focus. When Chrysler was in deep financial trouble in the early 1980s and might have gone out of business or been purchased by Mitsubishi Motors, the case was treated like a national crisis and Chrysler became the beneficiary of federal loan guarantees to help it through. But when Chrysler was purchased by Daimler in 1998, there was hardly any concern. And the financial problems of General Motors in 2005–2006 were treated like any business difficulty—something for the General Motors management to work our on its own. Automobile manufacturers, and their brand images, once regarded as icons of U.S. culture and economic prowess, today appear to be just corporations—as they should be. This positive trend was disrupted by the public and political outcry over the attempted purchase of Unocal (a relatively small U.S. oil firm) by CNOOC (a Chinese firm with majority ownership by the government), an embarrassing example of xenophobia discussed in chapter 2. In 2006, a similar outcry greeted DB World, a company owned by the Dubai government that had purchased P&O, a British firm with franchises to operate port services at six U.S. ports. In both cases, the foreign firms backed off without any legal action being taken. In the conclusion to the book, I consider further why this antiforeign reaction was wrong.

Other Capital Flows

Direct capital flows are the most visible form of international investment, but falling capital controls and advances in telecommunications have also led to a large increase in other forms of capital flows—involving bank loans, portfolio equity investments, bonds, derivatives, and other financial instruments. Chapter 1 shows how rapidly these have grown for European countries. The same is true for the United States. Until the 1970s (when restrictions on capital flows were being relaxed or removed by other industrialized nations), both the ratio of inflows and outflows of financial investments to GDP were less than 1 percent. Since that time, both have risen sharply, with inflows reaching 5–6 percent of GDP and outflows in the 2–4 percent range since the late 1990s.[9]

Keep in mind that these numbers represent net inflow and net outflow. Thus, they do not capture the increase in gross investment activity. That is, if Americans buy and sell foreign stock every day, but end up the year with only a small increase in their holdings compared to the previous year, it is only this final amount that is registered in the balance of payments. As capital controls have fallen in foreign countries, the daily volume of transactions, both buying and selling, has also increased dramatically.

Figure 3.3 adds up direct investment, other private-sector investments, and official exchange transactions, thereby showing the total capital flow out of and into the United States, again demonstrating the sustained increase in these flows relative to GDP. By 2004, the outflow was 7 percent of GDP and the inflow was just over 12 percent.

As financial markets around the world continue to develop, providing greater opportunities for U.S. investors to invest abroad and a broader number of foreigners to invest in the United States, there is every reason to think that these ratios will continue to rise. The same is true of direct investment—especially as the gradual liberalization of service-sector indus-

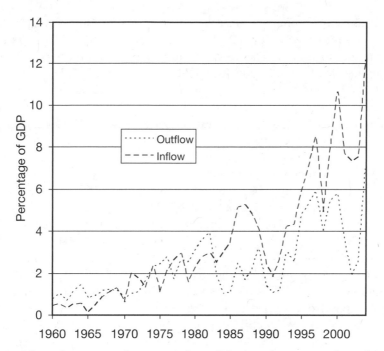

Figure 3.3 Total investment flows into and out of the United States as a share of GDP, 1960–2005. *Sources:* For balance of payments data, Bureau of Economic Analysis, U.S. Department of Commerce, available at http://www.bea.gov/bea/international/bp_web/ simple.cfm?anon=71&table_id=1&area_id=3 (May 10, 2005); for GDP data, Bureau of Economic Analysis, U.S. Department of Commerce, available at http://www.bea.doc.gov/ bea/dn/nipaweb/TableView.asp#Mid (May 10, 2005).

tries around the world opens greater opportunities for foreign firms to participate in these areas. Today, Americans deciding how to invest their 401(K) pension funds usually find that the financial institution chosen by their firm offers a considerable array of overseas funds. And the lesson of portfolio theory is to diversify into investments that do not have correlated returns—providing an incentive to add overseas investments as part of a prudent investment strategy. Financial liberalization, enabling more of these flows, especially in developing countries, remains a controversial question (taken up in the conclusion of the book), but the general trend should be one of continued liberalization as the financial sectors of developing countries become more robust over time.

International Education

One of the important ways in which the United States has become more connected with the world is through the flow of international

students—both foreign students coming to the United States and
U.S. students studying abroad. The U.S. Congress recognized the strategic
importance of international education immediately after the Second World
War when it established the Fulbright program in 1946. The Fulbright
program today sends some one thousand Americans abroad each year
while hosting roughly three thousand international students in the United
States.[10] However, the flow of international students today is vastly larger
than the numbers supported by the venerable Fulbright program.

Figure 3.4 shows the changes in the number of foreign students studying in the United States. From only 34,000 students back in the 1954–1955
academic year, the number reached 586,000 in the 2002–2003 academic
year, before dropping to 572,000 in 2003–2004. Back in 1954–1955, those
students represented only 1.4 percent of the total university student body
in the United States, but by 2003–2004 they represented 4.3 percent of
the total student body. The drop in 2003–2004 was a reaction to 9/11—
a combination of students choosing not to go to the United States and
more onerous visa rules that kept some students out. Finally, in 2006,
applications from abroad to U.S. graduate programs appeared to rise
from the previous year (up 11 percent in one partial survey) but remained
below the 2003 level.[11] Whether this upturn would yield a higher number
of actual students entering the United States at the undergraduate and

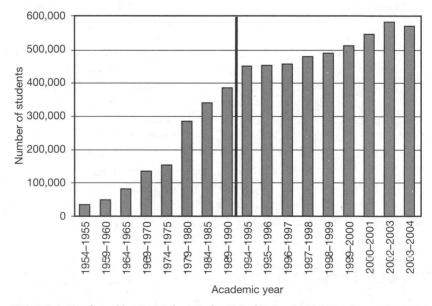

Figure 3.4 Number of foreign students in the United States, 1954–2004. *Source:* Institute
for International Education, *Open Doors 2004*, available at http://opendoors.iienetwork.
org/?p=28633 (May 9, 2005).

graduate levels, however, remained to be seen. The important point is that the actions to tighten up visa reviews had a noticeable impact on the number of students entering the United States from abroad.

The overall presence of international students in the United States might appear small as a share of the total student body, but in some graduate programs, such as engineering, foreign students are a very large part of the student body. The percentage of total Ph.D. degrees awarded to noncitizens is now close to 30 percent, in computer science it is close to 50 percent, and for engineering degrees it is over 50 percent.[12] Although these percentages have been stable since the early 1990s, the levels are very high and indicative of the importance of international students to graduate programs in the United States. On the one hand, U.S. graduate programs have become important for the training of students from around the world, especially in areas such as engineering; on the other hand, the programs themselves have become highly dependent on international students to provide revenue and lab assistants to maintain the high quality of the programs.

Students come to the United States from a wide variety of countries. As shown in figure 3.5, the top five countries of origin (India, China, Korea,

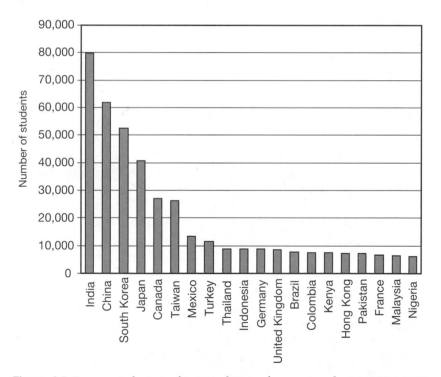

Figure 3.5 Foreign students in the United States by country of origin, 2003–2004 academic year. *Source:* Institute for International Education, *Open Doors 2004*, available at http://opendoors.iienetwork.org/?p=28633 (May 9, 2005).

Japan, and Canada) supplied 41 percent of the students in 2003–2004, and another fifteen countries supplied 30 percent, with the remainder coming from many more. For example, 62,000 students from China were studying in the United States in 2003–2004.[13] Although some of these students come from other developed nations, many of them are from developing countries, including (in the top-twenty list) China, Korea Taiwan, Mexico, Turkey, Thailand, Indonesia, Brazil, Colombia, Kenya, Pakistan, Malaysia, and Nigeria.

The number of U.S. students studying abroad has also risen. Admittedly, most of these students go for only a semester or one academic year, whereas most foreign students coming to the United States come for the duration of the degree program. As recently as the 1991–1992 academic year, only 71,000 U.S. students studied abroad, a number that had expanded to 175,000 by the 2002–2003 academic year.[14]

In a straight economic sense, the rapid rise in the number of foreign students has created a significant income source for U.S. educational institutions. The United States also has (or probably has) a surplus in our education trade because the number of foreign students coming to the United States exceeds the number of Americans studying abroad (although the size of the surplus depends on the relative expenditures on education here and abroad, as well as who does the spending—foreign students in the United States on Fulbrights or other scholarship assistance do not add to earnings from abroad). The role of foreign students is large enough so that when the number of foreign students dropped, U.S. universities were quick to complain to the U.S. government about what they perceived to be an excessive post-9/11 response to the problem of visas issued to potential terrorists.

The implications of international education are much broader than just the straight economic impact. Foreign students studying in the United States represent the elites of their home societies in many cases. Not all of them will form favorable views of the United States, but, for most, study in the United States is a very broadening experience. Most of them eventually return to their home countries and take both their education and their cosmopolitan attitudes with them. Moving into jobs in government and the private sector, they may not always agree with U.S. foreign policies, but they have a stronger understanding of U.S. society and know better how to manage mutually successful negotiations with the Americans.

Some portion of foreign students ends up staying in the United States. The United States has a long history of benefiting from foreign scientific talent—from Jewish scientists fleeing Nazi Germany in the 1930s to students being educated in the sciences in elite U.S. universities today. There are powerful reasons why these students excel—including the excellence of U.S. educational institutions and the combination of personal drive and perception of opportunity in the United States. The importance of the constant stream of bright students from abroad was, at least temporarily, forgotten in recent years in the zeal to keep out potential terrorists.

Americans studying abroad also provide important national benefits. As indicated in the section on direct investment, U.S. firms are investing more and selling more abroad, and these firms need a workforce with foreign experience and language skills to make them more effective managers in the corporate world. To be sure, multinational corporations can hire talent locally, but effective U.S. corporations also need internationally savvy U.S. managers.

In these ways, international education—of foreign students in the United States and of U.S. students abroad—has implications beyond the straight intellectual one of providing a better or more varied education. International education enhances knowledge of and experience with the outside world, reducing the sense of otherness about other cultures and policies, as well as providing a greater sense of humility about the superiority of one's own society. Hosting foreign students, therefore, enhances foreign familiarity with the culture and policies the United States (even if the reaction is not always one of admiration). The same holds true for Americans abroad—these students are an important resource for both the private sector and government—providing a larger supply of managers who can deal with an increasingly globalized business world and government officials who can handle relations with other governments on the basis of personal knowledge and understanding of their societies.

Energy

U.S. imports of oil and natural gas are a segment of U.S. trade that is a popular target for concern. Is the nation too dependent on foreign sources of energy and, especially, oil? Can or should the government do anything about this situation? As chapter 2 indicates, the short answer to these questions on a global basis is no. But let us look here at the specific situation of the United States.

The temporary Arab embargo of oil shipments to the United States and the subsequent tripling of crude oil prices by OPEC had a devastating psychological impact on Americans. I vividly remember sitting for several hours with a nearly empty gas tank in a long line of cars to buy gasoline in winter 1974, wondering if the station (or my car) would run out of gas before getting to the head of the line (they did not, and I made it). In reality, oil was not in short supply, but panic buying and misguided government policies to suppress price increases led to a situation in which some gas stations ran out of fuel and others severely limited opening hours. When OPEC raised oil prices again in 1979 the lines were generally shorter, but the psychological impact of the price shock was palpable. Americans' auto-dependent lifestyles suddenly became much more expensive and people felt as though they were at the mercy of greedy exporters, and especially Arab governments, with little love for the United States. As discussed in chapter 2, the 1980s and 1990s brought greater energy efficiency, diversification away from oil, and diversification of oil supplies away from the Middle East as new sources were developed. Anxiety faded but began to return by 2005 as tight demand-supply conditions pushed crude oil prices back up (although not to 1979 levels in inflation-adjusted terms).

To answer the question of how worried Americans should be and how foreign policy should respond, let us look at the facts. For most of its history, the United States relied on domestic sources of energy—wood, coal, oil, and natural gas. The fact that the nation was well endowed with energy resources was considered a national strength prior to World War II. However, since the middle of the twentieth century, the nation has outstripped its domestic energy resources and has become a net importer.

Figure 3.6 shows the changes in net imports of energy resources since 1950. At that time, the United States was still a small net exporter of energy resources (mainly coal). But rising imports of oil and (more recently) of natural gas have pushed the overall use of imported energy resources up. The trend was interrupted in the wake of the oil shocks of the 1970s, with a temporary drop from 23 percent (in 1977) to 10 percent (in 1982), but since then it has climbed once again, reaching 28 percent by 2003. This includes a high import share for petroleum, with imports supplying 66 percent of domestic demand by 2003. Furthermore, although natural gas imports remained fairly low (13 percent of total domestic demand in 2003), all expectations are that imports will rise rapidly in coming years.

The data in figure 3.6 actually do not give a complete picture of import dependency because the import data do not include uranium. As of 2003, electric power generated by nuclear power plants was 11 percent of total energy supply.[15] When nuclear energy was in its infancy, imports supplied most of the uranium supply, but as domestic mines came into production, the United States actually became a net exporter throughout the 1970s. By 2003, however, domestic production had dwindled and imports had returned to a high level—close to 100 percent of domestic consumption.

The main conclusion to draw from these data is that the United States is inextricably reliant on the rest of the world for a significant and rising

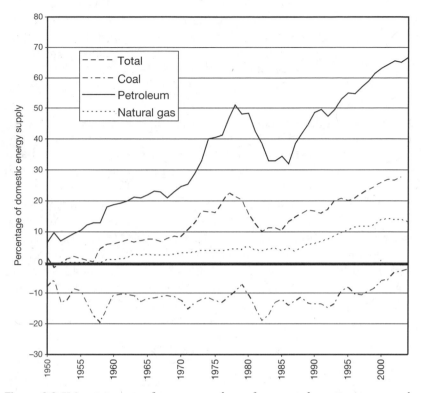

Figure 3.6 U.S. net imports of energy as a share of apparent domestic energy supply, 1950–2005. *Source:* Energy Information Administration, U.S. Department of Energy, available at http://www.eia.doe.gov/neic/historic/hsupply.htm (April 25, 2005).

share of its primary energy resources. Policies to reduce imports can affect this situation at the margin, but it is unrealistic to believe that different policies could produce independence on energy (at least until a time in the future when solar, wind, and other sources of primary energy become more important as the economy shifts away from fossil fuels). Therefore, Americans should accept the use of energy imports and consider how to reduce the accompanying sense of insecurity. Chapter 2 concludes that global oil and other energy markets work rather well, so worries over energy imports are overblown.

There are two substantive issues involved in energy supply: price and availability. On price, U.S. reliance on imports is irrelevant to what happens in the United States. Oil (and natural gas and uranium) trades in global markets, so the price in the U.S. market is determined by global supply and demand regardless of whether the nation imports all of its oil or none at all. After all, if the U.S. government tried to suppress the domestic price below the global level, U.S. companies would have an incentive to sell their supplies abroad rather than at home. To think, therefore, that Americans can buy independence from global price developments is illusory.

The second issue is availability—at any price. Is the nation at the mercy of foreign oil producers who can threaten U.S. economic well-being as a bargaining tool in foreign policy? The key factor in answering this question is the number of suppliers. A single supplier, or a very small number of suppliers, might be able to conspire to withhold sales—as the oil-producing Arab countries in the Middle East did in 1973. But U.S. imports match the pattern shown in chapter 2 for the world as a whole; the United States imports energy—petroleum, natural gas, and uranium—from a fairly wide variety of sources. Figure 3.7 shows, for example, the top suppliers of crude petroleum to the United States. In 2002, 95 percent of U.S. petroleum imports came from seventeen countries. Four of them stand out—Saudi Arabia, Mexico, Canada, and Venezuela—but each of these countries had 16 percent or less of the market. To be sure, the members of OPEC in total supplied 45 percent of U.S. imports. Chapter 2 shows, however, that OPEC has had only limited success in operating as a tight cartel. If oil were analyzed like any other product market, economists would conclude that it ought to operate in a

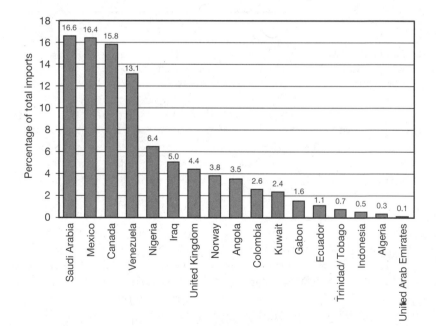

Figure 3.7 Sources of U.S. petroleum imports, 2002. *Source:* U.S. Department of Commerce, *Statistical Abstract of the United States: 2003* (Washington, D.C.: U.S. Government Printing Office, 2003), 590.

reasonably competitive manner, given the number of producers and the dispersion of production among them.

Diversity of sources also applies to other kinds of energy. For natural gas, the overwhelming source of imports has been Canada (87 percent of total imports in 2003). Should Americans worry about monopolistic behavior by Canadian producers? Uranium comes primarily from a set of seven countries (dominated by Canada, Australia, and Russia). These two sets of countries are different from the set of oil exporters—further reducing the risk in relying on imported energy in general. That is, although the suppliers of one kind of energy might try to collude, the possibility of alliances across kinds of energy is remote.

These data suggest that any single supplier or small group of suppliers of oil, or other types of energy resources, has only a limited ability to disrupt U.S. lives. The situation in winter 1974 seemed dire at the time, with gasoline shortages, inflation, and recession, but U.S. policy mistakes (suppressing the price of oil temporarily and then allowing general inflation to rise) were equally responsible. In the longer run, the opportunities to respond to the crisis through the policies considered in chapter 2 (such as conservation, switching suppliers, or substituting other forms of energy) meant that the pain of the disruptions was relatively short-lived. Should such a crisis strike again, Americans would undoubtedly feel that a catastrophe was occurring, but a mild recession and modest overall inflation for a brief time are all that should occur. This conclusion does not even take into account the limited ability of some of the key suppliers—particularly in the Middle East—to embargo exports of oil without seriously disrupting their own export-dependent economies (considered further in chapter 6).

Despite this upbeat conclusion, economists do recognize one serious problem in all these energy markets—the lag between changes in demand and the response of supply. Drilling for new sources of oil and gas, bringing these sources into production, and transporting the output all take time. Therefore, it is possible to have times when demand outstrips supply and prices increase—with or without deliberate actions by antagonistic supplier nations. The U.S. government can help moderate the negative impact of these price increases through the promotion of energy conservation, expansion of domestic supply, and release of stockpiles. But the main source of adjustment comes from the private sector, where both demand and output will adjust appropriately to price movements over time. In the interim, people feel the pinch of higher prices or even lower economic growth, but these diminish as markets adjust.

For all these reasons, the U.S. sense of anxiety and vulnerability stemming from imported oil is overdone. The very notion of independence from imported energy is illusory, at least for the next several decades. A greater reliance on domestic energy sources would not isolate the U.S. economy from global energy price developments anyway. Embargoes of supply used as a bargaining tool in foreign policy disputes are certainly possible—as in 1973—but they hardly threaten the U.S. way of life. In addition, no one should believe that possession of military might—and the threatened or actual use of it—matters very much in assuring the reliability of supply. Some believe that the invasion of Iraq is "all about the oil." That belief is probably incorrect, but if oil concerns fed at all into the decision to invade Iraq in 2003, it was a mistake.

U.S. Economic Performance

Finally, several aspects of U.S. domestic economic performance have important implications for international relations and the conduct of foreign policy: overall economic growth, macroeconomic imbalances (the current-account deficit), and the rising foreign ownership of U.S. government debt. Because the United States is such a large part of the global economy—roughly 25 percent of global GDP—the performance of the U.S. economy has a major impact on overall global economic developments and on the effectiveness of U.S. foreign policy.

Overall Performance

Despite the recession of 2001, U.S. economic performance has continued to be strong. In the ten-year period of 1996–2005, U.S. real GDP growth averaged 3.3 percent—higher than the 2.9 percent of the preceding decade (1986–1995). This acceleration was propelled by an improvement in productivity growth. This improvement is visible in crude terms in the performance of GDP per capita, the growth of which accelerated from an annual real increase of 1.7 percent in 1986–1995 to 2.2 percent in 1996–2005.[16] These are healthy rates of increase in overall affluence for a mature industrial nation.

Nevertheless, there are some worrisome signs. Despite the strong economic recovery since the recession of 2001, the public mood remains sour. Household income growth has been weak, income and wealth disparities have increased, some companies have reneged on pension benefits, and current and retired workers face cutbacks in corporate-provided health-care benefits. Just to give one example, indicators of income disparity in the United States have been widening for several decades, and U.S. income distribution is less equal than in any other industrialized nation.[17] People who are dissatisfied and anxious about their personal lives are more likely to support bad policy ideas such as protectionism.

U.S. economic performance also affects the government's ability to push its foreign policy initiatives—both international economic policies and diplomatic and security policy. Joseph Nye calls this "soft power"— power or influence that flows from national reputation and performance.[18] In one sense, the U.S. government has disproportionate influence over other countries simply because of economic size; governments that spurn U.S. policy initiatives may fear that their privileged access to the world's largest market might be jeopardized. This aspect of soft power should not be overemphasized, however. As any trade negotiator knows, foreign governments constantly push the boundaries of what they can get away with, knowing that the U.S. government's ability to reduce their access to U.S. markets is actually quite limited. Nor is it likely that the French or German governments felt that their opposition to the Iraq War would have any repercussions for their economic relationship with the United States. But size certainly matters if, for example, Middle East oil producers contemplate an embargo like that of 1973—if their actions push their largest export market into recession (thereby cutting demand for oil) they will end up hurting themselves.

Perhaps more important is the intangible impact of economic performance on reputation. Is the United States an enviable economic model performing so well that other governments are willing to listen to and accede to the policies pushed by the U.S. government? Americans seem to think that being "the land of opportunity" is a sufficiently powerful image for international status and reputation to remain high. Personal economic opportunity is indeed a powerful image, one that motivates a continuing flow of immigrants (both legal and illegal). But diplomacy and international negotiations are conducted by policy elites who are perfectly content to live in their own countries. For many of these people around the world, the highly visible flaws and problems producing the sour mood in the United States leads to skepticism or contempt. The United States is the only major industrialized nation without a national health-care system, and a significant minority of the population has no health-care insurance at all. The United States has greater income and wealth inequality than other major industrial nations—including a highly visible pool of very poor people. Workers in the United States face greater uncertainty in employment than in most other major nations. Although some of these images, such as job uncertainty or income inequality, may be a necessary corollary to being "the land of opportunity" and an economy that can respond flexibly to new challenges, they provide a distinctly negative image abroad—as I know well from many conversations in Japan and elsewhere in Asia over the past thirty-five years. The Japanese are reforming their own economy, but most of them have no desire whatsoever to be a clone of the U.S. economy and have great disdain for what they perceive as the unsavory aspects of U.S. capitalism. In the conclusion, I return to this issue of U.S. economic performance and what should be changed to maintain growth and reduce the social costs of flexibility and opportunity.

Macroeconomic Imbalances

A more technical issue is the large and increasing current-account deficit. Figure 3.8 shows changes in the U.S. current-account balance with the world.

In the balance-of-payments accounting framework, the current account includes trade in goods and services, repatriation of earnings on international investments, and unilateral transfers (that is, foreign aid grants and remittances). In accounting terms, for the balance of payments as a whole, what enters the country necessarily equals what leaves it. In addition

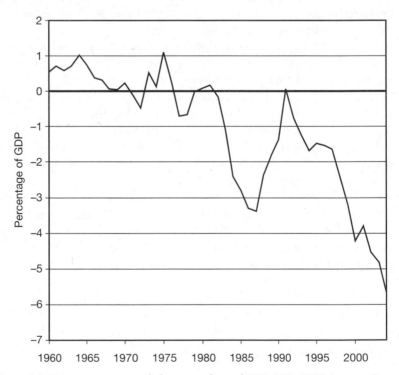

Figure 3.8 U.S. current-account balance as a share of GDP, 1960–2005. *Sources:* Current account data from Bureau of Economic Analysis, U.S. Department of Commerce, available at ttp://www.bea.gov/bea/international/bp_web/simple.cfm?anon=71&table_id=1&area_id=3 (May 10, 2005); GDP data from http://www.bea.doc.gov/bea/dn/nipaweb/TableView.asp#Mid (May 10, 2005).

to the items included in the current account, the balance-of-payments accounting framework includes capital flows (consisting primarily of direct investment, portfolio equity investments, bonds, bank loans, and the foreign exchange holdings of central banks). Therefore, if the nation has a deficit on the current account, then there will necessarily be a corresponding net inflow of capital. Conversely, if a nation has a current-account surplus, there will be an offsetting net outflow of capital. This is not economic theory but the simple reality of the accounting framework—the bottom line is zero. Put another way, if there is a U.S. current-account deficit, then the rest of the world chose not to buy as many goods and services from the United States as they sold to it, leaving them with a pile of dollars. Because they did not use the dollars to buy goods and services, they must have chosen to buy something else: financial and real assets that represent a capital flow.

Through much of the twentieth century the United States had a current-account surplus, but as figure 3.8 shows, the country has had a deficit since 1982. After a temporary surplus due to the Gulf War (with payments to the United States from Japan and elsewhere to help pay for the war), this deficit has increased dramatically as a share of GDP. The deficit was 6 percent of GDP by 2005—a number that may seem small but is very large for this particular economic balance. Some small nations have occasionally had current-account imbalances that are much larger (Greece in the 1970s once had a deficit on the order of 14 percent of GDP), but this is highly unusual for a large economy.

How did this happen? Economists have many competing explanations.[19] But the essence is to realize that an economy is a complex organism of many parts, with independent developments in each (which economists call exogenous factors) affecting the whole, and with the domestic economy interacting in equally complex ways with the rest of the world. Within an economy, savings, investment, the government fiscal balance, and the net balance with the rest of the world (the current-account balance and the offsetting movement of capital), all jockey up and down to balance out with one another. One way to view these interactions is to begin with domestic investment. Economies grow by investing in capital stock—such as factories, office buildings, houses, and roads. The money to finance these investments comes from savings, either domestic savings or savings from abroad. Societies that save more than they want to invest end up putting those savings into investments abroad (which shows up in the balance of payments as a current-account surplus and an offsetting net capital outflow). Those societies that want to invest more than they want to save end up absorbing savings from abroad to fill the gap (which shows up in the balance of payments as a current-account deficit and an offsetting net capital inflow). There is nothing wrong in depending on foreign sources of financing for domestic investment. However, economists worry that if the level of dependence on foreign financing rises to high levels, the situation may not be sustainable for very long because of the need to repay the foreign investors.

In the case of the United States, the past several decades show a level of domestic investment that exceeded the supply of domestic savings. There are several reasons for this, including a sagging household savings rate and an increased deficit of the federal government (making it a larger net absorber of domestic savings). As a result, since 1982 the United States has experienced the current-account deficit and net inflow of capital from abroad shown in figure 3.8. At the same time, some parts of the rest of the world have had more savings at home than investment, yielding current-account surpluses and the net capital outflow necessary to finance the U.S. current-account deficit.

The key question is whether this situation is currently sustainable—can the United States continue to experience a current-account deficit of 6 percent or more of GDP, or will it shrink? If it does shrink, how will this happen—will the process be orderly or disorderly? And, will there be international political consequences as well, especially if the process is disorderly? As is often the case, economists are sharply divided on the first two questions.

Without going into the technical details of the various arguments, some economists see no problem at all. Ben Bernanke, chosen by the Bush administration to be chairman of the Federal Reserve Board in late 2005, argues that as long as the rest of the world wants to save more than it invests (which he terms a global savings glut), the United States is naturally pushed toward a current-account deficit to absorb those savings.[20] Some economists outside the administration agree with Bernanke—notably Richard Cooper of Harvard University (who served in the Jimmy Carter and Bill Clinton administrations).[21] In this view, as long as the global savings are put to good use in real investment in the United States, everyone benefits and the situation is both stable and desirable. The United States gets additional capital investment to enable faster economic growth and the rest of the world gets a higher return on its savings than it could get at home.

The critics, however, argue that this view is wrong and self-serving because it conveniently absolves the U.S. government of responsibility for causing the size of the current-account imbalance or the need to change any policies.[22] In this view, what happens at home is just as important as what happens abroad, especially given the size of the U.S. economy relative to the rest of the world. The most noticeable change at home has been the rapid increase in the federal deficit since 2001, caused by the Bush administration's tax cuts and spending increases. Thus, the increase in capital inflow to the United States has not gone to finance private-sector investment (which would increase the productive capacity of the economy) but to finance the federal fiscal deficit. Private fixed-capital formation has been rather steady (at 10–11 percent of GDP), whereas the government-sector fiscal balance has moved from a surplus of 2.4 percent of GDP in 2000 to a deficit of 3.5 percent in 2004. Furthermore, within the private sector, the one area of investment that rose from 2000 to 2004 was housing—which does not have the kind of impact on productive capacity as nonresidential fixed investment. Therefore, the assumption that the U.S. is in a stable relationship with the rest of the world because money borrowed from abroad is being used productively (enabling economic growth and a sufficient return to pay back the foreign creditors) is not fully supported by the facts.

In addition, the notion of a world experiencing a savings glut is misleading. What has happened in the rest of the world (or those parts of the world with current-account surpluses and net capital outflows) is a decline in investment, not an increase in savings. For example, one of the principal surplus nations is Japan, where private-sector investment had dropped as the economy wrestled with stagnation and other economic problems over the past decade and where now the completion of economic adjustment and a rebound in the growth rate is causing investment to rise. Furthermore, a rapidly aging Japanese population is producing a decline in household savings. With a recovery in investment and declining savings, Japan should experience a falling current-account surplus over the next several years. Thus, Japan's recovery and similar shifts elsewhere in the world could well shrink the world's ability or desire to finance the continued high current-account deficits in the United States. Critics also note that much of the increase in the U.S. current-account deficit was not financed by foreign private-sector investors seeking a higher return on their money but by foreign governments amassing foreign exchange reserves to keep their currencies from appreciating against the dollar— an artificial policy-driven result rather than the stable outcome of market forces. This financing by foreign central banks eased after 2004 (because the Japanese government stopped intervening in foreign exchange markets), but remains substantial.

Finally, whereas the optimists talk as though the current-account deficit is stable at its current level, the pessimists note that the deficit has been rising as a share of GDP. Some predict that the consequences of Bush administration fiscal policies (such as making the 2001 tax cuts permanent) will be to push the deficit even higher—as far as 8–10 percent of GDP, an unprecedented level for a large economy.[23]

The optimists are certainly correct to argue that a current-account deficit is acceptable in principle, as long as it represents the international balancing of differing desires to save and invest around the world. But the critics are correct to point out that the United States is experiencing a deficit and capital inflow far larger than economists ever expected and that the flow is related in part to the rise in the U.S. fiscal deficit and therefore not contributing directly to the formation of productive capital stock. Financing the U.S. current-account through foreign governments building foreign exchange reserves—even if that factor has subsided from its 2004 levels—is also a sign that the situation is not stable. Therefore, the pessimists have the more convincing argument: the U.S. economy cannot continue its current trajectory of current-account deficits rising to and beyond 6 percent of GDP for any prolonged period of time.

Reducing the current-account deficit will require a combination of fiscal restraint and a falling dollar. Edwin Truman, a former U.S. Treasury Department official now at the Peterson Institute for International Economics, argues persuasively that such a combination, to bring the deficit down to about 3 percent of GDP, would be appropriate.[24] As the U.S. adjusts, of course, the rest of the world will necessarily need an opposite shift in policies—to stimulate domestic investment (perhaps with a more expansionary fiscal policy or lower interest rates) and appreciating currencies. Whether this can be done smoothly or will occur in a very disorderly manner with a crashing dollar remains in dispute among economists.

Finally, the importance of these developments for the central theme of this book is that they raise political questions. Large U.S. current-account deficits followed by a disorderly correction (with a U.S. recession and large currency fluctuations) imply that there will be a heavy strain on the international financial system and international trade. Will these strains produce a failure of the WTO and trigger a round of global protectionism—and associated political anger directed at those who choose protectionism? Will the financial strains from a crashing dollar and possibly sharp U.S. recession put an unbearable strain on the functioning of the IMF? It is not possible to answer these questions, and we can hope that the reduction in the U.S. current-account deficit does not produce such large negative economic outcomes; nevertheless, however unlikely major disruptions may seem, they are certainly conceivable.

Foreign Debt

Rising federal deficits and the lack of domestic savings to finance both these deficits and private-sector investments has led to a substantial increase in foreign holdings of U.S. federal debt. To fund its annual deficit, the federal government issues bonds, sold to the public. Foreigners have been major purchasers of those bonds in recent years, including foreign central banks. This has raised the question of whether those investors have gained leverage over U.S. policy because they could threaten to sell their bonds, a move that might cause U.S. interest rates to rise.

Figure 3.9 shows the share of publicly traded U.S. government debt held by foreigners. From 2000 to 2005, that share rose from 30 to 45 percent. A considerable portion of that amount was owned by foreign central banks—25 percent of publicly traded debt, or over half of the total foreign ownership.

On the surface, therefore, fears of political leverage gained by foreigners might seem justified, given the large percentage of U.S. federal debt owned abroad, and particularly the large share owned by central banks (that could act on the basis of their governments' policy decisions). But the first question we need to ask is how this debt is distributed among foreign owners. Figure 3.10 shows the distribution of ownership among the top foreign owners. In general, ownership is very broad, with investors in most countries owning less than 2 percent of publicly held debt.

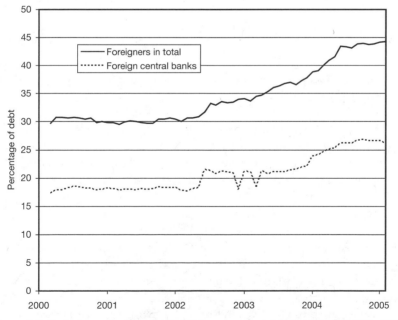

Figure 3.9 Percentage of publicly traded U.S. government debt held abroad, 2000–2005. *Sources:* U.S. Department of the Treasury, available at http://www.publicdebt.treas.gov/opd/opdhisms1.htm; http://www.publicdebt.treas.gov/opd/opds012004.htm; http://www.ustreas.gov/tic/mfh.tx; http://www.ustreas.gov/tic/mfhhis01.txt (May 10, 2005).

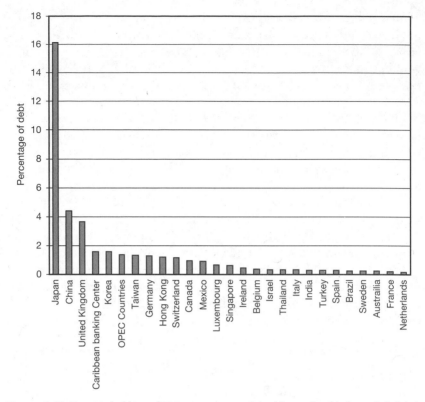

Figure 3.10 Foreign holders of U.S. government debt (share of publicly traded debt), 2004. *Source:* U.S. Department of the Treasury, available at http://www.ustreas.gov/tic/mfhhis01.txt (April 27, 2005).

Only three countries have significant ownership: Japan (16 percent), China (4.4 percent), and the United Kingdom (3.7 percent). For Japan and the United Kingdom, this ownership is a combination of private-sector owners and the central bank; for China, the central bank is presumably the only owner. If there is any question of leverage, therefore, it is really only these three countries that have gained it.

Of these three, the distinctiveness of Japanese ownership is quite startling, having amassed an amount of U.S. Treasury debt instruments far in excess of investors from any other country. The holdings by China and investors in Britain are small in comparison, although perhaps a 4 percent holding is enough to cause havoc in U.S. financial markets if the holdings were suddenly dumped. No one seems to worry about the British, but concern over the ability of the Japanese or Chinese to use their Treasury bond holdings for political leverage over policies ranging from trade negotiations to Washington's support for Taiwan is a recurring theme at Washington think-tank conferences.

The question, however, is: do these holdings really imply an increase in the leverage of these governments over policy decisions by Washington? Probably not, for three important reasons. First, in the case of the Japanese, much of the debt is held by private-sector owners, who probably could not be mobilized very easily to join in a government policy-driven decision to sell a large block of U.S. Treasury debt. Second, neither the Japanese nor the Chinese central bank made these purchases to gain leverage over the U.S. government; they made them to keep their currencies from appreciating. Therefore, a large sale would undermine this objective. The exchange-rate motive in buying Treasury debt has been quite powerful for the Japanese government for the past three decades. Although scenarios in which some other policy objective outweighs this desire to restrict currency appreciation are conceivable, they are unlikely. Third, U.S. financial markets are broad and deep. Should either the Japanese or Chinese central bank choose to sell a large block of their holdings, it is unlikely that either one of them would have more than a very temporary impact on U.S. interest rates. As interest rates on Treasury bonds and bills go up, other investors—both in the United States and from around the world—would be inclined to shift funds into the Treasury market. Meanwhile, the money the Chinese or Japanese pull out would need to be invested somewhere else, pushing interest rates in those markets down and further encouraging other investors to shift their own funds away from those markets into the U.S. Treasury market. This optimistic conclusion does not prevent Japanese government officials (including the prime minister) from hinting occasionally that they do possess leverage and might sell their holdings, but this political bluster should not be taken at face value.

THIS chapter has sketched out a number of ways in which the U.S. economy is now much more deeply interconnected with the rest of the world than in the past. U.S. individuals and corporations live in a very different environment than half a century ago. Because these interconnections are driven largely by technology and economic rationality, they should be here to stay. The U.S. economy will probably become even more open to trade in goods and services as barriers continue to fall and international competition extends to more industries. And until some new technological breakthroughs occur, the United States will continue to import primary energy resources. In the service sector, flows of students should increase as more of the world's population can afford to travel abroad for education. Because managing direct investments abroad is much easier today for both U.S. and foreign firms, the pattern of increased relative importance of both outward and inward direct invest-ment will continue. Portfolio and other forms of international investment will also continue to rise in relative importance as global capital controls diminish, technology evolves, and investors around the world become more savvy about international investment opportunities.

These rising interconnections with the world have had an impact beyond the narrowly beneficial economic benefits that economists usually discuss. If the United States wants to foster a world in which the political and economic elites of other countries have an informed, cosmopolitan view of the world (and perhaps with some of them even holding a favor-able view of the United States), then the rising flow of international stu-dents to the United States is important. In similar fashion, foreign direct investment helps to enmesh the investing countries in a new relationship with the United States. For example, back in the 1980s, some Americans talked about the danger of selling the country to the Japanese. But the reality is that Japanese firms, and the expatriate managers who came with them, became embedded in U.S. society. This gave them a stake in lobby-ing their own government to keep the bilateral relationship healthy. But foreign firms can do more than champion favorable policies toward the host country. U.S. firms investing in China, for example, are a force for positive change within China (better employment conditions, stronger rule of law, and better protection of intellectual property rights)—despite the uproar in 2006 over the behavior of Google and others in submitting to Chinese government demands on Internet censorship.

Meanwhile, some aspects of U.S. interconnections with the world are the subject of anxiety without much justification. Reliance on imported sources of primary energy does not make the nation dangerously dependent on suppliers who could cause havoc with the U.S. economy—nor would a lack of reliance on imports insulate the economy from global demand-supply developments. Similarly, foreign holdings of U.S. gov-ernment debt do not really give foreign governments leverage over U.S. foreign policy—only three governments hold enough to matter, and they have very good reasons not to dump their holdings.

Although the economy as a whole has performed quite well over the past decade, there remains a darker underside that undercuts both domestic public support for open economic engagement with the rest of the world and overall U.S. influence in global affairs. At home, workers losing jobs to outsourcing, or losing health-care and pension benefits as their employers chop benefits in response to international competitive pressures, find little reason to support liberal trade policies. And the image of an uncaring government presiding over a widening disparity between wealthy winners and the rest of society undermines U.S. soft power in the world. Meanwhile, the unsettling increase in the current-account deficit brings the United States closer to a day when there could be a very messy correction, with recession, sharp dollar depreciation, and slowdown or recession in other parts of the world that could severely strain or break the trend toward more open markets and free flow of capital. In the conclusion to this book, I return to the importance of facing up to these domestic issues as a nontraditional but critical component of strengthening U.S. foreign policy.

4. THE EUROPEAN UNION

The story of the countries of Western Europe that make up the European Union dramatically illustrates the basic theme of this book, that fundamental economic changes since the mid-twentieth century have had a profound impact on international relations. In spring 1945, much of Europe was a scene of grim devastation, with many cities reduced to rubble, tens of millions of people dead, millions of refugees, economic output severely reduced, and hunger rampant. Given the ferocity and extent of the human carnage that characterized the war, a new cycle of retribution, animosity, and renewed conflict would have been a plausible scenario. Indeed, such had been the outcome of the First World War, when heavy reparations levied on Germany contributed to economic chaos, the rise of the Nazis, and the outbreak of the Second World War. Instead, something quite different happened. A handful of visionary leaders sought to bring their nations together economically, in the belief that removing trade barriers and increasing economic interdependence would create a mutual embrace that would suppress nationalistic competition and conflict. That vision led eventually to the European Union, a group of twenty-seven nations (with more knocking on the door for admission as of 2007), with a subset of twelve tied together by a common currency. The path to the European Union of today has been a long one, with many doubts and setbacks along the way. Indeed, doubts and worries continue at the present time.

Western Europe has prospered and has become a sufficiently cohesive economic whole that a descent back into conflict is difficult to imagine. Of course, as with all human institutions, it is conceivable that the cohesiveness of the European Union could come undone. The end of the Cold War has contributed to this worry—much as it has for the Bretton

Woods institutions discussed in chapter 2—by removing some of the glue of political will that had underwritten the earlier determination to band together economically. This chapter takes up these issues.

The focus of this chapter is very limited, concentrating on the economic aspects of the European Union rather than on either the varied experiences of individual member countries or the political and security aspects of the European experience. Those topics are interesting but less germane to the purposes of this book. To be sure, although the European Union has brought economic integration (and even a common currency for a subset of its members), it remains a collection of sovereign nations, with separate languages and many national or regional differences. The story of each individual member is worth exploring, but to do so would require another book. Instead, this chapter explores the basics of the European Union as an economic institution and the implications of those developments for our themes.

The History of the European Union

For people across much of Western Europe, the Second World War was a ferocious and bloody tragedy of monumental proportions. Excluding the Soviet Union, some 6 million soldiers and 8 million civilians lost their lives in Europe, or 4 percent of the total population. The losses in the Soviet Union were larger, with 9 million soldiers and 19 million civilians perishing, a stunning 14 percent of the population.[1] Millions more were either wounded or barely surviving as refugees. The brutal behavior of soldiers on all sides (but especially on the Eastern Front), the cold-blooded extermination of Jews (and other "undesirable" elements of society), and the carpet-bombing of cities provided ample grounds for bitterness and a desire for revenge.

However, in the next several years, a number of visionary figures developed a liberal vision for Western Europe—building on the concept that a region with lower economic barriers and a closer economic interdependency might suppress a reemergence of nationalistic competition and conflict. In particular, the founders of European integration were very explicit about the need to bring Germany into a close economic embrace with the rest of Europe (and particularly France) for the sake of preventing future European wars. Jean Monnet of France is often regarded as the father of European integration; he was the author of the Schuman Plan of May 1950 (named after Robert Schuman, the French foreign minister—and former prime minister—for whom Monnet worked) that led to the initial step of integration. But there were others whose ideas and actions contributed to the process, including Austrian economist Friedrich von Hayek, William

Röpke (a German economist who fled to Switzerland when Hitler rose to power and remained there the rest of his career), and Ludwig Erhard (a West German economic minister under the occupation in 1948).[2]

The Schuman Plan called for what became in 1951 the European Coal and Steel Community (ECSC). This was actually a very modest step, involving only six nations and focusing only on a common policy for coal and steel production, but it was taken with the intention of "setting up...common foundations for economic development as a first step in the federation of Europe."[3] Table 4.1 shows the seminal developments in European integration since that humble beginning.

In 1957, the Treaty of Rome formally expanded the role of the ECSC, creating the European Economic Community (EEC). The EEC was to preside over the removal of trade barriers among the member states, forming a common market, the nickname by which the EEC was generally called. By the late 1960s, most internal tariffs and quotas had been successfully removed. In 1967, the institutions of the EEC were strengthened and several separate bodies were unified, creating a single central bureaucracy (the European Commission), a Council of Ministers, and a European Parliament (initially a rather toothless legislative body but important symbolically nonetheless). The members of the Parliament were originally selected by the national legislative bodies of the member states, but this was changed in 1979 to a system of direct elections.

Table 4.1 History of the European Union[a]

1951	Formation of the ECSC with six members
1957	The Treaty of Rome transforms the ECSC into the EEC
1967	The institutions of the EEC are transformed, creating the European Commission, a Council of Ministers, and the European Parliament
1973	The first round of expansion of membership, with Britain, Denmark, and Ireland joining
1979	Elections for the European Parliament changed from selection by national parliaments to direct election
1986	Single European Act (SEA) calls for a single European market by 1992 through removal of nontariff barriers
1992	The Treaty of Maastricht transforms the EEC into the EU with expanded areas of cooperation, including the planned EMU
2002	EMU goes into full effect, with a common currency for twelve of the EU members.
2004	A major membership expansion occurs with ten new members added, mainly from Eastern Europe.
2007	Romania and Bulgaria become members.

Source: European Commission, "Europa—The EU at a Glance: The History of the European Union," available at http://europa.eu.int/abc/history/index_en.htm (April 4, 2006).
    [a] ECSC, European Coal and Steel Community; EEC, European Economic Community; EMU, European Monetary Union; EU, European Union.

Meanwhile, an initial round of expansion in membership occurred in 1973, adding Britain, Denmark, and Ireland. This was a significant development because Britain was the third largest economy in Europe and because of the tendency of the British—living in an island nation sitting just a few dozen miles off the coast of the continent—to remain aloof and contemptuous of continental affairs. Arguably, pulling Britain into the EEC was just as significant as initially pulling in Germany. Table 4.2 shows the complete history of membership expansion. The biggest expansion came in 2004 when ten additional countries were admitted, mostly from Eastern Europe, bringing total membership to twenty-five. As of 2006, several others were engaged in negotiations to join, with Bulgaria and Romania becoming members in 2007 and negotiations underway regarding Croatia and Turkey.

Table 4.2 European Union Membership

	Date of Entry	Member of European Monetary Union?	Member of NATO?
Belgium	1951	Yes	Yes
Germany	1951 (1990)	Yes	Yes
Italy	1951	Yes	Yes
France	1951	Yes	Yes
Luxembourg	1951	Yes	Yes
Netherlands	1951	Yes	Yes
Denmark	1973		Yes
Ireland	1973	Yes	
United Kingdom	1973		Yes
Greece	1981	Yes	Yes
Spain	1986	Yes	Yes
Portugal	1986	Yes	Yes
Austria	1995	Yes	
Finland	1995	Yes	
Sweden	1995		
Cyprus	2004		
Czech Republic	2004		Yes
Estonia	2004		
Hungary	2004		Yes
Latvia	2004		
Lithuania	2004		
Malta	2004		Yes
Poland	2004		
Slovenia	2004		
Slovakia	2004		
Romania	2007		
Bulgaria	2007		

Sources: The European Commission: "Europa—The EU at a glance: The History of the European Union," available at http://europa.eu.int/abc/history/index_en.htm (April 4, 2006); NATO, "Welcome to NATO," available at http://www.nato.int/welcome/home.htm (April 6, 2006).

In 1986, the Single European Act advanced the goal of a single internal market by calling for the elimination of nontariff barriers, the opening of government procurement, and the harmonization of standards. The vision was to establish a fully unified market "embodied in the four freedoms of movement of goods, services, capital, and labor."[4] As of the mid-1980s, the EEC had failed to accomplish this vision, and the Single European Act was designed to clarify and codify the goals. Tariffs and quotas on merchandise goods were gone, but nontariff barriers (product standards and the like) remained, while little progress had occurred on liberalizing trade in service industries. Although the implementation was imperfect, some of these areas were liberalized by 1992, and others proceeded later in the decade. As a result of efforts to push the single market, intraregional barriers for service industries such as telecommunications and aviation were eliminated.

Airline deregulation occurred in 1997, with the result that intra-European airfares, which used to be abominably high, became amazingly low as new low-cost carriers entered the regional market and challenged the stodgy old national-flag carriers. The reduction of fares and entry of new no-frills private-sector airlines led to an explosion of intra-EU travel. Cross-border intra-EU passengers arriving or departing Germany, for example, rose 45 percent in the seven years from 1997 to 2004; for Britain the increase was an even higher 64 percent.[5]

The opening of intra-EU competition in the wireless telecommunications industry contributed to a wave of cross-border investment, with a series of regionwide acquisitions reshaping the industry. Vodafone and Orange (two new British firms dating back to the mid-1980s) emerged as dominant EU-wide players (albeit with Orange eventually being purchased by France Telecom). Deregulation of other sectors, however, lagged behind. As of 2006, the EU Commission was still struggling with the removal of national barriers in the electric power industry.[6]

The next major step for integration came in 1992, with the Treaty of Maastricht, which transformed the EEC into the European Union. By the 1990s, most trade barriers had already been eliminated, but the Maastricht Treaty extended liberalization to government procurement, service sectors, and movement of people, ratifying and extending the intent of the 1986 Single European Act. But the most ambitious consequence of the Maastricht treaty was the move to a European Monetary Union. The initial step toward monetary unification had begun with the European Monetary System (EMS) in 1979, designed to reduce fluctuations among member currencies. However, this mechanism proved vulnerable to variations in macroeconomic policy and inflation levels in the different member countries. Therefore, the Maastricht Treaty established a set of macroeconomic criteria that member states wishing to join the monetary union would be required to meet (such as a government deficit no larger than 3 percent of GDP) and created a single European Central Bank. The European Monetary Institute was set up in 1994 as an interim step toward a central bank, and the European Central Bank then replaced the Institute in 1999. The new unified currency (the euro) came into effect at the beginning of 1999 as an international settlement currency and was fully implemented in 2002, replacing the paper money and coins of twelve of EU members.[7]

In 2004, a major expansion of membership occurred (see table 4.2). More than a decade after the end of the Cold War, the European Union agreed to accept ten new members, with most of them (except Cyprus and Malta) from the former Soviet bloc in Eastern Europe. Indicative of the impact of joining, intra-EU air passenger traffic for Slovakia jumped 350 percent in just the single year of 2004 and traffic for the Czech Republic and Hungary rose 45 percent.[8] The decision to admit these ten new member countries was controversial; they were less affluent and had only recently converted to democratically elected governments. (I return to this problem later in the chapter.)

In 2005, the European Union devised a constitution that would have advanced political integration another step, but this effort failed to be ratified in some of the member states. The constitution would have brought member nations somewhat closer together politically by establishing an EU foreign minister. However, fears about the implications of the 2004 membership expansion (with enhanced competition from the new lower-wage member countries) appear to have left voters in no mood to endorse this modest move, and the constitution was turned down by voters in key EU states.

In addition to the initial desire to lock France and Germany together, another motivation for European integration was the Cold War. By 1947, the Soviet Union had consolidated its grip on the countries in Eastern Europe, installing communist regimes across the region and attempting to drive the Allies out of their occupation zone in Berlin. Winston Churchill's famous Iron Curtain speech of 1947 provided a symbolic beginning to this confrontation—as border fences between Eastern and Western Europe were going up, trade was largely choked off, and Eastern Europe became a political and military adversary for Western Europe. The founders of European integration were cognizant of the need to bury their own historic antagonisms in order to present a united front to the new military threat posed by the Soviet bloc. This legacy of the Cold War (from 1947 to the early 1990s) also helps to explain the popular ambivalence or opposition to the 2004 membership expansion; it let in countries that had been perceived as enemies for over four decades.

The United States played an active role in the European confrontation with the Soviet bloc, as the exhausted European nations needed U.S. military might to deter Soviet aggression. The result was the North Atlantic Treaty of 1949, which created the North Atlantic Treaty Organization (NATO). In addition to being a military alliance, NATO established a joint headquarters with a sizable bureaucracy to pursue joint defense policies. Membership in NATO is not entirely the same as in the European Union (see table 4.2); for example, Norway belongs to NATO but not the European Union.[9] Nevertheless, what matters here is that from 1949 NATO provided an institutional setting for European political and military cooperation (albeit with the United States as a major player) that somewhat paralleled the process of economic integration. Even though the Cold War ended in the late 1980s, NATO continues to exist, and, like the European Union, has expanded its membership to include countries in Eastern Europe that had previously been part of the Soviet bloc.

Positive Outcomes

Western Europe has prospered and integrated to a remarkable degree. Since the formation of the original ECSC, the liberal vision of Jean Monnet and others has been largely realized, with France, Germany, and a number of other countries locked tightly into a mutually beneficial economic interaction that has largely eliminated the possibility of renewed European conflict.

Growth

Figure 4.1 shows the growth of GDP per capita in the EU countries. Back in the 1960s, when some of these countries were either still recovering from the devastation of the Second World War or benefiting from the newly lowered trade barriers with their European neighbors, per capita GDP grew considerably faster than in the United States—4.0 percent for the fifteen countries that were members prior to the recent 2004 membership expansion and 4.6 percent for the original six members of the ECSC, versus 2.5 percent for the United States. Since the mid-1970s, growth in GDP per capita has been very close to that of the United States. Mature industrial nations do not experience rapid increases in GDP per capita, so the roughly 2 percent growth rate in Europe and the United States from 1980 to 2000 is what economists consider a successful performance. The lower growth in the 2001–2003 period reflects the recession that hit industrial nations in 2001, which affected per capita income growth somewhat more in Europe than in the United States. Overall, however, this figure shows that the members of the European Union

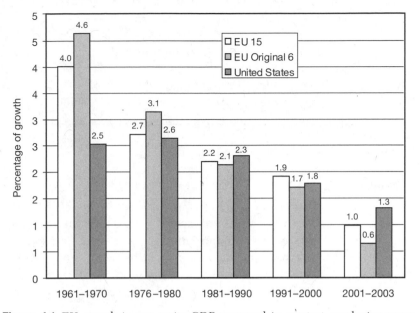

Figure 4.1 EU growth in per capita GDP measured in constant purchasing-power-parity (PPP) international dollars, 1961–2003. Because the World Bank's series of GDP measured in constant PPP dollars extends back only to 1975, the 1961–1970 growth rate is measured at constant U.S. dollars. The Bretton Woods system of quasi-fixed exchange rates did not break down until 1971, so there was little distortion due to any changes in the exchange rate between European and U.S. currencies during this period. Note also that Germany is excluded in this period because the World Bank does not provide data for Germany (presumably due to the lack of data on East Germany for that period). *Source:* World Bank, *World Development Indicators 2005* (CD-ROM) (Washington, D.C.: World Bank, 2005).

have done quite well, with growth rates in overall economic output per person rising above that of the United States during a period of catch-up and then continuing to match growth in the United States thereafter.

The success of these countries in terms of rising affluence is important. For much of the past thirty years, the media story about European countries has been one of problems and failures—"Euro pessimism," "Euro sclerosis," inflation, economic stagnation, and the like. However, the reality is that affluence on a per capita basis has continued to rise at about the same rate as in the United States. Because we think of the United States as being a successful, growing economy over the past thirty years, we should regard the EU members as successful as well. Those readers familiar with European economic performance may be shaking their heads at this point because there is a bit of bad news here as well—the failure of GDP per capita to fully catch up with the level in the United States (an issue that I return to later in this chapter).

What was true for the original six members or the larger group of fifteen should also now apply to the ten members added in 2004. Participation in the large EU market should boost economic growth as these countries catch up with the more affluent members. The anecdotal evidence on dramatically rising passenger air traffic with the rest of the European Union for Hungary, Slovakia, and the Czech Republic is indicative of what should happen. Low wages will also attract investment—from both other EU members and the rest of the world—to produce goods for the European market.

Trade

The purpose of European integration was to promote increased trade, and figure 4.2 looks at the proportion of exports and imports that represents intra-EU trade. As is obvious from the data, that proportion has risen dramatically. Look first at the original six members of the ECSC. For them, the proportion of their imports sourced from other members of the original six doubled from 25 percent in 1950 to 50 percent by the early 1970s. Exports

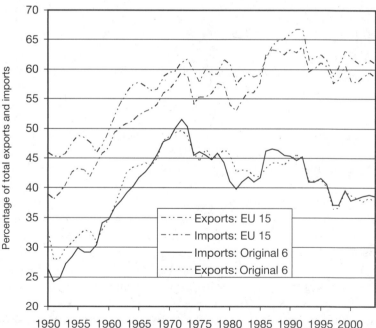

Figure 4.2 Intra-EU trade (share of total exports or imports), 1950–2005. *Sources:* International Monetary Fund, *Direction of Trade Statistics March 2006* (CD-ROM) (Washington, D.C.: IMF, March 2006); *Direction of Trade Statistics Historical, 1948–1980* (CD-ROM) (Washington, D.C.: IMF, 2002).

destined to the other six also rose, from 30 percent in 1950 to 50 percent by the early 1970s. Since that time, these percentages have drifted down, as the expansion of EU membership broadened their trade relations (that is, relative to trade among the original six, they have experienced rapid expansion of trade with the newly added members, such as the United Kingdom).

For the broader membership of the fifteen countries in the European Union prior to the most recent expansion, a similar and longer-lasting trend occurred (keep in mind that nine of these countries were not members originally, so there was a progressive effect as more of them became members and their trade barriers fell). In this case, imports sourced from the fifteen EU countries rose from just under 40 percent in 1950 to a peak of 64 percent in 1990 before subsiding slightly to 60 percent. Exports follow a similar pattern.

What these trade data show is that European integration had exactly the effect that its founders hoped it would. The nations of Western Europe that belong to the European Union have seen their trade among themselves expand to high levels, creating a set of mutual (and mutually beneficial) trade dependencies. This holds as well for the two core countries, France and Germany. For that pair, the share of imports that each sourced from the other tripled from 6 to 18 percent in the years from 1950 to the mid-1970s (subsiding a bit thereafter to around 13 percent as their trade patterns shifted a bit to the new members of the European Union).

The story so far has been about an increasing *portion* of trade among members of the European Union. However, at the same time that these nations were trading more intensively with one another, they were also trading more with the rest of the world, paralleling the global trend identified in chapter 1. In all cases, the members of the European Union experienced substantial increases in the ratio of total imports (that is, intra-EU imports plus extra-EU imports) to GDP, in some cases dramatically. For Germany, the World Bank did not report this ratio until 1971, when it was already undoubtedly higher than back in the 1950s. But even for Germany, the ratio has almost doubled since that time, to 32 percent by 2002. The smaller countries, such as Luxembourg (128 percent) and Belgium (80 percent), have high levels that are distorted by their role in passing goods through the country, but even for them it is instructive that as European trade as a whole has expanded, their role as pass-through points has expanded as well. Other countries, such as Spain, show an even more dramatic change. Prior to its membership in the European Union (Spain joined in 1986), imports were a relatively low 7 percent of GDP, but that share more than quadrupled to 30 percent by 2002.

The rise of intra-EU trade has been so strong, that we should wonder about what has happened to the trade relationship between these countries and the world outside the European Union. Figure 4.3 shows a strong rise in imports as a share of GDP, but how much of that is accounted for by the strong rise in intra-EU trade? *Trade diversion* refers to the removal of trade barriers causing a group of countries to trade more among themselves, often at the expense of what had formerly been their imports from the rest of the world. Whereas firms inside the bloc benefit, competitors outside are disadvantaged (because their goods still face tariff barriers). Could trade diversion have been sufficiently pronounced in the European Union that their non-EU imports have not risen over time? U.S. and Japanese firms, for example, felt for a long time that the formation of the EEC in the 1950s worked to their disadvantage. In the 1980s, it was common to speak of "fortress Europe"—especially because the Single European Act promised to erase even more internal barriers (thereby increasing the diversion effect).

However, the answer to the question about the impact of diversion is negative. Although trade diversion is certainly a factor, as shown in the rising share of intra-EU trade relative to total trade, these countries have

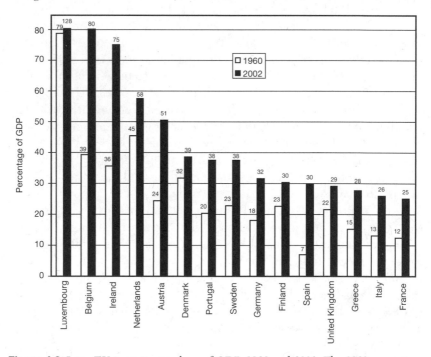

Figure 4.3 Intra-EU imports as a share of GDP, 1960 and 2002. The 1960 percentage for Germany is actually for 1971, the earliest year for which the World Bank provides this indicator for Germany. The 2002 figures for Luxembourg is 128 percent, and for Belgium 80 percent. *Source:* World Bank, *World Development Indicators 2005* (CD-ROM) (Washington, D.C.: World Bank, 2005).

also become more exposed to the outside world, albeit to widely varying degrees. Figure 4.4 shows changes in the ratio of the imports of EU
members from the rest of the world (that is, extra-EU imports) as a ratio
to GDP. The first thing to notice is that in 2002 exposure to the outside
world varied, from a high of 27–28 percent for Austria, Belgium, and
Denmark to a low 9 percent for Spain and Sweden. Austria sits on the
geographical edge of the European Union, as does Belgium (a major port
of entry for goods coming into the European Union by sea from elsewhere
in the world) and perhaps Denmark (a close neighbor of nonmember
Norway). Spain, which had not had a high ratio of imports to GDP prior
to joining the European Union, has obviously opened itself up to its EU
partners, but has not become much more exposed to the rest of the world
(although its lack of change is a bit of a puzzle given the strong increase
in exposure to the outside world of its next-door neighbor Portugal). But
the larger point is that, for most of these countries, there has been an
increase in the ratio of imports from the rest of the world to GDP; even
as these nations have become more integrated among themselves, they
have also opened up to the outside world.

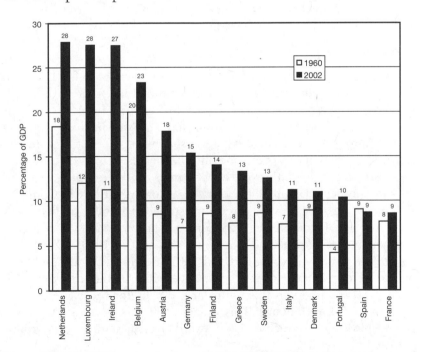

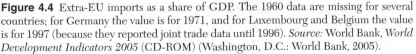

Figure 4.4 Extra-EU imports as a share of GDP. The 1960 data are missing for several
countries; for Germany the value is for 1971, and for Luxembourg and Belgium the value
is for 1997 (because they reported joint trade data until 1996). *Source:* World Bank, *World
Development Indicators 2005* (CD-ROM) (Washington, D.C.: World Bank, 2005).

Why did this happen despite the apprehensions about Fortress Europe? One explanation is that the Single European Act and the Maastricht Treaty shifted authority over trade policy from individual member states to the EU Commission. Despite the fact that the commission had formal authority over trade policy since 1969, member states continued to maintain separate policies on nontariff barriers. When the EU Commission consolidated control over trade policy at the end of the 1980s, it turned out to be more liberal than some of its individual member countries.[10] To give just one example, individual EEC members had imposed different unilateral restrictions on the imports of Japanese automobiles, ranging from no restrictions in Ireland to a 10 percent market-share limit in Britain and a miniscule two thousand cars per year in Italy. These individual limits were eliminated by a common policy that phased out all quantitative restrictions on Japanese automobiles in the 1990s.

The total story, therefore, is one of increasing integration among EU members and an overall rise in the importance of trade as a share of GDP, driven by both the elimination of trade barriers among EU members and a gradual decline in their barriers to imports from the rest of the world. Today, these countries are heavily integrated with both themselves and the outside world through trade.

Direct Investment

Just as these countries have become more open to trade, they have also experienced an increase in inflows of direct investment, although the rise is more recent. Figure 4.5 shows the inflow of direct investment using data from two sources. Obtaining a picture of what has happened to the European Union as a whole is somewhat difficult, due to the expanding membership over time and the lack of a common currency. As in previous figures, this one concentrates on the experience of the fifteen European Union states (EU-15). However, the EU Commission itself does not provide direct investment data on a unified basis prior to 1994. Therefore, figure 4.5 uses data from the IMF balance-of-payments data to extend the view back to the 1980s. Even with these data, problems abound. Until 2001, Belgium and Luxembourg published joint balance-of-payments data, not available from the IMF, so the IMF numbers in this figure are actually for the EU-15 minus Belgium and Luxembourg. This deletion matters because these two countries were major recipients of inward investment during the frenzy at the end of the 1990s.

With these caveats in mind, figure 4.5 shows a steady rise in the exposure of the EU-15 to inward direct investment, somewhat similar to the experience of the United States discussed in the previous chapter. Until the early 1990s, inward investment (from all sources including other EU

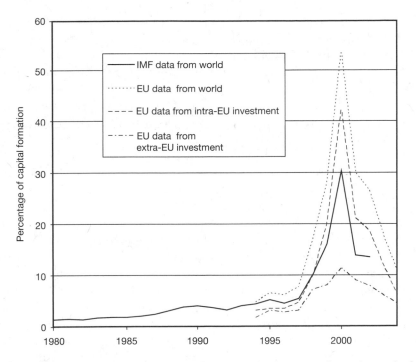

Figure 4.5 Foreign direct investment in the European Union as a share of gross fixed capital formation, 1980–2005. The IMF data for the total inflow of direct investment exclude Belgium and Luxembourg (until 2001, Belgium and Luxembourg had a joint publication on balance-of-payments statistics, not available on the IMF data set). *Sources:* International Monetary Fund, *International Financial Statistics* (CD-ROM) (Washington, D.C.: IMF, March 2005); Eurostat, available at http://epp.eurostat.cec.eu.int (April 11, 2006).

countries) rose a bit, but was in a range of 1–3 percent of total domestic capital formation—not a high level. From 1995 until 2000, a surge of investment occurred, driven by both the IT bubble (which affected the United States as well) and the implementation of the EU single-market policy. The emergence of the single market made cross-border acquisitions more attractive as firms sought to assemble EU-wide businesses. The story of the telecommunications firms Vodaphone and Orange mentioned earlier is a part of this story. (The disparity between the IMF and EU data in showing the spike in investment up to 2000 is due in large part to the absence of the data for Belgium and Luxembourg in the IMF data.)

Since 2000, overall investment inflows have plummeted, but as of 2004 they were still above the levels of the early 1990s. Further declines from the 10 percent of total domestic capital formation level of 2004 are unlikely—a relatively permanent shift has occurred in the openness of European markets to cross-border investment flows. As the after-effects of the collapse of the IT bubble fade, it is likely that direct investment inflows will stabilize or rise again.

Figure 4.5 also shows what happened to intra- versus extra-EU invest-ment flows. The effort to build a European common market from the 1950s through the 1980s did not include much of a rise in intra-EU cross-border investments. Trade barriers fell and intra-EU trade expanded, but intra-EU investment was not high—only 3 percent of domestic capital formation for the EU-15 as a whole in 1994, when the EU investment data series starts. Since then, both intra- and extra-EU direct investment has exploded, although the bulk of the bubble up to 1999 was due to intra-EU investments. Nevertheless, by 2004, both intra- and extra-EU investments were higher than they were prior to 1995, with just over half of the investments from within the European Union (5.9 percent of domestic fixed-capital formation) and a bit less than half coming from outside (4.3 percent).

What can we conclude from these investment numbers? Like the United States, the EU-15 were not exposed to high levels of cross-border inward investment until the 1990s. To be sure, some U.S. firms had been investing in Europe since the 1950s, but the vast bulk of investment in European countries was purely domestic. We might expect that the effort to build a more open European market would have biased cross-border investment heavily toward other members of the European Union, but even this drift was modest until the 1990s. The vigorous steps in the 1990s to consummate a true single market, however, created a more enticing market for invest-ment, both by other EU firms and by those outside the European Union. This greater attractiveness was distorted upward in the late 1990s by the IT bubble (during which European telecommunications and airline services were deregulated), but even postbubble, direct investment flows are rela-tively high—both among EU members and with the outside world.

Monetary Union

The commitment of at least a subset of EU members to participate in the unified currency is a remarkable development. As put by one U.S. economist at the time without overstatement: "European Monetary uni-fication...is a process for which there exists no historical precedent."[11] As the European Monetary Union (EMU) took shape, economists and political scientists debated whether the new system would work and whether it made any real difference to either Europe or the world. This development was so audacious and difficult that some outside observers with long experience in Europe, such as Richard Cooper or Martin Feld-stein, economists, remained unsure if it would succeed.[12] At the opposite end of the spectrum, C. Fred Bergsten (assistant secretary for Interna-tional Monetary Affairs in the Carter administration and founder of the Peterson Institute for International Economics) predicted the euro would be a major currency that would rival the U.S. dollar in global transactions.[13] The doubters turned out to be wrong, although the euro is not quite as significant in the global financial system as Bergsten predicted. Still, the creation of this new currency was a very major development for Europe.

The movement toward a single currency began back in 1979 and took over twenty years to consummate. The original agreement (the EMS) attempted to reduce the currency fluctuations among EU members, with participants committed to keeping their currencies within a band of 2.25–6.00 percent around declared benchmark exchange rates. This system met with limited success due to the wide variations in monetary policy and inflation rates among member states. Some members in the 1970s and 1980s pursued more restrictive monetary policies to hold inflation low (especially West Germany), whereas others followed more expansionary monetary policies with higher inflation (such as Italy). Some authors, however, do credit the EMS with reducing inflation across the European Union and setting the stage for an eventual single currency.[14]

The inherent problem in any scheme to coordinate among floating currencies is that each country has its own central bank and faces distinctive domestic conditions and political pressures in setting monetary policy. Faced with problems in the EMS, the Delors Report (named after Jacques Delors, president of the European Commission at the time) of 1989 recommended a single currency, a proposal adopted in the Maastricht Treaty of 1992. To ease the transition, the treaty imposed goals for inflation and central government budget deficits. Whether Italy, with a large government deficit and generally higher than average inflation in the European Union, would meet the Maastricht requirements was a matter of some concern over the course of the 1990s. Despite the speculation, the Maastricht Treaty guidelines were met, and the euro came into existence for twelve member states. Britain, the third largest economy in the European Union, opted to remain outside the system (as did Denmark and Sweden). In 1999, the new common currency (the euro) went into effect as a currency for international settlements, and it replaced national paper currencies and coinage in 2002.

One reason the creation of a single currency seemed unlikely is that the only way to have a truly unified currency is to have a single central bank. As previously noted, the problem with the predecessor EMS system was the continued existence of individual national central banks that could not be counted on to pursue identical monetary policies. But a single central bank raised questions of which government would end up with the dominant power. As it evolved, the European Central Bank is widely acknowledged to be heavily influenced by the Germans. For decades, German monetary policy had emphasized low inflation, even at the expense of economic growth. This history led to skepticism about whether other member governments would agree to join a system that would probably lean toward low inflation. Nevertheless, this has been the outcome.

The changes in inflation are shown in figure 4.6. In the 1970s, the average consumer price inflation in the twelve countries that eventually adopted the euro rose (as it did in other industrial nations due to the impact of the large oil price increases in 1973 and 1979). In addition, the dispersion of inflation (the variance, in the parlance of economists) also increased, shown simply in this figure as the maximum and minimum inflation rates among the twelve countries in each year. Back in 1970, average inflation was just under 5 percent, whereas the maximum (Ireland in that year) was 8 percent and the minimum (Greece) was below 3 percent; but by 1980, the average had swelled to 13 percent with a maximum of 15 percent (Greece, which moved from lowest to highest) and minimum of 6 percent (Luxembourg). Since then, the average fell and the dispersion shrank, so that by 1999 the average consumer price inflation level was only 1.5 percent, with a maximum of 2.6 percent and a minimum of 0.5 percent.[15]

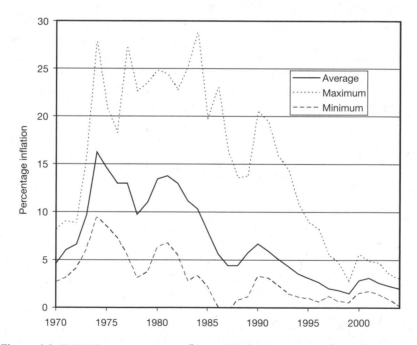

Figure 4.6 EMU-12 consumer price inflation, 1970–2005. German inflation data are not included in this data set until 1992 (after reunification). *Source:* International Monetary Fund, *International Financial Statistics* (CD-ROM) (Washington, D.C.: IMF, March 2005).

From the standpoint of this book, the importance of the establishment of the euro lies in what it shows about the willingness of at least twelve members of the European Union to surrender a piece of their national sovereignty to a new central bank. Whether the British or the Scandinavians will deign to join is an important question, but it is less important than the simple astonishing fact of the existence of a new currency uniting much of Europe.

Problems

European efforts to move forward with economic integration have been fraught with doubts, major political battles, and frequent setbacks. The situation today is little different. Because institutions can be undone, we should worry about the direction in the future. Could poor economic performance lead to tensions among EU members that cause them to pull apart? Might the ambitious expansion of membership to Eastern European countries in 2004 prove to be the undoing of the European Union due to wide divisions in national interest between the EU-15 and the new twelve? Does the failure to adopt the EU constitution in 2005 portend a trend toward the unraveling other ties? Let us look briefly at each of these questions.

Poor Economic Performance

One of the puzzles of European economic performance is why these countries have not closed the gap with the United States in terms of GDP per capita. After a period of rapid growth in the first few decades after the Second World War, most of the members of the EU-15 have remained at a level of 75–80 percent of the level of U.S. GDP per capita, when the comparison is made using the World Bank's purchasing power parity exchange rates. As figure 4.7 shows, most of these countries were at about the same percentage of the U.S. level in 2003 as they were in 1975. Only two—Luxembourg and Ireland—show dramatic gains. Luxembourg is very small, which makes success easier to achieve than for a large country. Ireland has succeeded as the result of thorough economic reforms that attracted large inflows of foreign direct investment. But the failure of the major countries—Germany, France, Britain, Italy, and Spain—to close the gap with the United States has been a disappointment.

The explanations for this failure have generally focused on the continued excessive regulation of these economies. Firms are reluctant to hire because of regulations that make it difficult to terminate employees during recessions, and generous unemployment and social welfare systems make unemployment a reasonable alternative for many. Agricultural policies subsidize inefficient

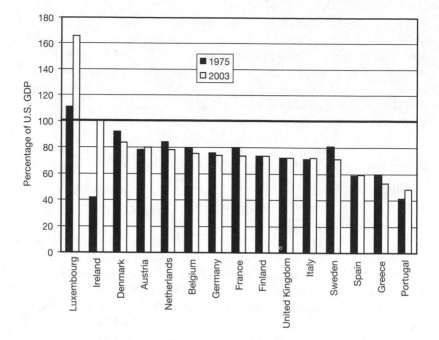

Figure 4.7 EU-15 GDP per capita as a percentage of U.S. level, 1975 and 2002. *Source:* World Bank, *World Development Indicators 2005* (CD-ROM) (Washington, D.C.: World Bank, 2005).

farms and inhibit imports of lower-cost agricultural products from abroad. The process of industry deregulation has proceeded, but much remains to be done. Almost every day, the media presents stories of economic problems or failures in the European Union, and economists explain why economic performance has not lived up to its potential.[16]

However, these shortcomings should be kept in perspective. First, our measures of GDP per capita and adjustments for purchasing power parity are very imprecise. As a result, it is not entirely clear whether these countries are really less affluent or whether our measures are simply inaccurate. Japan, too, has been stuck at roughly 75 percent the level of U.S. GDP per capita for the past two decades. Yet in neither Europe nor Japan does a casual visitor have any real sense of being in countries with noticeably lower income levels.

More important, the problems and failures of economic reform or performance do not appear to be driving the EU members apart. From the outside, the EU states appear to be constantly bickering among themselves and complaining about poor performance. France even faces some domestic violence by poor immigrants who have not been well integrated into an economy that has a high unemployment rate; the British love to rail against Euro-bureaucracy. Nevertheless, economic performance has been sufficient to satisfy the member countries that their membership is worthwhile.

The more difficult question to answer is: What would happen in the face of a deep recession or a very sharp divergence in economic performance? A disaster on the order of the 1930s depression could tear the euro asunder and perhaps undo the single market. But at least these governments are locked in a close dialog on macroeconomic issues. Finance ministers, for example, meet monthly—with back-to-back meetings for the full EU set of ministers and then for the twelve members of the EMU.[17] Furthermore, the very existence of the European Union and the European Central Bank diminishes the probability that individual governments will make the kind of foolish policy decisions that characterized both macroeconomic and trade policies of the industrial nations at the beginning of the Great Depression. They may bicker, but each year that goes by, the more ingrained the habit of cooperation becomes and the less likely they are to walk out in anger. Therefore, the possible impact of a severe economic downturn deserves some mild concern, but its occurrence is unlikely and the extent of its negative impact on the European Union far from obvious.

Resistance to Integration

The story of European integration is not as smooth as the earlier discussion in this chapter suggests. Even among the older members of the European Union, there are signs of strain, along with concerns about the implications of expansion of the membership. But these concerns do not pose much of a problem. The deep economic integration that has already occurred is an important reality, and some of the concerns that have appeared in the media are overdrawn.

As a consequence of the effort to create a single market, intra-EU direct investment has risen. However, by 2006, there was concern that member governments were "throwing up a raft of barriers" to discourage the takeover of local firms by suitors elsewhere in the European Union.[18] In 2006, the French government intervened to prevent the acquisition of a French electric power utility by an Italian firm, and the Spanish government did the same to prevent the purchase of an electric utility by a German firm.[19] What is difficult to discern is whether these protectionist moves were a blip in a continuing story of integration or a more serious unraveling of the five decades of progress toward a truly unified market. Given the progress in opening telecommunications and aviation to EU-wide competition and investment, however, the resistance on the issue of electric utilities appeared to be more of a blip than a trend.

A new feature in the debate over open markets concerns the recent and future expansion of membership. Through the 1990s, membership in the European Union had been confined to countries that had belonged to the Western bloc during the Cold War and generally was limited to relatively affluent, industrialized nations (with Greece and Portugal at the bottom end of the income scale). As noted earlier in this chapter, these states were motivated by a desire to create lasting peace among themselves and to band together in the face of the Soviet threat. These two goals—to overcome a violent past and to band together against the Soviet bloc— provided powerful motivators for progress on economic integration.

The 2004 membership increase, however, brought in countries in Eastern Europe that were former members of the Soviet bloc and that were less affluent than the existing members of the European Union. As indicated earlier, this expansion was somewhat controversial, typified by the French media decrying the possible inroads of Polish plumbers. Other nations, however, remained eager to join. Romania and Bulgaria were formally admitted in January 2007, and Croatia hoped to be admitted within another year or two.[20] But membership for other Balkan states that wanted to join—Serbia, Montenegro, Bosnia, Herzegovina, and Albania—appeared more problematic. Turkey (a country that has wanted to join the European Union for several decades) presents another difficult case—an Islamic country considered by many to belong to the Middle East rather than deserving to be part of Europe.[21] Its effort to join was on hold at the end of 2006.

Figure 4.8 shows GDP per capita in 2003 for the members added in 2004 and 2007 (Bulgaria and Romania), plus for those negotiating entry (Croatia and Turkey), measured as a percentage of the level of the United States at purchasing power parity exchange rates (as in figure 4.7). Whereas the EU-15 members were mostly in a range of 70–80 percent of the U.S. income level, these other countries are lower. Of the members added in 2004, the most affluent (Slovenia) was only as affluent as the poorest of the EU-15 (Portugal), at just over 50 percent the U.S. level; the poorest (Latvia) was only 28 percent the U.S. level. The countries admitted or seeking entry in 2007 were lower still, ranging from Croatia (30 percent) to Turkey (18 percent). These data explain some of the sense of the anxiety that the enlargement of the membership has aroused in some groups in the more affluent, older members. By way of comparison, think about the issue of Mexican economic integration with the United States. Mexico's GDP per capita was 24 percent the level of the United States in 2003, and that led to fears of Mexico sucking jobs away when the North America Free Trade Area (NAFTA) was formed in the mid-1990s.

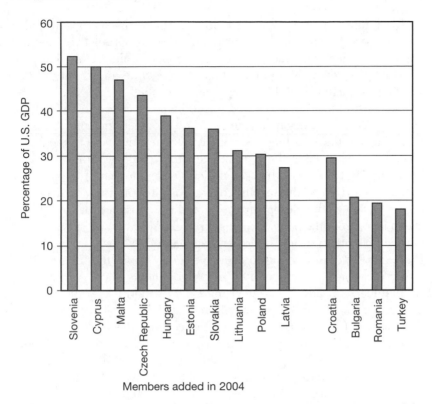

Figure 4.8 New and proposed EU members' GDP per capita as a percentage of the U.S. level, 2003. Data for Slovenia are for 2001. *Source:* World Bank, *World Development Indicators 2005* (CD-ROM) (Washington, D.C.: World Bank, 2005).

How the stresses and strains from EU expansion will play out remains to be seen. Nonetheless, the 2004 expansion appeared to be going smoothly as of 2006. The requirements of openness should have a very positive economic benefit on the new members, accelerating their growth and reducing the disparity in income levels over time. But there is no guarantee that the earlier members of the European Union will accept competition—and workers—from the new members willingly.

The Failed European Constitution

In 2005, the European Union attempted another step toward integration when a draft European Constitution was drawn up and submitted to the member states for ratification. Because the constitution was not intended to forge the European Union into a real nation, the overall impact of the European Constitution would have been more symbolic than real. However, the constitution did include the establishment of an EU foreign minister, which would have tilted the European Union further toward a common foreign policy. Despite its relatively modest implications, however, the draft constitution was almost five hundred pages long—a length almost guaranteed to generate uncertainty, confusion, and suspicion about its contents and meaning.

The constitution was submitted to the member countries for ratification, and a dramatic negative vote in France doomed the constitution to failure, a vote that was followed shortly by a negative vote in the Netherlands as well (leading the EU ministers to formally withdraw the proposal later in the year). Much of the opposition appeared be symbolic rather than driven by the specifics of the constitution itself. Anxiety over the expansion of the European Union and the prospects of an influx of cheap labor from the east was one source of opposition (despite the fact that labor mobility from the lower-wage countries being added to the European Union was going to occur with or without the constitution), a fear embodied in derogatory French comments about having "Polish plumbers" invade the French market.[22] Opposition to the Brussels bureaucratism was also a perennial popular theme that worked against the constitution (with the length of the constitution itself providing a convenient political image for those opposed to the EU bureaucracy). As one German newspaper sympathetic to the constitution put it, "the EU constitution is studded with technical terms, unwieldy sentences and bureaucratese, not to mention that it is an epic 500 pages."[23]

At the time, the defeat of the constitution led to a predictable comments about crisis in the EU process. There is no doubt that the failure of the constitution was something of a setback to EU integration, but it was hardly a crisis, and it perhaps served as a useful lesson to proponents of deeper integration about the speed with which their national voting publics could be brought along. Therefore, we should not read very much into the defeat of the constitution. Furthermore, the constitution was mostly about strengthening the political aspects of integration, not the economic side, and so makes little or no difference for the broad benefits flowing from economic integration.

THE history of European integration is a remarkable one. Since the breakup of the Roman Empire, Europe experienced frequent wars and constantly sifting political boundaries. In the twentieth century, the two world wars brought these conflicts to a shockingly high level of death, destruction, and barbarous actions. The subsequent Cold War held the prospect of a conflict that would be much worse, turning the continent into a nuclear wasteland. Frightened by both the past and the possibilities for the future, determined individuals and governments forged a new pattern of economic cooperation explicitly designed to lock former enemies together into an economic embrace that would be so strong and beneficial that a return to mortal conflict would be averted. The process of achieving this goal has not been easy, occurring in fits and starts from the original ECSC to today's European Union. At each step along the way, doubts abounded. But the landscape of Europe today is amazingly different from the beginning of the 1950s. Although the single market concept is not entirely in place yet, it has progressed very far. Students and workers move relatively freely through the European Union, and competition in many industries is wide open. French farmers may occasionally create a splash by blocking trucks coming in from Italy with inexpensive wine, but the European Union has accommodated farmers with subsidies like the rest of the industrialized parts of the world.

Meanwhile, twelve of the members have accepted a unified currency. Not only does this move involve a remarkable willingness to cede national sovereignty to a regional central bank (dominated by the Germans no less), but it involves a willingness to abandon powerful psychological symbols of that national sovereignty—distinctive national paper money and coinage. Germany without the Deutschmark, France without the franc, or Italy without the lira seemed unimaginable in the recent past. Even the names of these currencies seemed closely linked to national identity. Although Britain remains aloof, the future expansion of the euro zone appears likely.

The story of Europe, however, is not without at least some areas of mild concern. Because the institutional structures of the European Union were created by human beings, they can be undone by human beings. Nevertheless, the extent of integration is now so far advanced and the rules for entry so rigorous that it is increasingly difficult to imagine the European Union foundering. Failure to pursue economic deregulation more vigorously may condemn most members to be stuck a bit below the U.S. level of affluence—but even that failure implies a continued growth of GDP per capita at the same rate as a United States that has been quite successful.

Overall, therefore, the story of Europe is one of successful economic transformation with huge positive geopolitical implications. The accomplishments of the past half century are substantial and should not be obscured by the tendency to look for problems and failures. As a result of growing affluence and the strong economic benefits flowing from intra-European economic integration, armed conflict in Europe, which so bedeviled the world in the twentieth century, is now a matter of history.

5. EAST ASIA

The East Asian economic experience since the mid-twentieth century has been nothing less than astonishing. In 1950, a war raged on the Korean peninsula as North Korea attempted to forcibly reunite the politically divided peninsula and South Korean and UN (mainly U.S.) military forces fought back. The Chinese civil war had just ended the previous year with a communist victory, separating mainland China from the rest of the region and initiating a tense military standoff with the remains of the Kuomintang forces that had fled to Taiwan. Japan was just beginning to recover from the huge physical and human devastation of the Second World War and was still occupied by U.S. military forces, and its future economic and security behavior remained in considerable doubt. Indochina was in the middle of a revolutionary war against the French colonial regime, a conflict that would re-ignite as the Vietnam War, lasting until 1975 and eventually involving the civil war and massive genocide in Cambodia in the 1970s. The Netherlands had just acknowledged Indonesian independence the previous year after four bloody years of revolution. Burma (now Myanmar) had just achieved independence in 1947, whereas Singapore and Malaysia would not become independent until 1957. East Asia was seething with actual and potential conflict while locked in a morass of poverty.

Today, peace has reigned across the region for almost thirty years (since the end of the Vietnam War and a brief 1979 border war between Vietnam and China), and the region has been generating some of the highest economic growth rates in the world for several decades. Japan underwent a quarter century of high growth starting in the early 1950s, bringing it into the ranks of the advanced industrialized nations by the mid-1970s—a position it maintains today. China embraced a process of cautious but largely continuous market economic reforms since the early 1980s that unleashed high economic growth. Symbolic of its new attitudes about interacting with the outside world, China joined the WTO in 2001. Although dangerous tensions on the Korean peninsula are building again today, the armistice has prevailed since 1953 and South Korea has experienced its own economic miracle. Taiwan has become another successful middle-income economy and is the source of large amounts of investment flowing into China, even though political tensions remain. In the 1980s, a number of Southeast Asian economies joined the bandwagon of rapid economic growth and opened up their economies to trade and investment to a considerable extent. In the 1990s, even communist Vietnam began economic reforms.

Developments in East Asia powerfully illustrate the positive impact of economic development discussed in chapter 2. Economic growth and international economic engagement have transformed the region in ways that no one could have imagined in 1950. Japan, China, and a number of the smaller developing countries have prospered through international trade and investment, leaving them with little reason to engage in military adventurism. However, the region also contains two of the most dangerous hot spots in the world: North Korea and the Taiwan Strait. Both of these problems are legacies of the Cold War, with the United States championing of Taiwan as the legitimate Chinese government until the 1970s and the Korean War ending in a stalemate causing the United States to maintain military forces in South Korea ever since. China still wants political control over Taiwan, whereas some Taiwanese yearn for recognition as a legitimate nation-state (having long ago dropped the pretension of being the legitimate government of China). North Korea may no longer seriously dream of conquering South Korea in a renewed war, but it is now sufficiently fearful of its own survival that it has pursued the dangerous path of developing nuclear weapons. These two potential conflicts are driven by highly emotional nationalistic feelings. Nevertheless, the rising opportunity cost of armed conflict helps deter military action by China against Taiwan, and the prospect for outside economic help may yet deter North Korea from further nuclear development. But there is no guarantee that peaceful outcomes will prevail.

This chapter considers both the evidence of the positive outcomes driven by economic development and the remaining problems. A principal goal of this discussion is to refute the neo-realist school of international relations, which argues that the economic rise of China is necessarily a security threat to the United States because relative shifts in economic status have generally been accompanied by tension and conflict in human history. Although the course of its development certainly bears watching, there is no reason to treat Chinese economic growth as a problem.

The experiences of Japan, China, and now other parts of the region show that rapid economic development and relative shifts in economic size and affluence can occur without actual conflict or debilitating tension. When we look around the world, it is the East Asian experience that provides some of the strongest evidence for the argument I make in chapter 2 concerning the positive impact of growth and interdependence in leading governments away from military action. This chapter focuses on Japan, China, and the countries that belong to the Association of Southeast Asian Nations (ASEAN). The economic story of other economies in the region is equally dramatic, including South Korea, Taiwan, and Hong Kong; nevertheless, these three additional examples are left out of this chapter to avoid an overly long discussion. The chapter also takes a sober look at the North Korea and Taiwan-China issues and other areas of actual or potential conflict in the region.

Japan

Japan's modernization began early. Not long after a revolution that unified the country under a new central government in 1867, the new leaders switched from a simple desire to hold the Western imperial powers out of Japan to embracing the economic institutions and technology of the West. The nation had come far enough along the economic development route by 1941 that the government believed it could successfully attack the U.S. military forces in the Pacific. The causes of the Pacific War were complex, but a key trigger was oil. The U.S. government embargoed the export of oil in 1941 in a move to apply leverage on the Japanese government to withdraw its military forces from China. Unwilling to comply, the Japanese government decided to secure oil by the conquest of Southeast Asian oilfields and refining plants in Indonesia and Singapore. Because the conquest of Southeast Asia would expose Japan to a flank attack by the U.S. navy, the perfectly logical conclusion was to initially knock out U.S. military capability in the Pacific—and seek an armistice once Southeast Asia was firmly in Japanese control. This strategy was based on the belief that pacifist feelings in the United States were sufficiently strong that the U.S. government would accept an armistice rather than face a difficult war. That belief turned out to be catastrophically wrong.[1]

Japan was devastated by the war—losing its colonies, several million of its citizens, a large part of its economic infrastructure, and the downtown areas of many of its major cities to both massive fire bombings and two nuclear bombs. The allied occupation of Japan in 1945 was almost entirely a U.S. affair, bringing with it demilitarization, a new democratic constitution written by the Americans, the breakup of large business conglomerates, and many other reforms. The occupation was entirely peaceful, but whether the reforms would yield a stable or prosperous Japan was certainly in some doubt in the late 1940s.[2]

From that uncertain beginning, the Japanese experienced the first of the East Asian economic miracles. From 1950 to 1973, the average annual real economic growth rate was over 9 percent. From the devastation of the Second World War, Japan reached the ranks of the advanced industrial nations by the mid-1970s, as shown in figure 5.1. Measured in purchasing power parity terms, the Japanese had reached 40 percent of the level of per capita GDP of the United States just prior to the war. That level dropped to only 11 percent in 1945, but rose to 70 percent by the 1970s; it is around 75 percent today—a level similar to France.[3]

Economists tend to focus on the various economic problems that Japan has faced since the beginning of the 1990s that lowered economic growth. However, these problems do not diminish the dramatic story of Japanese economic success since the 1940s. Although the problems of the 1990s were relatively serious, the economy did not experience any major economic crisis—growth was very low (just over 1 percent annually) but

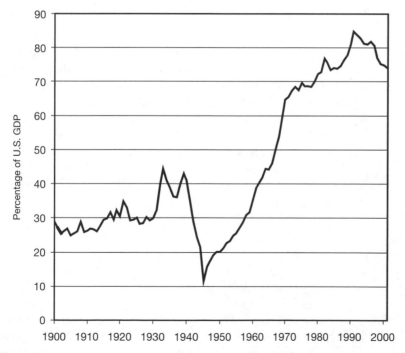

Figure 5.1 Japanese GDP per capita as a percentage of the U.S. level, 1900–2001. *Source:* Angus Maddison, *The World Economy: Historical Statistics* (Paris: OECD, 2003)

positive. As any visitor to Tokyo quickly realizes, Japan is one of the major centers of global affluence. And by 2006, the economy appeared to be shaking off its dozen years of sluggishness.

This record of extraordinary accomplishment was achieved without any ability to project military power, without the array of colonies that Japan had acquired in the first half of the twentieth century, and with the heavy use of imported raw materials—especially oil. Adopting the imperialist rationale of the Western powers, Japan had grabbed Taiwan (1898), Korea (1911), and Manchuria (1931) and then conquered much of mainland China itself (1937) and most of Southeast Asia (1941) during the war. Secure access to raw materials and food provided one important official rationale for this land grab, along with arguments about needing land for an expanding domestic population. After the war, all these possessions were stripped from Japan and several million Japanese colonists were returned home. High economic growth provided jobs and rising incomes for all, including those repatriated at the end of the war. If ever there was an example to prove that colonial possessions are unnecessary to provide growth and prosperity, post–World War II Japan is that example.

Raw Material Imports

Without its colonial possessions, the Japanese economy was left dependent on imports for a variety of critical raw materials, including for almost 100 percent of the petroleum it needed. Table 5.1 presents self-sufficiency data for a variety of products. The self-sufficiency ratio shows the percentage of domestic consumption of a product that is supplied by domestic production. For petroleum, the self-sufficiency ratio had always been low, but for some other materials such as food, lumber, copper, lead, zinc, and coal the previous relatively high levels of self-sufficiency declined sharply from 1960 to 2000, largely as Japanese high-cost domestic mines were closed, leading to a sharp decline in domestic ore production.

Even the heavily protected agriculture, fishing, and timber industries have been opened gradually to imports, bringing a decline in self-sufficiency. Some agricultural products—rice in particular—remain heavily protected from imports, and the negotiating process to convince Japan to reduce its barriers has been very difficult. But those difficulties and the continuing heavy protectionism on such products as rice should not obscure the fact that even in agriculture the self-sufficiency ratio has fallen. The overall facts of the agriculture situation are especially interesting because government officials in the Agriculture Ministry, politicians representing rural areas, and farm lobby groups use some of the same rhetoric as U.S. politicians do in talking about the need for energy

Table 5.1 Japanese self-sufficiency ratios for selected primary commodities, 1960–1985

Year	Agriculture and Fisheries	Lumber	Crude Petroleum	Coal	Iron Ore	Copper Ore	Lead Ore	Zinc Ore
1960	93	91	2	80	8	16	48	59
1965	85	75	1	79	3	16	45	37
1970	81	97	0	46	1	19	32	39
1975	78	38	0	23	0	10	29	35
1980	70	33	0	21	0	6	22	37
1985	75	37	0	16	0	1	16	22
1990	72	28	0	7	0	0	6	10
1995	68	21	0	5	0	0	5	8
2000	63	19	0	2	0	0	4	6

Sources: Kazuo Sato, "Japan's Resource Imports," *Annals of the American Academy of Political and Social Science* 513 (January 1991): 79; Statistics Bureau, *Japan Statistical Yearbook 2004* (Tokyo: Ministry of Public Management, Home Affairs, Posts and Telecommunications, 2004), 256, 286–87, 470–71; Organization for Economic Cooperation and Development, *Source OECD* (online data bank), available at http://www.titania.sourceoecd.org/vl=2779842/cl=18/nw=1/rpsv/home.html.

independence. Despite the rhetoric, the actual policy on agriculture has drifted slowly toward permitting more imports. Fear mongering about the dangers of dependency on foreign food may be good for politicians, but the policy reflects a modicum of rationality about the benefits of international trade.

Due to the postwar constitution's revocation of the use of military force, Japan has not had the option of using its military to provide a sense of security for its raw material supply. Yet the nation has managed extremely well, despite that fact that the overall economy relies much more on imported raw materials and foodstuffs today than even a few decades ago. The way in which the government has managed the anxieties that often accompany such high degrees of reliance on imported petroleum and other raw materials include the following:[4]

• Stockpiling inventory in Japan. For petroleum, the government established quasi-public corporations in the late 1970s to increase domestic oil stockpiles.
• Policies to promote conservation and increased efficiency. Laws in the 1970s, for example, mandated improved energy efficiency for consumer appliances.
• Diversification of foreign suppliers. For a time, Japanese dependence on oil from the Persian Gulf region declined, although it rose again in the 1990s. When the U.S. government briefly embargoed the export of soybeans (mainly to Japan) in 1973 in a misguided attempt to stop the rise of domestic prices, the Japanese government embarked on a plan to foster

production of soybeans in Brazil and import them (a plan that eventually faded as faith in U.S. reliability as an exporter gradually returned).

• Diversification to alternative raw materials. Electric power generation shifted from oil-fired plants to coal and nuclear energy, accelerated by government policies to promote nuclear energy.

• Foreign aid and other foreign policy initiatives to maintain good relations with suppliers. Indonesia, an important non-OPEC source of oil and natural gas has long been a top recipient of foreign aid from Japan. For a time in the late 1970s, the Middle East was the major recipient of foreign aid from Japan.[5]

• Direct investment in overseas extraction of resources. In the 1970s, the Japanese made major investments in Australian iron-ore mines, Japanese firms have purchased grain elevators in the United States, and the government created a quasi-governmental oil company to explore and invest in overseas oil fields.

Of course, many of these policies are no different than those in other countries, including the United States, as discussed in chapters 2–3. As figure 2.2 shows, the United States actually experienced a larger relative improvement in energy efficiency since the 1970s, having started from a position of much lower efficiency than Japan. However, even the more modest improvements in Japan mean that energy consumption in Japan per unit of GDP is still lower than in the United States. Some of the policies were foolish—the government-owned Japan National Oil Company was recently disbanded after a decade of poor investment decisions and financial losses. But the point is that this combination of responses left the government and the public willing to tolerate the relatively high ratio of imports of a wide variety of raw materials and agricultural products.

Could we argue that the uncertainty associated with reliance on imports of raw materials was lowered by U.S. global hegemony? That is, does U.S. naval power (by protecting the sea-lanes) or overall military power (by discouraging raw material exporters from behaving badly) serve as a public good for Japan by providing Japan with the benefit of reliable imports of raw material at no cost? No. The claim about U.S. protection of sea-lanes has already been discussed in chapter 2. As for other aspects of U.S. hegemony, the claim hardly seems plausible. Indeed, in 1973, when the Japanese government first realized the potential dangers of import dependency in the wake of the Arab-Israeli War, the danger appeared to stem precisely from U.S. policy. That is, the Japanese government was targeted as a U.S. ally and included in the short-lived Arab oil export embargo that fall. The Japanese government scrambled to disassociate itself from the U.S. policy position on Israel to placate its oil providers.[6] Since that time, the Japanese government came to realize that, although it may be dependent on raw material imports, Japan was such an important market for sellers of raw materials that it had independent bargaining power. Thus, it was the power of Japan as an importer and its array of other policies to cope with the uncertainties of supply from abroad, and not any umbrella established by the United States, that enabled the government to face import dependence with little anxiety.

The Japanese government was so confident in the success of its coping strategy that the initial response in 1990 when Iraq invaded Kuwait was bewilderment at the intense U.S. anger. From a Japanese perspective, the key issue was whether Iraq's possession of Kuwaiti oil fields would make much difference in the price and availability of oil, and the conclusion was that it would not. Furthermore, the government was reluctant to be dragged by the U.S. government into the very complex world of Middle East politics—doing so could damage relations with oil-exporting nations. In contrast, Prime Minister Koizumi strongly supported the 2003 U.S. invasion of Iraq (at least rhetorically; constitutionally Japan could not send soldiers for combat) and later sent some five hundred soldiers to participate in noncombat activities in the occupation. This more recent decision, however, was motivated by the memory of the tension in U.S.-Japanese relations over Japan's reluctant support for the Gulf War and not any new calculus about oil supply politics.

Trade and Investment Policy

The history of policy on trade offers a different lesson. U.S.-Japanese tensions on trade disputes over much of the thirty-year period from the early 1960s to the mid-1990s often appeared serious and led to concerns that the overall bilateral relationship might unravel. The answers to the questions of why and how these tensions were contained are important for understanding how the global trade policy system works and how a reluctant liberalizer like Japan behaves in such a system.

After the Second World War, the Japanese government erected stiff barriers to both imports and inward foreign direct investment. Like many governments, the concept adopted by the Japanese was import substitution—fostering the development of domestically owned industries to manufacture products previously imported. Although such policies usually fail, a number of industries in Japan managed to thrive behind the import and investment barriers, notably the automobile and electronics industries. Meanwhile, rapidly growing exports—aided by trade liberalization in Japan's principal export market, the United States, and elsewhere—were a core part of industrial policy.

Because Japan was an ally in a tense Cold War Asian setting, the U.S. government tolerated those barriers from the late 1940s through the 1950s. Beginning in the early 1960s, however, the U.S. government started a thirty-year period of pressure to open Japanese markets. From a U.S. perspective, the continuing stiff Japanese trade and investment protectionism at the same time that Japanese products were rapidly penetrating U.S. markets was increasingly offensive (a feeling heightened by a growing U.S. trade deficit with Japan after the mid-1960s). At times, the visible tensions generated in that process led to speculation that U.S.-Japanese relations would dissolve. This sense of anxiety was voiced most strongly during the George H. W. Bush administration and the first term of the Clinton administration because the Cold War had just come to an end.[7] From a neo-realist perspective, the glue of the Cold War that held Japan to the United States was gone, and rivalries over trade would come to the fore in a repeat of the commercial competition among great powers a century earlier. However, nothing of the kind happened for several important reasons.

First, the Japanese government played a very carefully calculated bargaining game within the context of the existing international trade environment. That is, the government attempted to keep domestic markets as closed to imports and investment as possible, but recognized that there were limits to what it could get away with. Therefore, whenever tensions on the U.S. side rose, concessions were usually forthcoming— just enough to keep the U.S. government satisfied. At times, actual trade sanctions were imposed by the United States, but other than textiles (mainly in the 1950s and 1960s) and steel (subject to periodic U.S. import restrictions from the 1960s to the present), these measures have been relatively few (including color television sets during 1977–1979, automobiles during 1981–1985, and short-lived retaliatory tariffs on a variety of products due to a lack of Japanese enforcement of an agreement to open the semiconductor market in 1987). These did relatively little economic damage to Japan, and certainly none of these episodes generated successive rounds of counterretaliation. Indeed, in some cases (automobiles, for example), the Japanese government willingly restricted exports to the United States for a period of time to avoid tighter restrictions that might have resulted from congressional action.

These actions by the United States and Japan might seem to be contrary to international trade rules, given the emphasis on bilateral deals and de facto quotas under the name of voluntary export restraints. But is important to realize that the GATT/WTO framework is a relatively loose one and that this was especially true during the years of pressure on Japan. A number of U.S. negotiations with Japan were handled in a bilateral setting but always in a manner that was GATT-consistent (that is, whatever concessions the Japanese offered pertained to all trading partners, not just to the United States). The voluntary export restraints on automobiles and some other products certainly violated the spirit of the GATT, but they were not technical violations at the time (because GATT rules did not prohibit exporting nations from imposing restrictions on their exports). Thus, both governments played fast and loose with GATT rules—Japan with its opaque nontariff barriers and the United States with its imaginative use of loopholes to single out Japan for protectionist action. But both governments avoided overtly flouting the GATT. More important, each government worked to tighten some of the rules during the Uruguay Round of the GATT (which concluded in 1993 and created the WTO) in areas where it felt the other side had been an egregious manipulator of rules in the past. The "voluntary export restraint" loophole was plugged by the Uruguay Agreement (something that the Japanese and Europeans pressed for in the negotiations). Japan's use of safety standards on agricultural products was limited by a new requirement to demonstrate the scientific need for and validity of the standards (something that the United States pressed for). And more recently, Japan and others have tried to scale back the scope of U.S. antidumping rules in the Doha Round of WTO negotiations. A number of the negotiating sticks that the U.S. government employed in negotiations with Japan in the past, therefore, are no longer used. Rather than railing against the WTO, the U.S. government has accepted this constraint on its negotiating options with reasonably good grace.

Second, as unfair as Japanese protectionism seemed to U.S. companies adversely affected by it, enough U.S. firms benefited from economic interaction with Japan that the broader bilateral relationship was not likely to spin out of control. Even during the rather intense period of negotiations in 1993–1995 (the Clinton administration's Framework Talks with the Japanese government), what business lobbies wanted was completed negotiations, not failure followed by retaliatory action. Angry voices in U.S. society desiring punitive retaliation against Japan were few.

Third, the dynamics of negotiation, coupled with the Japanese government's own sense of economic self-interest gradually led to markets that were more open. Although the pace of change has often been discouragingly slow, a number of past problems were resolved and today there are fewer complaints by U.S. firms concerning the terms of access to Japan. That is, instead of totally obstructing liberalization, which would have undermined the global trading system, self-interest led the Japanese government in the direction of opening markets.

Even today, Japan stands out for a relatively low level of imports and inward direct investment. Imports are less than 10 percent of GDP, no higher than 40 years ago, although manufactured goods are a higher share and raw materials a lower share of imports today. Foreign direct investment continues to be only about 1 percent of gross domestic capital formation (well below the level of other industrialized nations or the global average), despite a rash of highly visible acquisitions by foreign corporations in the late 1990s. What matters, however, is that foreign firms are more satisfied with the conditions of access to Japanese markets than in the past, making them less likely to complain to the U.S. government.

Japanese trade and investment behavior leads to two important conclusions. First, the reason that disputes did not spin out of control was because of economic interests on both sides, not because of the U.S.-Japanese security relationship. That is, the U.S. government did not pull its punches because of fear of losing Japan as an ally, nor did the Japanese government make concessions out of any similar fear—although there are certainly a handful of episodes in which such concerns were expressed. What really kept the economic relationship under control was the existence of powerful economic interests on both sides that would have been damaged if disputes had led to rounds of protectionist retaliation and counterretaliation. This conclusion is the opposite of the conventional wisdom in the past—that the importance of the security relationship constrains behavior on trade policy. There are certainly anecdotes of occasions on which U.S. officials concerned with the bilateral security relationship specifically tried to undercut pressure on trade issues.[8] However, had this interpretation of what kept economic issues from spinning out of control been generally true, then bilateral relations in the 1990s should have been worse than they were because the Cold War and the overriding importance of the security relationship disappeared.

Second, global institutions—the GATT and now the WTO—worked. This statement may seem an odd one given the fact that many bilateral trade disputes from the 1950s through the early 1990s proceeded outside the GATT. However, as previously noted, neither the United States nor Japan so abused the system as to cause a collapse of the global framework. Furthermore, the agreements on opening Japanese markets that resulted from bilateral bargaining were always formally on an MFN basis (that is, they applied to all of Japan's other trading partners), even if all participants knew perfectly well that the Americans would be informally favored in the outcomes. And, as already discussed, the new WTO resulted in tighter rules restricting the ability of the U.S. government to use unilateral retaliatory protectionist actions as a bargaining tactic against countries such as Japan, as well as limits on Japan's ability to use nontariff barriers such as safety standards to protect domestic markets. The U.S. government did not initially support the proposal for creating the WTO, but it acquiesced as a necessary element of bringing the Uruguay Round to a successful close, and it has used the new WTO dispute-resolution rules actively in cases involving Japan and other countries.

JAPAN is a preeminent example of a nation that adapted to the new global economic paradigm since the mid-twentieth century. The government embraced the concept of growth without colonies, learned to live with high import ratios for critical raw materials, and manipulated the international trade rules to protect its home markets while making enough concessions to prevent the U.S. government from abandoning the GATT/WTO system out of frustration. All of this was achieved with a constitutional prohibition in place on using military force to resolve international disputes. Back in the 1970s, many Japanese were fearful of the consequences of depending on imports of raw materials and food, but those fears are largely absent today. The farm lobby still fulminates about the need to avoid the danger of relying on imported foodstuffs, but even this lobby is gradually losing its power (as farmers decline in number and redistricting slowly reduces their voting power).

China

The story of the change in China and its relationship with the world over the past three decades is a dramatic one. After almost a half century of bitter, lethal civil war and war against Japan, the victorious communist Chinese leaders in 1949 found themselves in the Soviet economic bloc and largely excluded economically from the rest of the world. The disastrous Great Leap Forward of the late 1950s (an ill-conceived inward-looking attempt at domestic economic development—think of import substitution run amok) and the equally traumatic Cultural Revolution of the late 1960s left China impoverished and isolated compared to its noncommunist Asian neighbors, which were growing and industrializing vigorously. But beginning with the diplomatic thaw with the United States in 1972, the death of Mao Zedong in 1976, and the decision by Deng Xiaoping in 1979 to initiate economic reform, China began to emerge from its isolation. As Nicholas Lardy, an economist, puts it, the Chinese government "increasingly has staked its legitimacy on its ability to deliver sustained improvements in consumption and living standards to the Chinese people."[9] Economic reform at home in the direction of a market-based economy and opening up to trade and investment have been key elements in the government's approach to delivering these sustained economic improvements.

The World Bank estimates that China grew at an annual average real rate of 5.3 percent from 1961 to 1979 (keeping in mind that the quality of the economic data in this period is suspect, so this growth rate may be inaccurate and more likely to be overestimated than underestimated). From 1980 through 2003, the average growth rate was 9.4 percent— the highest in the world for this period of time (although this number may also be overestimated), comparable to the Japanese experience of 1950–1973.[10] Economic reforms unleashed private economic activity, and the role of state-owned enterprises declined. The urban landscapes of Beijing, Shanghai, and Guangzhou have been radically transformed in the past two decades. When I first visited Shanghai in 1987, the area visible across the river from the old Bund district (the pre–World War II center of foreign investment) was largely farmland and woods; today this is the Pudong district, a whole new city and industrial zone of several million residents that is considered part of the heart of modern Shanghai. The Chinese economic growth experience has been quite different from the earlier Japanese one because the government has embraced both a higher dependence on trade and a greater openness to inward direct investment.

International Trade

The transformation of trade is nothing short of stunning. As shown in figure 5.2, from a level only 2 percent of GDP in 1970, both imports and exports rose to exceed 30 percent of GDP by 2003. Despite the fact that China still maintains substantial tariffs and other barriers to imports, these data represent an astounding expansion of exposure of a large continental economy to international trade. On the export side, the shift is also remarkable, especially because the success in export markets is driven to a considerable extent by foreign firms investing in China (discussed later in the chapter). The contrast to the Japanese experience is obvious; in China, the decision to engage in trade with the world, to gradually lower import barriers, and encourage inward direct investment made a material difference in the role of international trade in the economy.

Chapter 1 explains that the preponderance of economic research concludes that more open trade is beneficial for growth. The facts that Japan grew rapidly from 1950 to 1973 behind a wall of import and direct investment barriers that held imports to 10 percent or less of GDP and had exports that ranged from 10 to 14 percent of GDP suggest that growth and exposure to trade need not be closely connected. However, Japan in the 1950s was a very different economy than China in the 1980s; Japan had a strong corporate sector with skilled managers and engineers, the product of successful industrialization since the 1870s. As a result, domestic Japanese firms were able to acquire technology and build their own industries more easily than has been the case in China, where

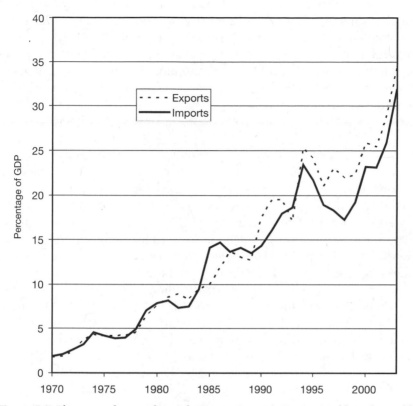

Figure 5.2 Chinese trade as a share of GDP, 1970–2005. *Source:* World Bank, *World Development Indicators 2005* (CD-ROM) (Washington, D.C.: World Bank, 2005).

manufacturing was dominated by inefficient, bureaucratic, state-owned enterprises. Even today, there are weaknesses in both overall management skill and the ability to assimilate and adapt foreign technology.[11] Therefore, China had a more critical need than Japan to open its economy to imports to help drive the economy toward greater efficiency.

As part of the process of opening the economy, the Chinese government made a strategic decision to join the GATT in 1986. Negotiations dragged on for many years—reflecting a variety of factors, including U.S. ambivalence about admitting China, the diplomatic disruption following the Tiananmen Square massacre, and an escalating set of demands from the U.S. government and others for market-opening concessions as the price of admission. Nicholas Lardy, the leading expert on this issue, argues that China agreed to far more extensive liberalization measures than other developing nations joining the GATT/WTO.[12] Despite the stiffness of the demands, the negotiations with the United States and other leading members of the WTO were finally successful and China became a member at the end of 2001. The accession of China—the world's most populous nation—to the WTO was a major victory for the coverage and robustness of the global economic system. China became embedded in the principal global trade organization, its markets became more open, and the WTO itself became a more inclusive and legitimate global institution.

Direct Investment

A somewhat similar story of expansion applies to foreign direct investment. From close to zero in 1981, the flow of inward direct investment expanded slowly to 3 percent of total fixed capital formation by 1990 and then exploded to 15 percent by 1995 before subsiding to 8 percent by 2003—still a relatively high level.[13] The decline in this percentage has occurred because the denominator (total domestic fixed-capital formation) has expanded very quickly, not because the amount of annual investment has fallen. Indeed, in 2004, the officially reported flow of direct investment into China was $54 billion.[14] As with many statistics in China, there are some doubts about the accuracy of these numbers. In 2004, 36 percent of inward investment was from Hong Kong, some of which is believed to represent "round-trip" investment by Chinese investors laundering investment money through Hong Kong firms in order to take advantage of various financial incentives provided to foreign investors. Nevertheless, the general conclusion that inward investment is a substantial share of annual fixed investment remains, a conclusion to which any visitor to China can attest.

Much of the investment is in the manufacturing sector, and initial rules on inward investment restricted foreign firms' access to the domestic market for their output, with the result that foreign-owned firms accounted for about one-half of China's exports by 2000.[15] For computers, foreign firms generated 75 percent of exports in 2003, and in electronics and telecommunications equipment they generated 71 percent.[16] Thus, although 8 percent of total domestic fixed-capital formation may seem like a low number, the concentration of foreign direct investment in areas such as export manufacturing gives foreign firms in China a critical importance in the overall economic growth and development process. That the Chinese government permitted this to happen when the government had pursued over thirty years of near autarky and had regarded the United States, Japan, and Europe as enemies from 1949 until the 1970s is remarkable. The contrast to Japan—a nation that has been a formal military ally of the United States since 1952 but that has maintained stiff barriers on inward investment through the 1970s and still attracts relatively little investment—is also remarkable.

Taiwanese firms are among the largest investors in China, and as many as 1 million Taiwanese live in China managing these investments. Investments include successful Taiwanese electronics firms that combine their design capabilities with production facilities on the mainland.[17] Thus, despite political tensions concerning Taiwan's ambiguous international status and occasional outbreaks of belligerent posturing by both the Taiwanese government (hinting at a declaration of independent sovereignty) and the Chinese government (claiming sovereignty over Taiwan and threatening the use of force should Taiwan declare independence), trade and investment has blossomed to a remarkable degree.

Trade and Investment Problems

The commitments made by the Chinese government as the price for joining the WTO include many that have yet to be enforced with any vigor, especially in the area of protection of intellectual property rights. By 2005, disputes over intellectual property rights were becoming a key issue in U.S. government policy toward China and fed into overall U.S. anxiety about the implications of expanding economic relations with China.

However, there are three important points to keep in mind when considering the problems of implementation of Chinese WTO and broader problematic behavior in business dealings. First, we can expect that the pattern will be much as it was with Japan. That is, problems and disputes will continue for many years and the tensions will occasionally appear to be quite strong. Other than tariffs—which are clear and measurable and usually fall as promised—the implementation of commitments can be delayed, only partially implemented, or offset by countermeasures that require further government-to-government negotiations. U.S. frustration with Japan over such problems was often intense, as discussed in the previous section of this chapter. The same will be true with China. Nevertheless, as with Japan, the economic interests of both governments should be sufficiently powerful that mutually acceptable solutions will be worked out, even if those fall short of completely satisfying U.S. firms. And U.S. government officials will have the same desire to reach a settlement—no bureaucrat or political appointee really wants to be known as the person who failed to reach an agreement and caused a broader deterioration of economic relations.

Second, in contrast to relations with Japan, U.S. firms have a much stronger vested interest in China and, therefore, a stronger interest in resolving problems rather than simply seeking retaliation. U.S. firms are more deeply connected to China through exports and direct investment than they were to Japan during the years of disputes with Japan, so their vested interest in keeping the relationship functioning is much stronger. When Japanese imports increasingly penetrated the U.S. market from the 1950s through the 1980s, those products were almost exclusively produced by Japanese-owned firms. U.S. firms felt little compunction in seeking retaliation for perceived bad behavior by Japanese firms because the Americans had so little at stake in Japan, either through exports or direct investment. In China, in contrast, imports are three times higher as a share of GDP than in Japan, and the inflow of direct investment is also much higher. Many U.S. imports from China are produced by U.S.-owned factories in China. This reality means that U.S. firms benefit from their presence in China, giving them a strong incentive to prevent trade and political disputes from spinning out of control. Of course, to the trade hawks in Washington politics this situation is not desirable. Phil English, a congressman from Pennsylvania who headed the Congressional Steel Caucus in 2005, complained that the U.S. government was reluctant to properly confront China because "many companies are depending on Chinese inputs and on imported goods to sell at retailers."[18]

In principle, keeping a lid on trade disputes is desirable, but it is important to realize that some issues are legitimate, especially the sorry state of protection of intellectual property in China. The lack of enforcement exacerbates the theft of intellectual property because the perpetrators believe that they will not be punished. Violations range from pirating CDs, DVDs, and computer software (relatively easy to do in any country) or imitating brand-name fashion items to more complex copying of sophisticated manufactured products (such as pharmaceuticals) and manufacturing processes. Indeed, there was one case in 2005 in which General Motors alleged that the Chinese virtually copied one of its automobile models. Even when the government does act to protect intellectual property, the results are not always satisfactory—as in a 2004 case where China's State Intellectual Property Office overturned Pfizer's patent in China on Viagra.[19]

What should be the reaction to these problems? First, it is important to recognize that cutting China back out of global economic flows in angry retaliation for misbehavior in areas such as intellectual property is not a realistic or desirable option. To that extent, Representative English was correct—U.S. firms and consumers are intertwined with China in ways that inhibit U.S. policy responses. But this should be welcomed rather than lamented. First, as any economist would argue, imports from China are good for the U.S. economy. But in addition, protectionist moves would damage the Chinese economy (in the theoretical, although unlikely, case in which other large trading partners join with the United States in isolating China), an outcome that would have a highly negative impact on the attitudes and broader foreign policies of the Chinese government. To put the matter crudely, there is no surer way to turn China into an enemy than to whack it too hard over trade problems. That is not to say that the U.S. government cannot afford to be determined and sharp in dealing with trade issues, just that the scale of the effort needs to be kept at a moderate level.

Second, it is important to realize that intellectual property violations are an old game—what is happening in China is little different from what has happened in all developing countries (including the United States in the nineteenth century). When technology is relatively easy to steal and when the owners of intellectual property charge high prices for legitimate access, firms in developing countries have an incentive to ignore the rules. Governments and firms in developing countries see little incentive in protecting foreign-owned intellectual property if they can get away with stealing it without retribution. The only real solution is to patiently encourage better enforcement and wait for firms to stop stealing technology as they develop further and have their own technology or brand name to protect.

Third, intellectual property theft is related to price. The purpose of intellectual property rights is to provide an incentive to create new products and technologies. But the risk to society is that those monopoly rights generate excess profits and delay the spread of useful technologies more broadly through the economy. Patent and copyright laws are an imperfect attempt to walk the line between too little protection (discouraging innovation) and too much (slowing the spread of innovations). What Americans might view as an acceptable price at home for products protected by these monopoly rights is often viewed as much too high in developing countries, providing a further incentive to simply steal the technology. Even for the U.S. government, there remains a fine line in dealing with countries such as China between standing up for important U.S. corporate interests (interests that have become more significant as the economy has become more knowledge-intensive) and simply helping greedy monopoly holders of patents and copyrights to extract excess profits from the rest of the world.

WHERE does this discussion leave us? The large story of China is that deliberate decisions to open the nation to trade and investment have deeply embedded the Chinese economy in the world economy. China has made enormous moves in opening its economy to trade and investment, symbolized by its joining the WTO in 2001 and by the high ratios of both exports and imports to GDP. U.S. and other foreign firms have responded to the opening and are now heavily involved in the Chinese economy. But problems remain both in the implementation of commitments made by China on joining the WTO and in the broader questions of the rule of law and business ethics. Dealing with these problems requires attention by the U.S. government and other members of the WTO, with continuous negotiations and pressure on the Chinese government. This process, however, needs to be a measured one; as in all negotiating games, there is always the danger of pushing too hard and causing the other party to stop playing.

Except under extreme circumstances, however, the Chinese government is likely to continue to play the game—making enough concessions or positive responses to foreign complaints to keep its principal economic partners from imposing retaliatory protectionist measures. Industrialization and economic growth depend to a large extent on continuing the flow of exports, imports, and inward direct investment. Imports bring critical machinery and components necessary for the growth of the manufacturing sector, as well as consumer products containing technology or having other attributes unavailable at home. Exports play an equally critical role, providing the foreign exchange earnings needed to buy imports (although China currently exports considerably more than needed to pay for imports—leading to complaints from the United States about the level of the exchange rate). For investment, it is important to point out that China does not need inward investment on a net basis—the Chinese economy generates an extraordinary rate of domestic savings (over 40 percent of GDP) that can be mobilized to finance domestic investment. But lacking technology, managerial skills, and quality control, the government has recognized that foreign firms could play a major role in creating a successful export industry—as they have. In these ways, opening the economy and becoming deeply intertwined with the rest of the world has played a strong positive role in the growth and development of the Chinese economy.

The broader consequence of these economic developments is to introduce a new and growing economic element into the Chinese foreign policy formation process. Back at the beginning of the 1980s, when the nation was largely isolated from the outside world, economic factors had no impact on foreign policy decisions. Today, these economic connections matter and appear to have a substantial impact on foreign policy because members of the government policy elite recognize the strong economic benefits that flow from the nation's international connections. Over the past several years, the government has moved to settle irritating border disputes with Russia, India, and Vietnam, and even negotiated a code of conduct for the disputed Spratly Islands.[20] The government permitted demonstrations by students against the Japanese in the spring of 2005, but moved to quell them and accept conciliatory moves by the Japanese government after a relatively short period of time. Even with Taiwan, flaring tensions in the spring of 2005 were quickly ended and the Chinese government extended its "charm offensive" to the opposition party in Taiwan.

An expansion of military expenditures, including the modernization of military equipment, coupled with continued claims of sovereignty over Taiwan, implies that uncertainty remains concerning the future behavior of the Chinese government. And the fact that the government is not democratic may indicate a greater reason for some concern about the future. But whether it is democratic or not, the Chinese government has made important decisions over the past three decades that have so thoroughly embedded it in the global economy that it would seriously jeopardize the economy's performance should it choose to pursue military action against Taiwan. Although the danger may not have entirely disappeared, certainly the probabilities have shifted dramatically.

Skeptics might argue that the government is only temporarily pursuing an open strategy—sucking in foreign firms and stripping them of technology—to build up the economy (and, thereby, the military) before returning to a more belligerent strategy in the future. But once foreign firms are as involved in the economy as they are in China, it is difficult to reverse direction. Plus, exports are even higher than imports; Chinese prosperity today and in the future depends on its ability to continue exporting goods to the rest of the world. The Chinese have discovered that the existing trade and investment system works to their economic advantage, so why jeopardize prosperity?

Southeast Asia

Most of the nations in Southeast Asia belong to the multilateral organization ASEAN. The members of ASEAN and the year they joined are listed in table 5.2. All the ASEAN nations are former European colonies with the sole exception of Thailand.

These nations did not achieve their independence until after the Second World War and in some cases not until the late 1950s (see table 5.2). Independence was often a bloody affair, beginning from insurgent groups in the 1930s, temporary military occupation by the Japanese, and renewed struggle against the returned European colonial powers after 1945. It is quite natural, therefore, that the newly independent governments of these nations would have a deep antipathy toward the West and would prefer to pursue domestic economic development behind high trade and investment barriers. What is remarkable about these nations, therefore, is their relative openness to both trade and investment.

Table 5.2 ASEAN members[a]

	Date of Joining ASEAN	Date of Independence	Colonial Power
Brunei	1984	1984	Britain
Cambodia	1999	1953	France
Indonesia	1967	1949	Netherlands
Laos	1997	1949	France
Malaysia	1967	1957	Britain
Myanmar	1997	1948	Britain
Philippines	1967	1946	Spain/United States
Singapore	1967	1963	Britain
Thailand	1967		Independent but effectively under Japanese control 1941–1945
Vietnam	1995	1954	France

Sources: Central Intelligence Agency, *The World Factbook*, available at http://www.cia.gov/cia/publications/factbook/ (February 23, 2006); Association of Southeast Asian Nations, "Overview," available at http://www.aseansec.org/64.htm (February 23, 2006).

[a] ASEAN, Association of South East Asian Nations.

Once the process of nation building was completed and the effects of the 1970s oil shocks over, growth was strong, as shown in table 5.3. Average growth for most was above 5 percent for the period from 1985 to 2003 (and keep in mind that these averages include the deep recession experienced by Indonesia, Malaysia, and Thailand in 1998, caused by the Asian financial crisis). With moderate population growth, GDP per capita has also grown rapidly—at rates of 3.4–5.0 percent for all but one. The laggard in the region has been the Philippines, dragged down mainly by the prolonged poor policies of the Ferdinand Marcos regime in the 1970s and 1980s. From 1989 (the end of the Marcos government) to 2003, GDP growth in the Philippines was a considerably higher 6.6 percent.[21]

Those countries that achieved independence, internal political cohesion, and an institutional framework for a market-based economy performed the best economically, with levels of per capita GDP (at purchasing power parity exchange rates) ranging from $3,000 to $23,000. In contrast, those that experienced periods of socialism—Vietnam, Laos, and Cambodia—experienced poor economic performance and became embroiled in internal strife. But once the conflicts were over in the 1980s, and economic reform began in the 1990s, their economic performance improved, bringing per capita GDP up to a level of $1,600–2,300. The World Bank does not have data on Myanmar, the problematic ASEAN member still run by a thuggish military regime with little economic reform. Nevertheless, the fact remains that overall this region has grown rapidly, fueled by political stability since the 1980s and market-based institutions.

Table 5.3 Economic growth in ASEAN countries[a]

	Average Growth 1985–2003		GDP per Capita	
	Real GDP (%)	GDP per Capita (%)	1985 ($PPP)	2003 ($PPP)
Brunei	n.a.	n.a.	n.a.	n.a.
Cambodia[b]	6.6	4.0	n.a.	1,963
Indonesia	5.0	3.4	1,769	3,175
Malaysia	6.1	3.4	4,729	8,986
Laos	5.6	3.0	966	1,662
Philippines	3.1	0.8	3,547	4,082
Singapore	6.3	3.8	10,826	23,127
Thailand	6.2	5.0	2,989	7,175
Vietnam	6.6	4.7	n.a.	2,353
Myanmar	n.a.	n.a.	n.a.	n.a.

Source: World Bank, *World Development Indicators 2005* (CD-ROM) (Washington, D.C.: World Bank, 2005).

[a] Per capita GDP in 1985 and 2003 is measured in constant purchasing power parity dollars ($PPP). ASEAN, Association of South East Asian Nations; n.a., not available.

[b] The average growth data for Cambodia are for 1994–2003; the World Bank has no data for Cambodia prior to 1994.

Trade

As these nations grew, they also became more open to international trade. Figure 5.3 shows the changes in the ratio of imports to GDP in four of the original ASEAN members. Singapore, a small city-state that, like Hong Kong, is a port through which goods pass to and from other nations, has a ratio of imports to GDP over 150 percent of GDP and does not appear in this figure. The others all show rising levels of imports. Indonesia, the Philippines, and Thailand now have ratios of imports to GDP of 25–60 percent, and Malaysia has reached 100 percent (however, this may be an artifact of bad data; or Malaysia, like Singapore, may play a major role in passing products to and from other nations). All four of these countries have trade barriers, but with these barriers declining, the level of imports in their economies has risen substantially.

The situation in the other, poorer ASEAN countries is somewhat more mixed. As shown in figure 5.4, Cambodia, Laos, and Vietnam have rejoined the global world since the end of the protracted military conflict in Indochina ended in the mid-1970s. The change for Vietnam and Cambodia has been dramatic, with imports now at 70 percent of GDP—with all of the increase coming after 1985. Laos had reached 50 percent of GDP, but the import ratio dropped in half to 25 percent from 2000 to 2003.

The one exception to this trade openness is Myanmar. Even though Myanmar has joined the ranks of ASEAN, it has become increasingly

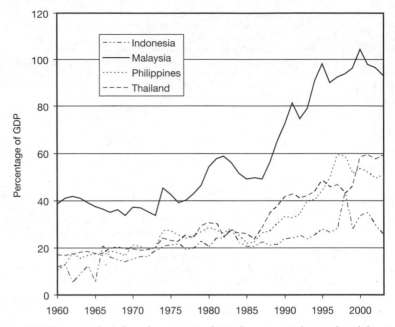

Figure 5.3 Imports of goods and services in the Indonesian, Malaysia, the Philippines, and Thailand as a share of GDP, 1960–2005. *Source:* World Bank, *World Development Indicators 2005* (CD-ROM) (Washington, D.C.: World Bank, 2005).

isolated economically, and it is probably one of the few nations in the world where the ratio of imports to GDP has actually fallen (to close to zero).

Trade flows within ASEAN have been enhanced by the signing of the ASEAN Free Trade Area (AFTA) agreement in 1991. AFTA is an imperfect free trade area, with each member reserving the right to continue to protect some favored products and industries, and its implementation has been slow. The pace of movement toward creating a common regional market has proceeded more slowly and less completely than in Europe (explored in chapter 4). Nevertheless, AFTA has lowered intra-ASEAN tariffs considerably. Some ASEAN members have also begun signing free-trade agreements with important trade partners outside the region, including with the United States, Japan, and Australia. Finally, ASEAN as a whole is implementing a free-trade agreement with China. With this proliferation of agreements, it is clear that the ASEAN countries (except Myanmar) have strongly embraced international trade and the benefits it provides. With falling intra-ASEAN barriers, moreover, the region has emerged as a successful regional manufacturing platform, despite concerns by regional governments about the relative inability of ASEAN to compete with China as a manufacturing base for foreign firms.

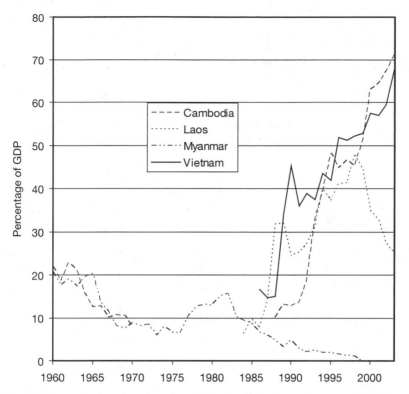

Figure 5.4 Imports of goods and services in the Cambodia, Laos, Myanmar, and Vietnam as a share of GDP, 1960–2005. *Source:* World Bank, *World Development Indicators 2005* (CD-ROM) (Washington, D.C.: World Bank, 2005).

As with China, it is easy to argue that opening up to trade has been good for ASEAN economic growth and development. Imports have provided these economies with needed industrial inputs and have pushed competing domestic industries to greater efficiency. Exports have also been a powerful driver of efficiency for any firm wanting to enter global markets. And the lowering of barriers (even if imperfect) within ASEAN has created a larger market and more competition across the region.

Direct Investment

The role of ASEAN as a manufacturing base is intimately related to inward direct investment. Figure 5.5 shows investment inflows as a percentage of gross domestic fixed-capital formation, as averages by decade since 1970 (which provides a clearer picture than annual numbers, which tend to fluctuate considerably). Singapore, an international financial center, has long attracted investment, although even there the ratio rose sharply to a remarkably high level of 63 percent in the 2000–2003

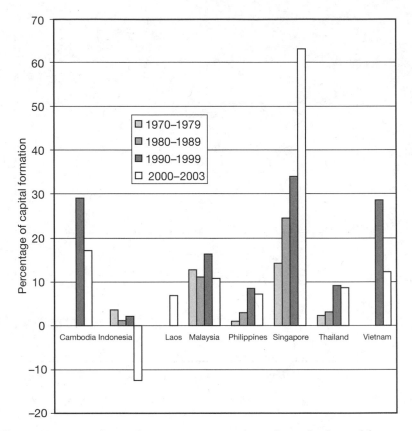

Figure 5.5 ASEAN foreign direct investment as a share of gross fixed-capital formation. *Source:* World Bank, *World Development Indicators 2005* (CD-ROM) (Washington, D.C.: World Bank, 2005).

period. Thailand, Malaysia, and the Philippines have fluctuated around 6–15 percent (roughly in the same range as China). Of the original ASEAN members, only Indonesia has failed to attract much foreign investment, and since 1998 foreign firms have been pulling out due to the continuing political uncertainty. Of the newer members, data are available for Cambodia, Laos, and Vietnam, all of which have attracted substantial amounts of investment since they began economic reforms.

Investments flowing into ASEAN countries have come predominantly from Europe, the United States, and Japan, much of it producing exports for the global market. The Japanese electronics industry has been especially visible in distributing production of components and finished products around the region.

Despite what we might expect to be a natural antipathy toward the West due to the history of colonization, the investment data indicate that Western firms are the dominant investors. Consider, for example, Malaysia. The long-time leader of Malaysia, Prime Minister Mahathir bin Mohamad (who served from 1981 to 2003), was a very outspoken anti-Western figure. Yet, even though he missed no opportunity for rhetorical diatribes against the United States and Europe and extolled Asian values, foreign direct investment has supplied 10–15 percent of Malaysian domestic capital formation since 1970. At one point, Prime Minister Mahathir championed a Look East policy, in which Japan rather than the West would be the favored economic model, trading partner, and source of direct investment. However, in the four years of 2001–2004, 21 percent of the inflows of direct investment were from Germany and 16 percent from the United States, with only 11 percent from Japan.[22]

THE openness of the ASEAN countries to trade and investment is a surprising development. Given their humiliating experience with Western imperialism, they had every reason to shun close ties with industrialized nations. For a time, some of them did pursue deliberate import substitution policies. But these governments have mellowed, and the level of trade and investment connection to the rest of the world is strong. Trade barriers and problems with investment certainly remain, but the direction of change in the past three decades has been to lower those barriers. These governments learned that they could accept trade and investment linkages without fear that they would jeopardize their newly won political independence.

Security Tensions

East Asia continues to harbor several potential security problems: the possible conflict with North Korea, the possible Chinese invasion of Taiwan, and Sino-Japanese tensions (and to a lesser extent, Japanese-South Korean tensions as well). These hot spots are driven to a large extent by noneconomic issues and are thus not directly part of the subject of this book. But they are evidence that the rising economic prosperity of the region and its increasing economic connections to the rest of the world are no guarantees that troubling security problems will disappear. Still, the economic trends of the region do have some positive bearing on these problems.

North Korea

The problem on the Korean peninsula is a relic of Cold War conflicts, a product of the division of the postwar occupation of Korea into Soviet and U.S. zones, the failed attempt of communist North Korea to forcibly unify the nation, and the armistice prevailing since 1953 that continues to leave the peninsula divided between a communist North and a capitalist (and now democratic) South Korea. The Cold War ended by 1990 and with it ended the subsidies from the Soviet Union that had helped to prop up the North Korean economy. Today, North Korea is a pit of poverty, stagnation, and isolation in a region that has grown much more affluent and open. When the Korean War broke out in 1950, North Korea was more affluent than the South, due to the concentration of Japanese colonial-period industrial investments in the North, but today the per capita GDP in South Korea is some ten times higher than in North Korea.

U.S. and South Korean forces remain deployed, but the prospect for another North Korean invasion is long gone—the North simply does not have the technology, resources, or training to successfully invade the South. Instead, a different problem has emerged. North Korea today is a small poor country in the midst of a region that has been growing and reforming for several decades, run by a despotic political regime increasingly worried that its own future and the independence of the country are in jeopardy. Rather than following the Chinese path of economic reform (although North Korea has tried this to some extent, but without much success, since 2002) and opening its economy to stimulate growth, North Korea chose to protect its independence by developing nuclear weapons (and thereby becoming even more isolated from the global economy), believing that these weapons will present a sufficient threat that the United States and other powers in the region will refrain from military action. The U.S. government, on the other hand, is adamantly opposed to the development of nuclear weapons by North Korea.

In 2004, a multilateral negotiation began, dubbed the six-party talks because they included North Korea, the United States, South Korea, China, Japan, and Russia. The talks proceed fitfully but resumed in the wake of a successful test of a nuclear bomb by North Korea during the fall of 2006, and an agreement was announced in February 2007. North Korea would shut down its single nuclear reactor, allow international inspectors to verify its closure, and disclose the full extent of its nuclear weapons development program. In exchange, the other five parties would provide fuel oil, the United States would begin bilateral talks leading toward diplomatic recognition, and Japan would begin bilateral talks aimed at diplomatic relations pending resolution of past abductions of its citizens. As of spring 2007, implementation of this agreement was still uncertain, as is often the case in dealings with North Korea. The very first step of shutting down the reactor was delayed pending release of funds belonging to North Korea in a bank in Macao that had been frozen under pressure from the U.S. government in September 2005.

The 2007 agreement was certainly a step in the right direction and represented an engagement with North Korea that was far more productive than the Bush administration's peevish refusal to negotiate during the 2001–2003 period. But the foot dragging by North Korea in implementing the agreement raises the question of why the offering by the United States and other parties was so meager. Other than a modest amount of fuel oil, all that North Korea gained was a promise to begin further talks that might bring further benefits. The incentive for North Korea to comply with the agreement, therefore, was rather limited—getting future discussions with uncertain outcomes in exchange for shutting down its nuclear weapons development program. Suspicion concerning North Korean intentions biases the United States and other parties from offering more than a sequential process of cautious steps, but a more substantial offer might produce better results.

Why not put a substantial economic package on the bargaining table? To be sure, Kim Jong Il is an outstanding example of a despotic leader running a highly dysfunctional and repressive regime. The world would be well rid of him and his government. But at what cost? The North Koreans would certainly lose a war, but they have had over a half century to dig their forces into the ground and would inflict heavy casualties while hostilities last. Furthermore, if North Korean military forces do have functioning nuclear weapons, they might actually use them, inflicting many more casualties. The only feasible alternative to a costly war is to coax out this paranoid regime: offer a guarantee not to attack, and offer to provide substantial economic assistance in exchange for its dropping the nuclear weapons development program. There is at least a chance that the offer of foreign aid, assistance in setting up foreign investment zones, and similar policies would overcome North Korean paranoia.[23] Dealing with the North Korean government is certainly extremely difficult, as it plays its limited negotiating cards for maximum advantage. But the obnoxiousness of the government's behavior should not obscure the desirability of a peaceful outcome, and that outcome may well require a more generous package of incentives. South Korea, on its own, reached an agreement several years earlier to build an industrial park across the border in North Korea, but this venture is very modest. It may serve as a test case, but it hardly represents the kind of opening up that is needed to draw North Korea into a more productive engagement with the world.

Taiwan Strait Tensions

The possibility of a Chinese invasion of Taiwan is the other major danger scenario in East Asia. In 1949, Chiang Kai-shek and his Kuomintang (KMT) fled the mainland to Taiwan at the end of the prolonged Chinese civil war. Refusing to admit defeat, he declared that his government in Taiwan continued to be the legitimate government of China. That fiction (with the backing of the United States) lasted until the 1970s, when the major powers finally recognized the People's Republic of China (PRC). The government in Taiwan eventually stopped pretending that it was the legitimate government of China, but it has remained in an uncomfortable limbo since—neither a province of China nor an independent Taiwan. Meanwhile, the PRC government continues to want Taiwan back. Although the history of Taiwan's political relationship to the mainland is ambiguous, the territory was part of China in the 1890s when it was ceded to Japan in the wake of the Sino-Japanese War, and Taiwan was formally returned to Chinese control in 1945 when Japan was defeated. From 1949 to the present a stalemate has prevailed, with periodic threats from China but no action.

Under normal circumstances, it is difficult to imagine China invading Taiwan. However, the one potential trigger is for Taiwan to declare itself a fully independent, sovereign state. Today Taiwan is formally recognized by very few governments, and it is officially represented in multilateral organizations (such as the Asian Development Bank, WTO, and the Olympics) under various euphemisms, such as Chinese Taipei. This ambiguity has existed now for several decades without serious incident. But should Taiwan reject the ambiguity and declare itself a sovereign state, that action could provoke a Chinese military attack.

An emotionally driven attack on Taiwan in the face of its attempt to declare full independence is certainly conceivable. However, the opportunity cost for China is much higher today than in the past. Although I have not included Taiwan in the earlier discussions in this chapter, it is important to recognize that Taiwan has been a highly successful economy, growing rapidly over the past half century. That growth has made the economy relatively affluent, with a GDP per capita around $15,000 and a highly successful manufacturing sector that plays a significant role in global trade in electronics and some other industries. With Taiwan serving as a major trading partner for China and as the source of large amounts of direct investment, war would destroy the goose that laid the golden egg. Furthermore, military action against Taiwan would undo China's profitable economic engagement with the rest of the world, and especially with the United States. If China's leaders are committed to bringing continued growth and rising household income to underwrite their political legitimacy, then invading Taiwan would suddenly undo their goals. To be sure, a realist might argue that the invasion of Taiwan would serve the purpose of rallying the public behind the regime—and some of the saber-rattling by the government in the past several years may well have been motivated by this goal. But we must wonder how long the domestic political benefit of invading Taiwan would last, even if the attack were successful and short. Having Taiwan back in the fold would certainly enhance the reputation of the Chinese government, but if severe sanctions by the United States and others then caused the economy to go into a recession, that support could be undone very quickly. Such calculations might not prevent an attack, but we must believe that a substantial part of the Chinese political leadership understands these dangers and will voice a policy of restraint on Taiwan.

Japanese-Chinese and Japanese-Korean Tensions

In recent years, diplomatic relations between Japan and China, and between Japan and South Korea, have deteriorated. Realists see this as the inevitable conflict between a major power (Japan) and its rapidly rising neighbors (China and South Korea). The story, however, is more complex.

From the 1970s to the late 1990s, Japan adopted a benign policy toward China. The Japanese government extended large amounts of foreign aid (of roughly $1 billion per year), encouraged Chinese trade and investment by Japanese firms, and moved more quickly than other major powers to restore normal relations after the Tiananmen Square massacre. For its part, the Chinese government played a game of reminding the Japanese of their wartime atrocities whenever it wanted more foreign aid or other economic favors.

In the case of South Korea, relations have not been close since the end of the Second World War. The Japanese had forced Korea into colonial status in 1911 and ran their new colony in a rather brutal fashion, despite considerable industrial investment. Land was forcibly removed from Korean farmers and given to Japanese colonists; people were forced to adopt Japanese names and use the Japanese language; and during the war, thousands of women were forced by the Japanese military into prostitution to service the Japanese army and thousands of men were shipped to Japan to work in mines and factories in slavelike conditions. However, in the 1990s relations appeared to be improving. During a bilateral summit meeting, the Japanese government offered an official apology for the colonial period, which was accepted by the South Koreans as a step forward. In 2002, the two countries jointly hosted the World Cup soccer tournament.

Relations began to deteriorate with China in 1998 when the Japanese government refused to extend an apology to visiting Chinese Premier Jiang Zemin similar to the one offered to Kim Dae Jung a few months previously. But the main problems between Japan and the other two countries have occurred in the period since 2001, after Junichiro Koizumi became prime minister. He made six trips to Yasukuni Shrine during his tenure (ending in September 2006)—a former state-run Shinto shrine that houses the spirits of Japanese war dead, including Class A war criminals (those tried and executed by an Allied tribunal after the Second World War for conspiracy to wage aggressive war). Official visits to this shrine are applauded by the political right wing in Japan and universally condemned by Japan's neighbors, especially South Korea and China. Prime ministers have generally avoided going to the shrine (Nakasone went once in the 1980s and then stopped in the face of Asian protests), so Koizumi's persistence—visiting once a year—was regarded by the Korean and Chinese governments as insulting to Asian sensitivities and as pandering to Japanese right-wing groups. Meanwhile, the Japanese government engaged in other provocative actions. In 2001, the Ministry of Education approved for use in the school system a right-wing history textbook that whitewashed war issues (although it was adopted by very few schools). Various Japanese politicians made anti-Chinese or anti-Korean statements in public, such as claiming that Korea had voluntarily become a colony of Japan or that the Nanjing massacre in 1938 was a fabrication. And Prime Minister Koizumi made unapologetic statements about his right to visit Yasukuni Shrine. In 2005, the Japanese government protested when it discovered a Chinese submarine lurking in Japanese coastal waters. Japan and China have contested ownership of a small rock in the East China Sea (called Senkaku in Japanese and Daiyou in Chinese, and occupied by Japan); Japan and South Korea dispute ownership of a small island (called Dokto in Korean and Takeshima in Japanese, and occupied by South Korea). In spring 2006, the Japanese government threatened to send a "survey team" of coast guard vessels to the vicinity of Dokto/Takeshima, and the South Korean government threatened to send its navy to stop them (with both sides backing off after several days of threats). In addition, as discussed in chapter 2, there is a dispute over the Chinese-Japanese boundary in the East China Sea in an area containing oil and gas deposits.

The Chinese responded to the provocations in kind—with antagonistic official complaints; a refusal to engage in bilateral summit meetings with Prime Minister Koizumi; bad behavior by spectators at a Chinese-Japanese soccer match in 2005; and several days of anti-Japan demonstrations in spring 2005, during which a few stones were tossed at the Japanese consulate in Shanghai.

Does all this not sound very juvenile? The only substantive issue has been the boundary dispute in the East China Sea because it affects rights

to oil and gas deposits. The rest is simply nationalistic posturing and deliberate insults. Why is this happening and where might it go?

First, in realist terms, some Japanese take umbrage at the rise of China.
From the mid-1980s, the Japanese basked in the self-image of being
the de facto, informal leaders of East Asia, although what this meant
in any operational sense is unclear. But after about 2000, much of the
talk in Asia (just as in the United States) was about the rise of China
rather than about Japan. The sense of being a leader began to slip away
from the Japanese, and some reacted with petulance. For example, in
2001 the Chinese government offered to negotiate a free trade area with
the ASEAN, forcing the Japanese government to somewhat reluctantly
make a similar offer, and they smarted from the image of following in the
wake of the Chinese leadership initiative.

Second, Japanese society appears to have moved in a somewhat more
conservative direction. With the passage of time and generational change,
people became tired of listening to reminders about past atrocities from
the Chinese and Koreans. On the fringe is a hard-line right-wing nationalism that would like to restore the honor, glory, and militarism of the
past, but this movement remains on the fringe. The Chinese are quick
to point to these right-wing groups and predict a return to the Japanese
militarism of the 1930s and 1940s, although this seems very unlikely.
For most, the feeling seems to be more one of being fed up with being
asked to apologize for the past. The contrast with Germany and its
postwar reconciliation with the rest of Europe is sharp. The Japanese
have not confronted their past in the way the Germans have, nor has
there been much formal regional dialog about reflection, contrition, and
reconciliation.

Third, some Japanese have the same misgivings about rising Chinese
military expenditures that some Americans have. What is puzzling about
this anxiety is that China has never threatened or attacked Japan in
recorded history (the only Chinese invasion—in the thirteenth century—
was by the Mongolians when they ruled China). Therefore, why the
Japanese should feel that Chinese military power is a threat to Japan is
unclear, but the feeling is a real one for some.

Fourth, the Japanese government perceived both the ambivalence of
the Bush administration toward China and the administration's desire
to strengthen U.S.-Japanese security ties. Encouraged by the sense of
close relations with the administration, Japanese political leaders felt that
they had the political cover to antagonize China and South Korea without
censure from the U.S. government or perhaps even with the administration's tacit approval. Some political leaders in Japan certainly dislike
China and Korea—often out of simple prejudice—and reveled in the

chance to express their views publicly without admonition from Washington. When President Bush visited Japan, South Korea, and China in fall 2005, for example, the White House made a point of not criticizing Japan's behavior. The official U.S. position was that other Asian nations should let bygones be bygones, as the United States had done with Japan. Although this is a good idea in principle, this approach explicitly ignored the recent provocations by the Japanese government—raking up bygones themselves. Thus, the U.S. approach essentially endorsed Japanese behavior—a mistake that the U.S. government finally appeared to recognize in 2006 when it began to put quiet pressure on all parties, including Japan.

What does all this imply for the large themes of this book? Japan and China have a rapidly expanding economic relationship. China is now Japan's largest trading partner (surpassing the United States), and Japanese firms have been roughly as active as U.S. firms in investing in China. Japan also has close economic relations with South Korea (especially because the Koreans gradually eliminated restrictions on the imports of Japanese consumer electronics and other products over the course of the 1990s). We would expect that this economic glue would cause both sides to be more mellow in their statements and diplomatic actions. Japanese businesses appeared to think that this was not necessary. They largely refrained from criticizing or pressuring Prime Minister Koizumi to be more conciliatory (probably out of fear of a right-wing backlash against their firms) on the dubious grounds that the "cold" diplomatic relations were not affecting the "hot" economic relations. At some point, however, those tensions could spill over in the form of greater hostility toward Japanese investment in China or perhaps less willingness to tackle intellectual property problems relating to Japanese firms.

Nevertheless, the economic glue does appear sufficiently strong to prevent an escalation to a more serious deterioration. It is, for example, difficult to imagine armed conflict over the East China Sea boundary dispute. The same is true of relations with South Korea. The underlying determination to prevent these tensions from spinning out of control were evident in fall 2006. As soon as Shinzo Abe replaced Koizumi as prime minister, he made a conciliatory trip to Beijing and Seoul. Known as an outspoken nationalist, he recognized the need to step back from the string of provocations. We may also guess that the Japanese business community made this need clear to him in return for their political support in the jockeying to replace Koizumi that summer. Equally instructive was the willingness with which the Chinese and South Korean governments accepted Abe's overtures. On all sides, therefore, there appears to be sufficient glue from deep, mutually beneficial economic ties to bring political leaders back to a less tense engagement.

———————

OVERALL, the story of East Asia since the mid-twentieth century has been an amazing positive tale of growth and increasing engagement with the rest of the world. From a war-torn region experiencing anticolonial revolutions and caught up in the titanic struggle of the Cold War, the region has become the major center of growth and development in the world. As these countries opened their borders to trade and investment, they have become locked into a pattern that has pushed them in a peaceful direction. China's decision to seek membership in the WTO, and the eventual willingness of the United States and other powers to permit this to happen, may be the single most important foreign policy action in the world in the past decade. Engaging in aggressive military action against their neighbors would disrupt all the benefits these countries have obtained through trade and investment. Even Japan, which colonized and invaded large parts of East Asia in the first half of the twentieth century, learned how to prosper without its colonial empire and to rely on imports for a substantial portion of its raw materials.

Nonetheless, potential conflict remains a possibility in the case of North Korea's nuclear weapons program and tensions between Taiwan and China. As I suggest in this chapter, however, even these problems have an economic component that gives some cause for hope. The other area of tension in the region—between Japan and its immediate neighbors South Korea and China—is far less serious. Although these relations may not be truly cordial in the future, the rapprochement under Prime Minister Abe indicates that all sides fundamentally understand the benefits flowing from their economic ties.

6. AREAS OF POVERTY

The previous three chapters sketched out the situation in economically successful parts of the world. In contrast to their economic prosperity and adaptation to the international economic framework, other regions have either remained trapped in poverty or have not succeeded very well in their attempts to grow and industrialize. These problems could be the biggest sources of tension and conflict that will affect U.S. foreign policy in the next several decades. The situation, however, is complex; although there are plenty of serious problems, there have been positive developments as well. This chapter reviews both these improvements and the continuing serious dilemmas.

Poverty does not paint a pretty picture—the images of poverty in the media are often discouraging scenes of despair, disease, malnutrition, and violence. Nevertheless, the economic performance of the developing world has been improving, particularly in the past ten to fifteen years. Economic growth has accelerated, the literacy rate is rising, population growth is down, domestic savings are rising along with fixed capital investment, trade has expanded, and inward direct investment is rising. These overall positive developments imply that the time is ripe for global attention on economic development. Done right, policy toward developing countries can help these countries remain on track to escape poverty.

However, not all of the developing world is doing better. At the bottom are a group of very poor countries that have not generated higher growth or industrialization for a variety of reasons: internal insurrection, poorly developed economic institutions, protectionism, rampant corruption, and other difficulties. Equally troubling are some other states that are highly dependent on the export of raw materials (and especially oil) and have bungled the use of their export earnings. These latter countries demonstrate the problem of premodern societies suddenly confronting the riches provided by the possession and export of an important raw material, principally oil. On the surface, they do not appear poor due to their large export earnings, but the economic record of these states is dismal, with large revenues feeding corrupt regimes while most of the population continues to live in poverty.

The poor countries of the world pose four problems. First, they can be the breeding grounds for international terrorism when economic failure is combined with religion, ideology, or other factors (as has been the case in Saudi Arabia, birthplace of Osama bin Laden). Second, even if they do not breed terrorism, poor countries provide a location for international terrorists to hide (e.g., Sudan and Afghanistan). Third, many of these countries have been wracked by internal conflict (e.g., Democratic Republic of the Congo and Rwanda). Even if those conflicts do not spill over borders, they present the developed nations with the problem of how to stop the violence, and they generate refugee problems that often do cross international boundaries. Fourth, some of these countries are the breeding grounds for disease—a problem that has a nasty habit of crossing international boundaries with considerable ease (as in the case of the spread of HIV/AIDS from sub-Saharan Africa to the rest of the world).

Before looking at the details, it is appropriate and important to note that the UN took a major step in 2000 in focusing global attention on the plight of poor countries. With the Cold War over and improved economic performance in some (but not all) of the developing world, Kofi Annan, the then-secretary general of the UN, pressed for a new commitment by the developed world to deal with these problems. The result was the Millennium Summit at the UN in September 2000, at which global leaders endorsed Secretary-General Annan's proposal. The declaration adopted was wide ranging—including such issues as human rights and democracy—but at the core was a set of commitments known as the Millennium Development Goals (see table 6.1). These include specific, measurable improvements to be accomplished by 2015. The UN reports annually on progress toward the goals.[1]

The UN has not been central to the story of this book, on the grounds that it is primarily an organization for international diplomacy and security rather than economics. The UN, however, has played an important economic role by establishing the Millennium Development Goals, and Kofi Annan deserves credit for spearheading this initiative. Although the UN does not have the defined economic role that the World Bank, IMF, or individual governments have in actually handling the specifics of foreign aid policy, these goals have created an important framework that guides the contemporary discussions of aid policy. With these goals in

Table 6.1 The millennium development goals

1. **Eradicate extreme poverty and hunger.**
    Reduce by half (from the 1990 level) the proportion of people living on less than $1 per day (measured in purchasing power parity terms).
    Halve (from the 1990 level) the proportion of the population that suffers from hunger.
2. **Achieve universal primary education.**
    Ensure that all children worldwide have the opportunity to complete a full course of primary education.
3. **Promote gender equality and empower women.**
    Eliminate gender disparity in primary and secondary education by 2005 and all levels of education by 2015.
4. **Reduce child mortality.**
    Reduce by two-thirds (from the 1990 level) the under-5 mortality rate.
5. **Improve maternal health.**
    Reduce by three-quarters (from the 1990 level) the maternal mortality rate.
6. **Combat HIV/AIDS, malaria, and other diseases.**
    Halt and begin to reverse the spared of HIV/AIDS by 2015.
    Halt and begin to reverse the incidence of malaria and other major diseases by 2015.
7. **Ensure environmental sustainability.**
    Integrate the principles of sustainable development into country policies and programs, and reverse the loss of environmental resources.
    Halve by 2015 the proportion of people without sustainable access to safe drinking water and basic sanitation.
    By 2020, achieve a significant improvement in the lives of at least 100 million slum dwellers.
8. **Develop a Global Partnership for Development.**
    Develop further an open, rule-based, predictable, nondiscriminatory trading and financial system.
    Address the special needs of the least-developed nations (free access for their exports, debt relief, and increased foreign aid).
    Address the special needs of landlocked countries and small island developing nations.
    Deal comprehensively with the debt problems of developing countries through national and international measures to make debt sustainable in the long term.

Source: United Nations, "Millennium Indicators," available at http://unstats.un.org/unsd/mi/mi_worldregn.asp (June 13, 2005).

mind, let us now look at the specifics of what has been happening in the developing world.

Improved Economic Performance

Economic development is a complex process. Growth requires political stability, rules enabling the creation of economic institutions (corporations, banks, markets, and the like), rule of law, property rights, savings and its deployment in capital investments, an educated workforce, and other factors. If getting all these elements right were easy, every nation in the world would be affluent. Some of the poor countries received large infusions of capital and institution building as colonies, but stumbled when they gained independence in the first three decades after the Second World War. In the absence of the crushing power of colonial overlords, ethnic and religious strife erupted in countries where the national boundaries were often the artificial constructs of the great powers and not the result of centuries of local conflict and political maneuvering. Despite such problems, the economic performance of the developing world has improved in recent years.

Economic Growth

The collapse of imperialism is now half a century in the past and the growth performance of the developing world has increased, on average, in recent years. The World Bank provides data for groups of countries by level of affluence—high, middle, and low-income—plus a smaller group of the least-developed nations.[2] Figure 6.1 shows changes in the growth in GDP per capita for these different groups. In a world where the less-affluent nations are catching up with the leaders, the growth rates for the middle-income, low-income, and least-developed countries should exceed those of the high-income countries. This is what happened to Japan in the twentieth century—and particularly in the first three decades after the Second World War—and what has been happening for the past two to three decades for China, South Korea, and a number of other East Asian nations, as discussed in chapter 5. Figure 6.1 shows that the middle-income countries (a group that includes the fast-growing East Asian nations) achieved this pattern in most of the five-year periods shown. But the low-income countries lagged behind from the 1960s through the first half of the 1990s (except for 1980–1984, when the growth in the high-income countries was diminished by inflation and recession following the 1979 oil price shock). These data imply that the gap in income levels between the low-income countries and the high-income industrialized countries actually widened from the 1960s until the mid-1990s—a discouraging trend. The least-developed countries fared even worse, although the data for this group date back only to 1980. In fact, for most of the period from 1980 to 1994, the GDP per capita for the least-developed countries actually declined in absolute terms.

Since 1995, however, the growth rates for GDP per capita in the low-income and least-developed nations have improved dramatically. The growth in income levels for both groups of countries is finally rising at a substantial 3 percent annual rate, exceeding the high-income countries and equaling the performance of the middle-income countries. Even

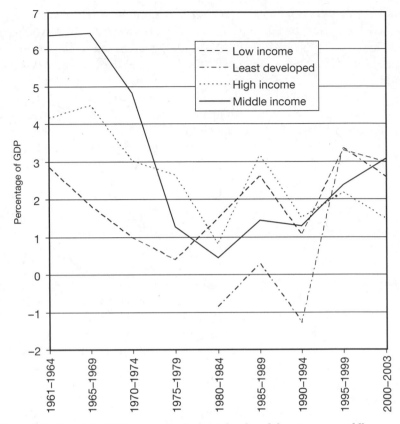

Figure 6.1 Growth in GDP per capita for least-developed, low-income, middle-income, and high-income nations, 1961–2003. *Source:* World Bank, *World Development Indicators 2005* (CD-ROM) (Washington, D.C.: World Bank, 2005).

though this favorable development began just recently—just over a decade ago—it is certainly encouraging.

Savings and Investment

Economic growth comes from several sources: more workers producing output, more capital equipment, and technological change (enabling more output for each worker or unit of capital). If the focus is on per capita output, then the extra output that comes from having more workers is irrelevant (although the increased output that comes from better-educated workers is not irrelevant, a factor considered later). This leaves capital and technology, which are often intertwined. Investing in additional capital stock requires money, which comes from savings. Individuals, for example, invest in a house by borrowing money from a bank, money that represents the savings of others. Businesses do the same, raising funds from the savings of others to invest in buildings and equipment. Although the savings needed to fuel investment do not necessarily need to come from inside one's country (if the government permits an inflow of investment from abroad), there is certainly a loose correlation between the domestic savings rate and capital investment.

Figure 6.2 shows changes in domestic savings expressed as a share of GDP. The high-income countries had a savings ratio of 25 percent in the 1960s, a level that subsequently declined modestly to 20 percent by 2003. The middle-income countries have been between 25 and 28 percent, putting them in a good position to mobilize those higher savings to fuel the more rapid expansion of capital stock and economic growth that occurred. The low-income countries, in contrast, began with quite low

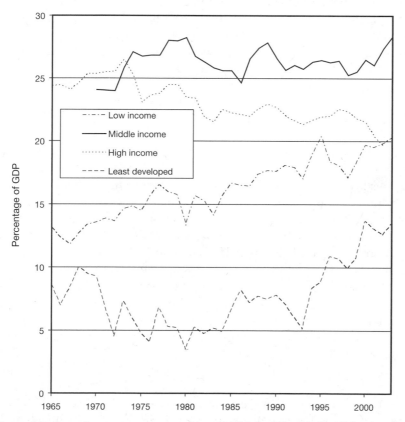

Figure 6.2 Gross domestic savings as a share of GDP for least-developed, low-income, middle-income, and high-income nations, 1965–2005. *Source:* World Bank, *World Development Indicators 2005* (CD-ROM) (Washington, D.C.: World Bank, 2005).

savings rates back in 1965, with a ratio of only 13 percent, but this rose quite steadily to 20 percent by 2003—the same level as the high-income countries. This is a major accomplishment. The group of least-developed countries had extremely low and falling savings rates, averaging only around 5 percent of GDP from 1970 to the mid-1980s. But even these countries experienced rising savings rates since then, reaching 13 percent by 2003—not high, but at least higher than before.

The next question is whether these societies have actually used their rising domestic savings—plus whatever money they borrowed from abroad—to fuel domestic investment in fixed capital—housing, government-constructed roads and other public infrastructure or private-sector factories, warehouses, and offices. Figure 6.3 shows the ratio of gross domestic fixed investment to GDP. As should be expected, the middle-income countries have had a high level of investment since 1975, ranging around 25 percent of GDP and outpacing the rate of investment in the more mature high-income countries (economies that are naturally growing more slowly and, therefore, do not need to spend as much of their GDP on fixed investment). The low-income countries had much lower investment ratios back in 1960—only 15 percent of GDP. But this level rose steadily, reaching 22 percent by 2003. Even the least-developed countries experienced rising investment levels, from only 10 percent of GDP in 1960 to 22 percent by 2003.

These data are quite encouraging. Low-income countries have clearly managed to increase domestic savings, and between the mobilization of those savings and borrowing from abroad, they have managed to increase domestic investment in fixed capital. Two important factors have helped produce this outcome: (1) the creation or expansion of financial institutions (mainly banks) to mobilize savings and lend to individuals and businesses for investment in new capital stock and (2) the improvement in property rights. Recall that Hernando de Soto, the Peruvian economist, argues that the lack of clear, legally enforced property rights has been a major obstacle to both savings and investment. These problems are clearly in decline, given the evidence of rising savings and investment rates. This trend toward higher savings and investment helps explain why the economic performance of poor countries has improved since the 1990s.

International Trade

Chapter 1 explains that greater openness to international trade is beneficial for economic growth. Most developing countries did not believe in this back in the 1950s, when the dominant concept was import substitution. According to this theory, poor countries should erect high barriers to

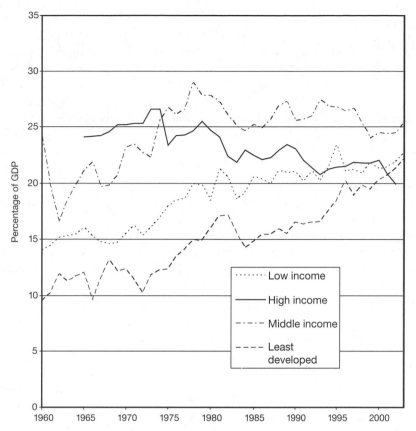

Figure 6.3 Gross domestic fixed capital formation as a share of GDP for least-developed, low-income, middle-income, and high-income nations, 1960–2005. *Source:* World Bank, *World Development Indicators 2005* (CD-ROM) (Washington, D.C.: World Bank, 2005).

imports in order to encourage and protect the development of domestic industries, which would not be able to compete against large established firms from abroad in the early years of their existence. Japan is often held up as an example of an economy that actually managed to make this theory work—experiencing explosive growth and productivity improvement behind a wall of high tariffs and quotas. Indeed, chapter 5 indicates that such policies were successful in Japan, at least in some industries. Japan, however, appears to have been a special case, with policies to encourage domestic competition and to encourage firms to reach a level of competitiveness at which they could penetrate foreign markets. The experience of most developing countries was quite discouraging; all they got were permanently inefficient industries, imposing a cost on the rest of society, which was forced to buy their expensive and often inferior products.

Figure 6.4 shows the changes in the ratio of imports to GDP for the low-income countries. From only 10 percent of GDP back in 1960, a level that was not far below the global average of 12 percent, the ratio of imports lagged well below the global average through the 1980s. Although the import ratio drifted upward in low-income countries, the world on average liberalized faster, and a wider gap opened up between the global average and the low-income countries. But since the late 1980s, the ratio for low-income countries has risen quickly and is now equal to the global average at 25 percent.

More imports also imply more exports. A nation's balance of trade (or, more precisely, the current-account, which includes goods, services, income on foreign investments, and foreign aid grants) reflects the big macroeconomic balances in the economy, as explained in chapter 3 in the case of the United States and its current-account deficit. The balance between domestic savings and investment, plus the government surplus or deficit, is the key variable. Although it is entirely possible for import

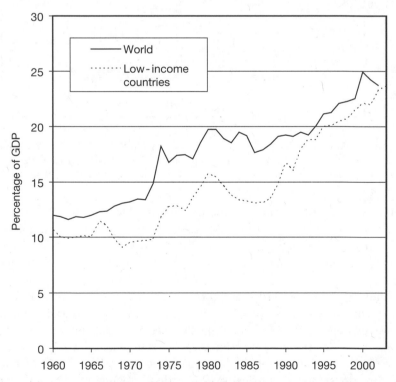

Figure 6.4 Imports of goods and services as a share of GDP for low-income countries and the world, 1960–2005. *Source:* World Bank, *World Development Indicators 2005* (CD-ROM) (Washington, D.C.: World Bank, 2005).

barriers to have complex domestic effects that might influence the level
of savings and investment, economists generally argue that a nation with
high import barriers to keep imports low will also probably experience
a low level of exports as well. Therefore, the greater exposure of low-
income countries to imports is associated with higher exports, shown in
figure 6.5. Back in 1960, low-income countries had an export ratio of only
8 percent, well below the global average of 12 percent. By 2002, the ratio
was up to 21 percent, still a bit below the global average of 24 percent but
not by as much of a margin.

The combination of rising imports and exports provides important
benefits for low-income countries. They have better access to the manufactured goods that they need to build their own economies—machinery,
components, construction equipment, and trucks and cars. Meanwhile,
exporting provides a powerful incentive for domestic industries to increase
quality and to control the cost of production because global markets are

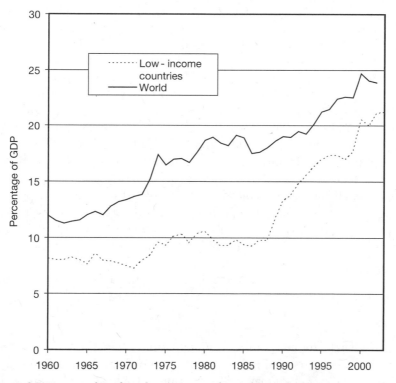

Figure 6.5 Exports of goods and services as a share of GDP for low-income countries
and the world, 1960–2005. *Source:* World Bank, *World Development Indicators 2005*
(CD-ROM) (Washington, D.C.: World Bank, 2005).

brutally competitive. The fact that low-income countries have become more exposed to both imports and exports, therefore, is encouraging and should be regarded as one of the causes of their accelerated economic growth since the mid-1990s. Recall, too, the international relations argument made in chapter 2; as these countries have become more exposed to trade, their governments are less likely to undertake aggressive actions against their neighbors because doing so would potentially disrupt their trade as their trade partners impose sanctions.

Foreign Direct Investment

In chapter 1, I show the sizable increase that has occurred in global flows of direct investment; in chapter 2, I explain why these flows are important both economically and for international relations; and in chapter 5, I show that the successful East Asian countries opened up to inflows of direct investment. Low-income countries in general have also become more open and have attracted more foreign direct investment. Figure 6.6 shows the changes in the share of domestic fixed-capital formation in these countries. Back in the 1970s, these countries experienced as much capital inflow as the world in general—which was very low. But when flows began to rise in the 1980s on a global basis, these countries lagged behind. For some, the problem was domestic political instability or corruption that scared off foreign investors. For others, the problem was falling raw material prices that discouraged foreign investors from developing mines or wells.

In the 1990s, investment began to rise in the low-income countries, just as it did on a global basis. These countries did not experience the spike in global flows at the end of the decade; that was driven by the temporary bubble in IT investment in the industrialized countries. Nevertheless, inflows of capital have risen to a level of 6–7 percent of domestic fixed-capital formation—considerably higher than the low 1–2 percent range from the 1970s through the 1980s. Although this is lower than, for example, in China—which is not included in the World Bank's set of low-income countries—recent inflows are not insignificant. These data provide further confirmation that, on average, these countries are moving away from import substitution policies and that foreign investors have responded positively to reductions in investment barriers.

Literacy

A critical factor in economic development is literacy. Farmers, factory workers, managers, and entrepreneurs all need to be able to read—to learn about new farming techniques, understand the instructions on bags of fertilizer, comprehend training manuals, read corporate memos, or learn about business opportunities. They also need to be able to

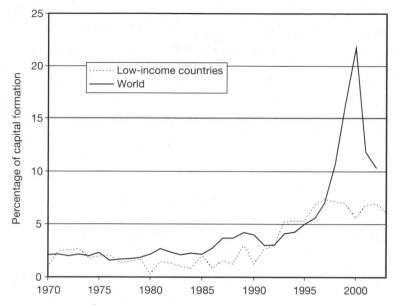

Figure 6.6 Foreign direct investment as a share of domestic fixed capital formation for low-income countries and the world, 1970–2005. *Source:* World Bank, *World Development Indicators 2005* (CD-ROM) (Washington, D.C.: World Bank, 2005).

write in order to cope with the requirements of a modern economy: filling out forms, communicating with customers, or applying for a loan. Economists use the term *human capital* to describe human attributes such as literacy or general education; like regular capital, human capital enables workers to be more productive. Literacy in the advanced industrial countries runs close to 100 percent, forming an important part of the human capital contributing to their economic performance. Literacy in the low-income countries rose from only one in three literate adults (or ~33 percent) in 1970 to 61 percent by 2001. The least-developed countries lagged behind this level, but experienced a similar growth during this time—from only 28 to 53 percent. Women in poor societies have lower literacy rates than men, but even these percentages have risen, so that by 2001 women's literacy was 48 percent in low-income countries and 42 percent in the least-developed countries. Thus, although the percentages still lag behind the advanced countries, the improvement in the past several decades has been substantial and the improvement continues.[3]

Literacy is a product of education. The data on education are spotty, but the available World Bank numbers show that the percentage of the relevant age cohorts completing primary school in low-income countries has risen from 65 percent in 1990 to 71 percent by 2002.[4] Other World Bank sources show that completion of primary school increased from 50 percent in 1990 to 59 percent by 2004 in sub-Saharan Africa and from 79 to 84 percent in the Middle East and North Africa.[5] Achieving 100 percent primary education by 2015 is one of the Millennium Development Goals of the UN (table 6.1), and the current upward trend is still insufficient to meet this goal. But the direction of change is clearly upward, underwriting the increase in adult literacy and assisting the bulk of the population in these countries to participate more successfully in economic development.

Population Growth

Prior to the Industrial Revolution, the birthrate was high, as was infant mortality. Over the past century, the spread of medicine and better medical practices caused the infant mortality rate to decline around the world, but the birthrate in many countries remained high. The result was a surge in population that often stymied efforts to raise the per capita income level; all the increase in economic output was simply spread across more people.

Figure 6.7 shows the changes in the total number of children expected to be born during a woman's reproductive lifetime given the actual births each year (known at the total fertility rate). Global fertility peaked at five children per woman around 1965 and declined to 2.6 by 2003. The high-income countries have been well below the average and even below the steady-state reproduction rate (about 2.1) since the mid-1970s. The low-income countries have been well above the global average—beginning at 6.2 children in 1960, but declining to 3.7 by 2003. The least-developed countries were even above this level, but they too experienced declines. Thus, although the rapid population growth in developing countries is not over, the danger of explosive population growth overwhelming economic growth has abated.

Even with falling birthrates, the proportion of children ages 0–14 in the total population of low-income countries has fallen more slowly due to reduced childhood mortality from disease. Thus, whereas this age cohort in the high-income countries declined from 28 percent in 1960 (a high ratio that was the result of the post–World War II baby boom) to 18 percent by 2003, it fell only from 41 to 37 percent in low-income countries. Still, the trend is downward, implying relatively fewer children for society to feed, clothe, and educate.[6]

THE picture of the low-income countries is mixed, but, on average, they show a number of encouraging trends, especially since the mid-1990s.

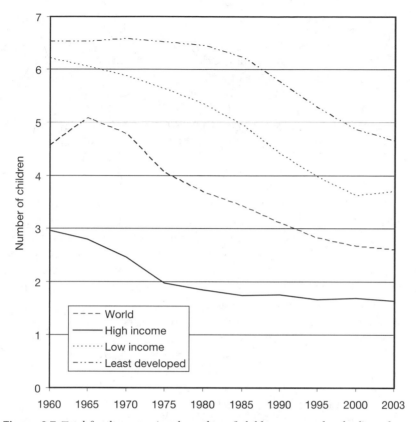

Figure 6.7 Total fertility rates (total number of children expected to be born during a woman's reproductive lifetime given the actual births each year) for least-developed, low-income, middle-income, and high-income nations, 1960–2003. *Sources:* World Bank, *World Development Indicators 2003* (CD-ROM) (Washington, D.C.: World Bank, 2003); *World Development Indicators 2005* (CD-ROM) (Washington, D.C.: World Bank, 2005).

Growth has picked up and finally exceeded that of the mature industrialized countries. Both savings and fixed investment have increased as a share of GDP, which should enable faster economic growth into the future. Trade—both imports and exports—has expanded as a share of GDP, and this should have a positive impact on growth. Foreign direct investment has increased, but the pattern is very mixed with some of the poorest countries still showing very low levels. Fertility rates have dropped, although they remain relatively high. Literacy has risen, although it remains relatively low for some countries. Altogether, these data add up to a more favorable situation for the developing world than at almost any point since they gained their independence.

Continuing Problems

The data in the previous section suggest that rather positive changes are occurring in the developing world. Although this is true, there are two major caveats: (1) averages mask wide variations and (2) even some nominally successful countries have serious problems that do not show up in these simple economic indicators. Anyone who has spent time in poor countries is confronted daily with the visible evidence of grinding poverty, disease, violence, and other problems that do not seem to match the overall data.

Economic Growth

The previous section noted that growth in GDP per capita in low-income countries accelerated in the decade since 1995. However, not all countries experienced that acceleration, and some even experienced declines. Table 6.2 displays data for those countries that experienced shrinking GDP per capita in the 2000–2003 period, when the low-income countries as a whole were growing rapidly. A total of thirty-seven countries with a combined population of 285 million people became poorer in this four-year period. Some do not represent much of a problem—the Bahamas, with a purchasing power parity level of GDP per capita of almost $16,000 simply hit a soft patch in growth. But others are clearly in deep trouble. Some of these countries are so small in population (e.g., the Seychelles or Kiribati) that they are merely blips on the global scene. Others matter more. Haiti has experienced falling income levels since 1980 and by 2000 had a GDP per capita of only $1,750. The Democratic Republic of the Congo has also seen falling incomes since 1980, with GDP per capita of only $700. Gaza and the West Bank experienced a steep 13 percent average annual decline in the 2000–2003 period. Uruguay, Côte d'Ivoire, Venezuela, the Solomon Islands, and Zimbabwe also experienced serious declines in income, with an annual shrinkage in GDP per capita of roughly 4–8 percent.

It should come as no surprise that some of these countries have experienced political upheaval—including civil war or major insurgencies in countries such as Côte d'Ivoire or a shift in government toward the left in Venezuela. Keep in mind that, although these particular countries collectively represent only about 5 percent of the global population, growth in low-income countries in general has been somewhat unpredictable, with some countries experiencing an encouraging spurt in growth only to shrink again under the impact of political unrest or bad policy. The Republic of the Congo (a different country from its neighbor, the Democratic Republic of the Congo), for example, had a growing GDP per

Table 6.2 Countries with shrinking GDP per capita, 2000–2003[a]

	Average Annual Change (%)				GDP/Population, 2000 ($PPP)	Population 2000 (millions)
	1980–1989	1990–1994	1995–1999	2000–2003		
Antigua and Barbuda	6.3	3.0	1.4	-0.1	9,728	0.1
Argentina	-2.1	5.6	1.2	-2.7	12,253	35.9
Bahamas	1.6	-2.0	1.4	-0.4	16,793	0.3
Barbados	1.8	-2.1	3.1	-0.5	15,323	0.3
Burundi	1.4	-2.6	-4.3	-0.5	601	6.8
Central African Republic	-1.6	-3.0	0.9	-2.4	1,160	3.7
Comoros	0.2	-1.4	-0.6	-1.0	1,625	0.6
Congo, Democratic Republic of	-1.1	-11.6	-4.7	-2.4	702	48.6
Côte d'Ivoire	-3.8	-3.4	2.5	-3.9	1,585	15.8
Dominica	6.3	2.2	2.6	-2.1	5,931	0.1
Eritrea	n.a.	14.3	1.6	-2.4	747	4.1
Gabon	-1.3	-0.4	0.1	-0.4	6,127	1.3
Guatemala	-1.5	1.3	1.5	-0.1	3,952	11.4
Guinea-Bissau	0.2	0.6	-2.3	-2.5	793	1.4
Guyana	-2.5	5.4	3.6	-0.3	4,043	0.8
Haiti	-1.5	-5.9	-0.6	-2.0	1,750	8.0
Israel	1.8	2.8	1.6	-0.3	20,615	6.3
Kenya	0.6	-1.2	0.2	-1.1	1,002	30.1
Kiribati	-5.1	1.4	4.7	-0.4	n.a.	0.1
Kuwait	-5.2	n.a.	-3.8	-0.2	15,743	2.2
Liberia	-7.1	-32.5	29.8	-2.8	n.a.	3.1

(Table 6.2—cont.)

	Average Annual Change (%)				GDP/Population, 2000 ($PPP)	Population 2000 (millions)
	1980–1989	1990–1994	1995–1999	2000–2003		
Madagascar	-2.3	-2.6	0.1	-0.9	822	15.5
Malawi	-1.5	-0.6	4.8	-1.4	599	10.3
Papua New Guinea	-1.2	6.2	-1.7	-2.7	2,386	5.1
Paraguay	1.0	0.3	-0.6	-1.6	4,613	5.3
Seychelles	1.2	3.2	3.5	-1.5	n.a.	0.1
Solomon Islands	2.5	1.4	-0.6	-7.6	1,881	0.4
St. Kitts and Nevis	6.5	4.0	3.8	-0.2	11,176	0.0
St. Lucia	4.3	5.8	1.1	-1.5	5,608	0.2
Syrian Arab Republic	-0.5	4.9	0.7	0.0	3,332	16.2
Togo	-0.6	-3.2	3.2	-1.1	1,578	4.6
United Arab Emirates	-4.5	-1.3	-1.5	-1.4	n.a.	3.2
Uruguay	0.1	3.6	1.5	-3.9	8,832	3.3
Vanuatu	-0.8	3.9	-2.1	-1.5	3,104	0.2
Venezuela	-2.9	1.7	-1.2	-4.8	5,632	24.3
West Bank and Gaza	n.a.	n.a.	-0.9	-13.2	n.a.	3.0
Zimbabwe	1.5	0.2	1.1	-7.8	2,577	12.7

Source: World Bank, *World Development Indicators 2005* (CD-ROM) (Washington, D.C.: World Bank, 2005).
[a] Per capita GDP/population in 2000 is measured in constant purchasing power parity dollars ($PPP). n.a., not available.

capita in the 2000–2003 period, but had experienced a decline from 1990 to 1999. Also keep in mind that some countries that probably ought to be in this table are missing simply because the World Bank has no statistical data for them, including Afghanistan, Iraq, North Korea, Libya, and Somalia.

Stepping back from growth, what about levels of income? One way of looking at this is to ask how many people live in extreme poverty—commonly defined as earning $1 or less per day. The World Bank estimates that in 1990, 28 percent of the world's population fell into this category. So, despite the improved growth discussed earlier, one in four people in the world still lives in dire circumstances. The UN Millennium Development Goal (table 6.1) is to bring this ratio down to 10 percent by 2015. As dramatic as this improvement would be, even incomes a bit over $1 per day are extremely low. Using the $1 per day metric, sub-Saharan Africa is the poorest region of the world, and it experienced a slight increase in the share of its population in this category between 1990 and 2001, from 44.6 to 46.4 percent—almost half of the total population.[7]

A similar conclusion emerges from looking at extreme poverty on a national basis. Table 6.3 lists the twenty-five poorest countries in the world, with GDP per capita measured at purchasing power parity exchange rates and ranked from most to least affluent. These levels of income look higher than might be expected because of the price adjustment. For example, GDP per capita in the Democratic Republic of the Congo in 2000 was only $89 at the market exchange rate, but domestic prices at that exchange rate were much lower than global prices; adjusting for the price difference brings the income level up to $730—much higher but still not very high (slightly less than $2 per day). Again, it is important to note that some countries that might be expected to show up in this table are missing due to lack of statistical data—including Afghanistan, North Korea, Somalia, and Myanmar.

The first important point to recognize about the countries in this table is that twenty-one out of twenty-five are in sub-Saharan Africa. To a considerable extent, the most serious poverty and economic development dilemmas facing the world are in this region. The second important point is that most of these countries have had serious problems with internal violence. The table shows the situation since 1995, with serious intrastate conflict occurring at some point since that time in fifteen out of the twenty-five countries on the list, excluding run-of-the-mill repression by the governments in power. Without getting into the detailed histories of these countries, it is not possible to say definitively whether extreme poverty breeds violence or the violence has kept them poor by stymieing growth. But the two—poverty and violence—are certainly intertwined.

Table 6.3 Political violence in the poorest countries, 1995–2005[a]

	GDP per capita (at $PPP exchange rates)	Internal Violence?	Details
Uganda	1,450	Yes	Resistance group in north
Central African Republic	1,310	Yes	Coup 2003
Nepal	1,280	Yes	Maoist insurgency
Rwanda	1,190	Yes	Some Hutu cross-border attacks since the end of the genocide
Tajikistan	1,100	Yes	Civil war to 1997; overthrow of government 2005
Burkina Faso	1,080	No	Not since about 1990
Chad	1,010	Yes	Sporadic rebellion in north
Mozambique	1,000	No	Peace since 1990
Kenya	980	No	Peaceful election in 2002
Guinea-Bissau	960	Yes	Military coup attempt and civil war in 1998; bloodless coup in 2003
Eritrea	960	No	2.5-year border war with Ethiopia
Congo, Republic of	950	Yes	Brief civil war in 1997; tenuous peace since 2003
Benin	950	No	
Nigeria	860	Yes	Recent violence in the Niger Delta region by insurgents
Niger	850	Yes	Coups in 1996 and 1999
Madagascar	810	No	
Yemen, Republic of	800	No	
Mali	780	No	
Ethiopia	770	Yes	2.5-year border war with Eritrea
Zambia	760	No	
Congo, Democratic Republic of	730	Yes	Ethnic violence and civil war since 1997
Burundi	680	Yes	Factional violence between Hutu and Tutsi
Malawi	590	No	
Tanzania	510	No	
Sierra Leone	450	Yes	Civil war 1991–2002

Sources: World Bank, *World Development Indicators 2005* (CD-ROM) (Washington, D.C.: World Bank, 2005); Central Intelligence Agency, *CIA World Fact Book,* available at http://www.cia.gov/cia/ publications/factbook/ (May 25, 2005).

[a] The twenty-five poorest countries in terms of GDP per capita in 2000 at purchasing power parity (PPP) exchange rates according to the World Bank's data, plus Afghanistan, Myanmar, North Korea, and Somalia.

Countries that were once wracked by civil war but have emerged from it
have fared much better economically once peace was established.

Mozambique provides an example of the possibilities once the violence
stops. Independence (from Portugal) came late for Mozambique in 1975
and was followed by a brutal civil war that lasted from 1977 to 1992. The
ruling party during this time was Marxist, but it abandoned its ideology
in 1989, adopted a new democratic constitution in 1990, and endorsed a
market-based economy. The World Bank has data on Mozambique back
to 1981, showing an average annual change in GDP per capita from 1981
to the end of the civil war in 1992 of –1.4 percent. But since the civil war
ended, annual growth has been 5.6 percent (1993–2003). Mozambique
remains a poor country, with a GDP per capita shown in table 6.3 of
only $1,000 in 2000 (and a higher $1,300 by 2005 according to CIA estimates). Mozambique continues to have other problems—among them, a
high birthrate, low literacy rate, and a high HIV/AIDS infection rate. But
clearly peace and economic reform have made a substantial difference in
economic performance.[8]

The violence in the poor countries discussed here has been internal. After all, people living in extremely poor countries rarely have the
income, mobility, or education to be able to participate in violent campaigns far from home. We could ask why internal violence in other
countries should matter to Americans—other than because of a sense
of moral compassion—for whom the current major problem is international terrorism and not African civil wars. After all, the U.S. government
was unable to muster a sufficient sense of moral distress to organize an
intervention in the Rwanda genocide in 1994. The worst problems the
advanced nations have faced in Africa are relatively minor on the scale
of global problems—for example, the death of a handful of U.S. soldiers
in Somalia in 1993, the bombing of two U.S. embassies by Al Qaeda in
Tanzania and Kenya, and the hijacking or killing of a few oil workers by
insurgents in Nigeria.[9]

The main impact of the recent Nigerian oil problems has been to discourage the activities of foreign oil firms, more to the detriment of Nigeria than the developed countries. But it would be dangerous to assume
that that the remoteness of these problems will necessarily continue
indefinitely into the future. After all, the radical Islamic movement in
the Middle East dates back only to the 1970s, and it had its first real
impact in the overthrow of the Iranian government in 1979. The embassy
attacks in 1998 were the first major operation by Al Qaeda, and its cells
were still active in the upheavals in Somalia in 2006. We need to ask
whether anger at continued poverty at home and the perception of the
unfairness of rich nations (with their trade protectionism; paltry foreign

aid; and other issues, real or imagined) will eventually spill over into a new round of international terrorist violence stemming from African countries. One sobering response to this question comes from Princeton Lyman and J. Stephen Morrison, two senior U.S. experts on Africa who write regarding the situation in Nigeria: "a potent mix of communal tensions, radical Islam, and anti-Americanism has produced a fertile breeding ground for militancy and threatens to tear the country apart."[10] They see a very real emerging terrorist threat there and elsewhere in sub-Saharan Africa—and especially in the countries in the Horn of Africa area, including Sudan, Eritrea, Ethiopia, Somalia, Djibouti, Uganda, Tanzania, and Kenya.

Trade

Although low-income countries on average have opened up to trade, those averages hide wide variations and some countries remain relatively less open. Figure 6.8 shows the ratio of exports to GDP for the same group of the twenty-five poorest countries identified earlier, ranked in descending order by their export-to-GDP ratios in 2003. Because the ratio of imports to GDP will show roughly the same results (as discussed

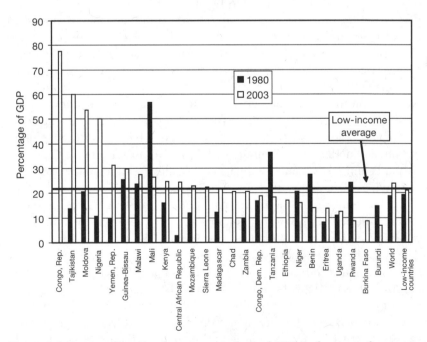

Figure 6.8 Exports of goods and services as a share of GDP in the twenty-five poorest countries, low-income countries, and the world, 1980 and 2003. *Source:* World Bank, *World Development Indicators 2005* (CD-ROM) (Washington, D.C.: World Bank, 2005).

earlier in looking at the averages for low-income countries), this figure suffices as an indicator of how involved in trade these countries are in terms of both exports and imports. Some of these countries have high ratios of exports to GDP because they are raw material exporters—a special dilemma considered later in this chapter. Others are below the global average and the low-income country average. Benin, Eritrea, Uganda, Rwanda, Burkina Faso, and Burundi are all under 15 percent.

These countries have followed the positive trend of rising trade exposure, at least between 1980 and 2003. But even here there are exceptions, including Mali, Tanzania, Niger, Benin, Rwanda, and Burundi. These countries have actually become less exposed to trade. Given the evidence of a positive relationship between trade openness and economic performance, this backward movement should be regarded as problematic.

Inward Direct Investment

The flow of direct investment has also varied a great deal by country, as indicated in figure 6.9. The encouraging news is that some countries among the twenty-five poorest have seen high levels of investment— Chad, Malawi, Moldova, the Republic of the Congo, Mozambique, and Mali all had ratios in the 2000–2003 period over 20 percent of domestic fixed capital formation and well above the 15 percent average for the world. Recalling our earlier discussion of Mozambique, this is an encouraging sign that peace and progress toward establishing a functional market-based economy have encouraged foreign investors to enter. These high levels of investment are all relatively new, as can be seen by comparing them to the 1980–1984 average; for example, Mozambique, in the midst of its civil war, at that time had no inward investment.

Most of the countries receiving above-average foreign capital inflows are raw material producers, where foreign investors have an incentive to accept corruption and uncertain political conditions if the potential profits from raw material extraction are sufficiently high. The Democratic Republic of the Congo, for example, attracted renewed foreign investment once its civil war, which began in 1998 and included foreign troops from Rwanda and other neighboring countries, ground to a halt in 2002. However, the country continues to suffer from corruption and renewed violence is certainly a possibility.[11] The incentive for commercial firms to invest in these corrupt countries because of the irresistible presence of raw materials is a vexing problem to which this study returns later.

Others in this group of countries, however, continue to lag well behind, with ten countries showing inflows of foreign direct investment of less than 10 percent of domestic fixed capital formation. Furthermore, in both the Central African Republic and Rwanda the inflow is actually

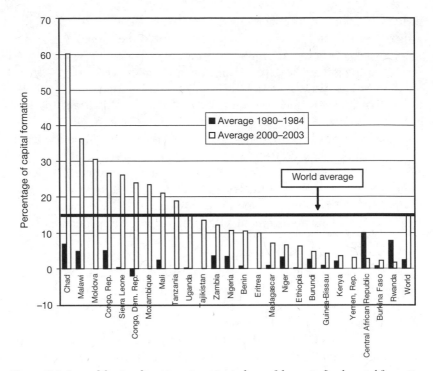

Figure 6.9 Inward foreign direct investment as a share of domestic fixed capital formation in the twenty-five poorest countries and the world, 1980–1984 and 2000–2003. *Source:* World Bank, *World Development Indicators 2005* (CD-ROM) (Washington, D.C.: World Bank, 2005).

lower than it was 20 years earlier. Thus, by no means are all nations benefiting from the overall increase investment flows in the world.

For some of the countries on this list with low inward investment levels, the problem is a lack of investor confidence because these countries lack internal political stability, do not meet the degree of legal and regulatory clarity that foreign firms deem necessary, or are exceptionally corrupt. Foreign direct investment occurs in a global market; corporations in the major investing countries use direct investment either to lower labor costs or as a means of effectively serving a local market, jumping over import barriers or producing goods and services that are not easily transported internationally. Given the limited funds that any corporation has to invest, investors weigh the advantages and disadvantages of particular countries. Low-income countries have discovered, therefore, that they are in a competitive global game to attract investment.

Perceptions of levels of corruption are available through the annual survey of business attitudes about individual countries published by

Transparency International. This survey asks businesses to rate countries on a scale of 1 (worst) to 10 (best). The industrialized countries in 2003 were in the range of 7–10 (with France and Spain on the bottom at 6.9, the United States in the middle at 7.5, and Finland at the top with 9.7). In contrast, fifteen of the twenty-five poorest countries were included in this survey, and these fell into the range of 1.4 (Nigeria) to 2.8 (Malawi), a very low level.[12]

Having a poor corruption rating does not prevent direct investment—as evidenced by Nigeria. The 1.4 rating for Nigeria is one of the lowest in the world (ranking 132nd out of 133 countries rated, with only Bangladesh ranking lower). But Nigeria possesses large deposits of oil and gas, which attracts investment despite the corruption. Although investment flows into Nigeria have not been large recently (10 percent of fixed capital formation in the 2000–2003 period, as shown in figure 6.9), they were much larger in the 1990s (15–40 percent of domestic fixed investment). This combination of raw materials and a venal government provides a witches' brew of corruption and wealth accumulation among the ruling elite, compounded by the acquiescence of the international corporate world. This combination is almost guaranteed to create ethnic strife and government repression.

Health

Poor countries also continue to suffer from poor health and poor health care. This is primarily a domestic problem, holding back economic growth and development by reducing productivity (sick people do not work or are less productive) or even decimating portions of the working-age population (through, for example, the HIV/AIDS epidemic). But health problems have a nasty habit of crossing national borders as well. Countries that have very poorly developed health-care systems are not in a position to stop the spread of new, dangerous viruses—and may not even be aware of their existence until they have become international problems. HIV-AIDS began in sub-Saharan Africa, and the region could now become a breeding ground for the new bird flu problem. In chapter 2, I suggest that such problems are unlikely to become global pandemics, but they are a serious concern nonetheless.

Table 6.4 provides a variety of health indicators for the twenty-five poorest countries. The situation is not encouraging. Health expenditures as a share of GDP are generally low (3–7 percent) and the low level of GDP per capita implies that the actual annual health expenditures per person are miniscule ($50–100). Immunization rates for common diseases such as measles remain short of 100 percent and are actually quite low in some countries (with only 35 percent of infants immunized for measles in Nigeria). The number of doctors is appallingly low in most of these countries—below 10 per 100,000 people in most of them. The fact that the number of physicians is high in Moldova and Tajikistan indicates that the paucity of doctors need not be related to the overall low income of the country. Access to improved water sources and improved sanitation also remains low—problems that exacerbate the spread of disease.

The foremost issue in recent years has been the devastating spread of the HIV/AIDS epidemic. A number of the countries in table 6.4 have adult populations that are 10 percent or more HIV-positive, all of them in sub-Saharan Africa (compared to 0.6 percent in the United States). There are additional countries not in this table (but still quite poor) that have even higher levels of HIV infection: Namibia (21 percent), South Africa (22 percent), Zimbabwe (25 percent), Lesotho (29 percent), Botswana (37 percent), and Swaziland (39 percent)—all in sub-Saharan Africa.[13] These are levels of infection on the order of the bubonic plague pandemics in Europe during in the Middle Ages. As was the case in Europe, infections and deaths on a large scale have economic, social, and political consequences. At the very least, the loss of a non-negligible portion of the adult population through this disease slows or disrupts the process of economic development and creates the social problem of caring for a rising number of orphans. In 2003, sub-Saharan Africa had an estimated 12 million orphans caused by the death of parents through HIV/AIDS, and this number was expected to increase to 15 million by 2010.[14] For the region as a whole, this amounts to roughly 4 percent of all children up to age 14, a not insignificant burden on these poor societies.[15]

The new concern is the spread of the H5N1 strain of bird flu, which can be transmitted from birds to humans (although not yet from human to human). Although this epidemic began in Asia—principally in Vietnam and China—infected birds have been discovered in Nigeria.[16] International health organizations have been involved in Nigeria, but to a large extent, the discovery and policy action to deal with this epidemic rest with the host governments. With only 27 doctors per 100,000 people (table 6.4), however, Nigeria is not in a good position to cope with any human outbreak of bird flu. Given what has already happened to the world with the outbreak and global spread of HIV/AIDS, the weak health infrastructure in the poor countries in both Asia and Africa should be a major concern.

Health has been a long-standing problem in developing countries and an emotionally appealing one, motivating humanitarian aid from rich countries. However, foreshadowing my policy recommendations of the next chapter, improving health alone is insufficient. Lowering mortality (especially infant mortality) without putting in place the other building

Table 6.4 Health indicators in the poorest countries[a]

	Health expenditure as a share of GDP, 2002 (%)	Health expenditures per capita, 2002 (PPP US$)	Adult population with HIV/AIDS, 2003 (%)	Immunization of infants against measles, 2003 (%)	Physicians, 1990–2004 (per 100,000)[b]	Population with sustainable access to improved sanitation (%)		Population with sustainable access to an improved water source (%)	
						1990	2002	1990	2002
Moldova	7.0	151	0	96	269	n.a.	68	n.a.	92
Uganda	7.4	77	4	82	5	43	41	44	56
Central African Republic	3.9	50	14	35	4	23	27	48	75
Rwanda	5.5	48	5	90	2	37	41	58	73
Burkina Faso	4.3	38	4	76	4	13	12	39	51
Kenya	4.9	70	7	72	13	42	48	45	62
Benin	4.7	44	2	83	6	11	32	60	68
Congo, Republic of	2.2	25	5	50	25	n.a.	9	n.a.	46
Nigeria	4.7	43	5	35	27	39	38	49	60
Mozambique	5.8	50	12	77	2	n.a.	27	n.a.	42
Chad	6.5	47	5	61	3	6	8	20	34
Yemen, Republic of	3.7	58	0	66	22	21	30	69	69
Madagascar	2.1	18	2	55	9	12	33	40	45

(Table 6.4—cont.)

	Health expenditure as a share of GDP, 2002 (%)	Health expenditures per capita, 2002 (PPP US$)	Adult population with HIV/AIDS, 2003 (%)	Immunization of infants against measles, 2003 (%)	Physicians, 1990–2004 (per 100,000)[b]	Population with sustainable access to improved sanitation (%)		Population with sustainable access to an improved water source (%)	
						1990	2002	1990	2002
Tajikistan	3.3	47	0	89	218	n.a.	53	n.a.	58
Guinea-Bissau	6.3	38	10	61	17	n.a.	34	n.a.	59
Mali	4.5	33	2	68	4	36	45	34	48
Zambia	5.8	51	17	84	7	41	45	50	55
Eritrea	5.1	36	3	84	3	8	9	40	57
Niger	4.0	27	1	64	3	7	12	40	46
Congo, Democratic Republic of	4.1	15	4	54	7	18	29	43	46
Ethiopia	5.7	21	4	52	3	4	6	25	22
Burundi	3.0	16	6	75	5	44	36	69	79
Malawi	9.8	48	14	77	1	36	46	41	67
Tanzania	4.9	31	9	97	2	47	46	38	73
Sierra Leone	2.9	27	7	73	7	n.a.	39	n.a.	57

Sources: United Nations Development Program, 2005 Human Development Report, available at http://hdr.undp.org/reports/global/2005/ (January 10, 2005); Central Intelligence Agency, CIA Factbook, available at http://www.cia.gov/cia/publications/factbook/rankorder/2155rank.html (March 7, 2006).

ᵃ The twenty-five poorest countries in 2002 measured by GDP per capita at purchasing power parity exchange rates using World Bank data; n.a., not available; PPP, purchasing power parity exchange rates.

ᵇ Most recent year of available data in this time range.

blocks for sustainable economic growth generates only higher unemployment and increased hunger. The title of a 2006 Council on Foreign Relations task force report says it all: *More than Humanitarianism: A Strategic
U.S. Approach toward Africa*. Although emphasizing the need for humanitarian assistance, this report calls for a broader effort to move African countries on to a path of successful economic and political development.[17]

Youth Unemployment

A serious consequence of poor economic performance and high birthrates has been high unemployment rates among young adults. Impres-
sionable, frustrated teenagers make ready recruits for radical religious
movements, antigovernment insurgencies, and terrorism. They are young,
idealistic, and sometimes very angry.

Figure 6.10 shows unemployment rates for various areas of the world
by age group. *Youths* here are defined as people between the ages of
15 and 24—teenagers and young adults just entering the labor market.
In all societies, unemployment in this age group tends to be higher than
the average—young people are often still at home or in school and may
have a more casual attitude about obtaining work (even if they are officially recorded in the statistics as looking and thereby qualified to be
considered unemployed).

In the industrialized countries in 2003, youth unemployment was 13
percent, a level considered a problem. This high rate was driven partly
by problems in the European labor markets, where a combination of
very generous welfare systems and rigid labor rules (making it difficult
for companies to fire workers during economic downturns) make firms
reluctant to hire new employees. East Asian countries—including the
high-growth countries discussed in chapter 5—had a youth employment
rate of only 7 percent because these countries tend to have more flexible labor regulations (except Japan, which has experienced higher youth
unemployment like the other industrialized countries).

In contrast, youth unemployment, in general, is higher in other parts
of the developing world. Northern Africa and the Middle East are the
worst, with a youth unemployment rate of 26 percent, more than one out
of every four individuals. Part of the answer is that unemployment as a
whole is higher in these parts of the world. However, in places such as
the Middle East, even the relative situation is worse. In the industrialized
countries youth unemployment was 2.4 times higher than adult unemployment, but in the Middle East it was 3.3 times higher (and in some
other areas, such as South Asia, the disparity is even higher).

Unemployment rates are tricky numbers. People who are not looking
for a job are not counted as unemployed. Some people may not want jobs,

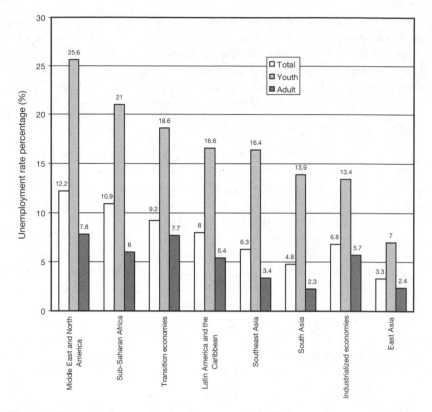

Figure 6.10 Regional unemployment by age group, 2003. *Source:* International Labour Office, "Global Employment Trends for Youth" (Paris: ILO, August 2004), 9 (fig. 3).

but others may have simply given up. Looking at employment figures, therefore, is just as important as looking at unemployment. The Middle East and North Africa fare poorly. In 2003, only 30 percent of youth ages 15–24 were employed, far below the global average of 47 percent and the lowest in the world. Even sub-Saharan Africa performed better—with 52 percent of youths employed. To make matters worse, estimates are that the Middle East and North African region is facing an 80 percent increase in the working-age population by 2020 as the rising numbers of children grow up—an explosion that could lead to even higher levels of youth unemployment.[18]

Is it any wonder that Al Qaeda and radical clerics in Iraq can find a ready supply of recruits? Even if those youths were not angry about the lack of a job, they are idle and available. Think of *West Side Story*, in which the hero Tony has left the Jets to take a job while the gang is run by his friend Riff, who leads the gang into fights with a Puerto Rican gang led by Bernardo. The Middle East has too many Riffs and Bernardos—young men in angry gang mode who are ready to take affront at every slight and engage in hormone-driven violent behavior—and too few employed, responsible Tonys.

Raw Material Exports

Last, we take up the bad news associated with countries that happen to posses and export raw materials. Table 6.5 provides some information on the thirty-one countries that had nonagricultural raw material exports (that is, minerals and fuels) in excess of 50 percent of total exports in 2000, ranging from 100 percent (Nigeria) to 54 percent (the Maldives and Cambodia). Most, but not all, of these countries are fuel exporters (petroleum and natural gas). And for all of them, total exports are a high share of GDP—ranging upward from 42 percent (the United Arab Emirates) to almost 100 percent (Guyana). Thus, to varying degrees, these countries are highly dependent on exports and those exports are dominated by raw materials.

At first blush, these countries appear to be in an ideal situation—simply dig or pump the resource out of the ground and sit back while the money rolls in. Better yet, get foreign companies to do the work and simply rake off a percentage. So what is the problem? An abundance of exportable raw materials can create three problems: (1) an underdeveloped manufacturing sector, (2) income volatility, and (3) conflict over the allocation of the new-found wealth. Overall, economists find that economies endowed with an abundance of raw materials grow more slowly than those with a paucity.[19] These problems associated with raw material abundance, therefore, have a real and distinctly negative impact on the fate of developing countries.

The first problem has been long recognized by economists.[20] Strong exports of oil or some other raw material tend to disadvantage other sectors of the economy by, for example, causing the exchange rate to be so strong that the domestic manufacturing industry has difficulty competing against imports. Saudi Arabia is a perfect example of this problem. Due to its enormous oil exports (40 percent of GDP), Saudi Arabia is a middle-income country, displaying the surface image of economic success. But Saudi Arabia has failed to develop a domestic manufacturing industry typical of middle-income countries. Middle-income countries have manufacturing sectors that have ranged from 20 to 25 percent of GDP from the 1960s to the present. This is a normal development pattern because successful developing countries recognize that they have a global competitive advantage in some aspects of manufacturing, due to

Table 6.5 Dependency on exports of minerals and fuel, 2000[a]

	Mineral and fuel exports (% of total exports)	Fuel exports (% of total exports)	Exports of goods and services (% of GDP)	GDP per capita (PPP constant 2000 international $)		
				2000	1990	2000–1990 (% change)
World	22	9	25	6,782	5,777	17
Nigeria	100	100	53	878	889	−1.2
United Arab Emirates	98	94	n.a.	n.a.	25,690	
Algeria	98	97	42	5,417	5,458	−1
Papua New Guinea	95	29	n.a.	2,386	1,925	24
Kuwait	95	95	58	15,743	n.a.	
Saudi Arabia	93	92	44	12,556	11,818	6
Qatar	91	91	n.a.	n.a.	n.a.	
Bahrain	90	73	88	15,870	14,303	11
Oman	88	83	58	12,491	11,634	7
Belize	87	n.a.	52	5,869	4,137	42
St. Vincent and the Grenadines	87	n.a.	53	5,398	4,626	17
Somalia	84	0	n.a.	n.a.	n.a.	
Turkmenistan	83	81	54	3,668	5,709	−36
Panama	83	7	68	6,254	4,525	38
Gambia	82	0	48	1,712	1,811	−5
Norway	81	64	47	35,132	26,334	33
Guyana	80	0	96	4,043	3,480	16
St. Lucia	80	0	53	5,608	5,076	10
Kazakhstan	79	53	57	4,594	5,716	−20
Honduras	78	0	42	2,500	2,513	−1
Vanuatu	77	0	n.a.	3,104	2,431	28
Ghana	75	8	49	1,963	1,634	20
Russia	75	51	44	7,242	10,309	−30
Tajikistan	74	14	81	803	2,320	−65
Angola	72	3	92	1,952	2,427	−20
Trinidad and Tobago	71	65	59	8,951	6,959	29
Moldova	64	0	50	1,290	3,754	−66
Dominican Republic	58	19	45	6,153	4,074	51
Bahamas	56	0	n.a.	16,793	16,982	−1
Maldives	54	n.a.	89	n.a.	n.a.	
Cambodia	54	0	51	1,758	n.a.	

Source: World Bank, *World Development Indicators 2005* (CD-ROM) (Washington, D.C.: World Bank, 2005).

[a] Those countries for which mineral and fuel exports are more than 50 percent of total exports; PPP, purchasing power parity exchange rates; n.a., not available.

low wages, and suck workers and capital into this sector for a number of years. In contrast, manufacturing in Saudi Arabia was only 5 percent of GDP back in the 1970s, and even with an increase over the course of the 1980s, it was only 10 percent by 2003; what appeared to be a move toward manufacturing in the 1980s stalled after the mid-1990s.[21] Thus, manufacturing remains at only half the level typical of middle-income countries. If Saudi Arabia were developing a successful service economy (which would be less vulnerable to exchange rates and imports than manufacturing), there would be no problem. However this has not happened; services are 40 percent of the economy (not an unusually high level), whereas oil and gas extraction is roughly 40 percent.[22]

Even Norway, which became an oil and gas exporter in the 1970s with the development of the North Sea oilfields, has experienced a shrinkage of its manufacturing sector, from 21 percent of GDP at the beginning of the 1970s to 11 percent by 2001—not much different from Saudi Arabia. But clearly Norway, which was already an advanced industrialized nation in 1970, has done what Saudi Arabia has not by running a highly productive services sector, which has been 60 percent of GDP. Granted, the mining (oil) sector expanded from 11 to 30 percent of GDP (1970–2003), which is sizable, although still smaller than that in Saudi Arabia. But the existence of a large services sector has helped to cushion the economy from fluctuations in the oil market, so that GDP per capita expanded by 33 percent in the 1990s, as shown in table 6.5.[23] Norway has also benefited from establishing an investment fund; its Fund for the Future invests a portion of the earnings from oil and gas exports, producing revenue for the government and the people to insulate the economy from exactly the kind of price fluctuations that I consider next.[24]

The second problem is the volatility of income due to global commodity price fluctuations. This problem is most easily visible for the oil exporters (because the non-oil exporters in table 6.5 sell a variety of commodities that have differing price cycles). Americans think of their country as being vulnerable to oil price increases, but pity the poor oil exporter, whose standard of living tends to fluctuate strongly as crude oil prices rise or fall. Figure 6.11 shows changes in real GDP per capita in five major oil exporting countries. (This figure leaves out Kuwait, which experienced a sustained drop in GDP per capita from the beginning of the 1970s due to a huge influx of foreign workers.) In order to show the cyclical pattern over time, this figure sets 1980 GDP per capita at 100, with GDP measured in local currencies adjusted for inflation.

The pattern is most striking for Saudi Arabia. GDP per capita more than doubled from 1965 to 1980 as oil prices soared in the 1970s, but then fell again by 45 percent. Today, the Saudis are little better off than they were forty years ago according to this crude measure of affluence. In dollar

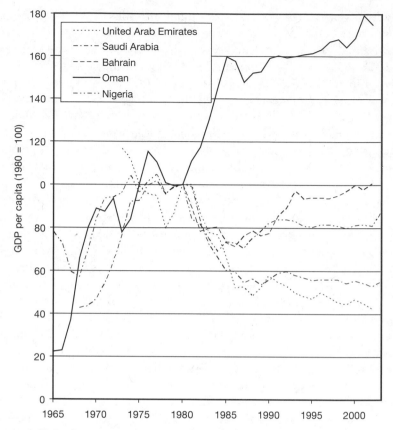

Figure 6.11 Real GDP per capita at purchasing power parity exchange rates in United Arab Emirates, Saudi Arabia, Bahrain, Oman, and Nigeria, 1965–2005 (1980 = 100). GDP is measured in local currencies adjusted for inflation. *Source:* World Bank, *World Development Indicators 2005* (CD-ROM) (Washington, D.C.: World Bank, 2005).

terms (at purchasing power parity exchange rates), the dollar value of GDP per capita in Saudi Arabia was $23,000 back in 1980, but by the late 1980s it was back to $12,000, where it stagnated until 2003. Since 2003, Saudi economic growth once again accelerated, driven by the rising price of oil. GDP growth ranged from 5 to 7 percent in the period 2003–2005. Nevertheless, it remains uncertain whether the government will promote sufficient economic social and political reform to enable the economy to escape the burden of its high dependence on oil exports.[25]

The data for the United Arab Emirates are not available as far back, but it, too, experienced more than a 50 percent drop in income levels after 1980. Oman (which began in the 1960s with a lower level of income than the others), however, has escaped this trap, with income experiencing a sustained increase despite the drop in oil prices after 1980, probably due to a more successful strategy of diversifying the economy beyond oil and gas, plus a policy of limiting the inflow of foreign workers. Bahrain lies in between—GDP per capita fell in the 1980s but managed to return to its 1980 level by 2003. Nigeria (the only African country considered here) shows the same cyclical pattern as Saudi Arabia, although less severe, with income levels rising by 40 percent up to 1980 and then declining by 20 percent.

The wide variety in experience shows how complex economies are; the price of oil, even for countries dependent on oil exports, is not the only factor at work in economic performance. Nevertheless, the rise and fall of GDP per capita for a number of major oil exporters who have an unusual dependence on those exports is striking and worrisome.

Consider again the experience of Saudi Arabia. As the nation was catapulted into relative affluence, some aspects of society did improve. Adult literacy, for example, has risen steadily from only 33 percent of the adult population in 1970 to 80 percent by 2003. Nevertheless, 80 percent literacy does not compare well with other middle-income countries, where the average is 90 percent.[26] Fertility, on the other hand, is closer to the experience of poor countries, with the total fertility rate remaining over five children per woman, although the number has dropped since 1982, when it was over seven. This pattern mirrors the world's poorest nations included in figure 6.7. The continued high birthrate, combined with the failure to build an economy broader than pumping oil and gas, exacerbated the youth unemployment problem considered earlier. These are the kinds of failures that reflect the inability of Saudi Arabia to insulate its economy from the fluctuations in oil prices.

The inability of countries such as Saudi Arabia to deal successfully with the wealth generated by oil exports can have serious negative consequences. Think about the fact that the 9/11 terrorists came from Saudi Arabia and the United Arab Emirates—two of the countries that had an especially huge increase followed by an offsetting collapse of GDP per capita. That degree of fluctuation would cause anger and frustration in any society. With the development of radical Islam, frustration in the Middle East found a particularly violent outlet.

Third, countries with a large dependence on raw material exports face the problem of wealth distribution. We might term this the Elvis Presley effect. Elvis was an enormously talented and innovative singer who came from a poor religious family. The sudden riches associated with pop stardom undid his life, and he died an early death from a drug overdose.

In similar fashion, the presence in a poor country of large deposits of oil and gas that can be easily exported creates sudden affluence in a society that—until the time of discovery and development of the oil and gas resources by foreign firms—had not been ready for economic development. The sudden wealth creates the appearance of economic success while actually having a corrosive effect on the society.

The elites running the society are provided with an overwhelming temptation to rip off the revenue for themselves so they can enjoy the lifestyle of the rich, leaving the rest of the society no better off. Recall the discussion in chapter 2 of the premodern association of wealth and the political control of land. What is happening in some oil-rich countries is no different—the political control of the land has provided the ruling elite with the opportunity to grab most of the revenues for their own benefit while the rest of the society remains relatively impoverished. The struggle in Iraq, for example, pitted the Shiites (who live predominantly in the south, where most of the oil deposits are located) and the Kurds (in the north, with some oil) against the Sunnis, who feared that the Shiites and Kurds would keep most of the oil revenues for themselves if they controlled the government.

Nigeria is another good example of this problem. The dictator of Nigeria from 1993 to 1998, Sani Abacha, is alleged to have siphoned off as much as $2.2 billion for himself, much of it stashed away in Swiss banks.[27] Abacha is gone, replaced by a new constitution and an elected government, but Nigeria still faces the problem of distributing wealth among feuding ethnic groups. Nigeria has some 250 ethnic groups, with four of them representing significant portions of the population (Hausa/Fulani at 29 percent, Yoruba at 21 percent, Ibo at 18 percent, and Ijaw at 10 percent).[28] In 2005 and 2006, insurgent groups operating in the Niger Delta area (where the deposits of oil and gas are located) stole oil and exported it on their own, and they kidnapped more than a dozen foreign oil workers in early 2006.[29] The local insurgents belonged to the Ijaw ethnic group, which felt it had been cheated, and with good reason, out of the wealth being pumped out of the ground where they live.[30] The current elected president, Olusegun Obansajo (who reaches the end of his term in 2007), on the other hand, is from the Yoruba ethnic group. The insurgents live in an area that, despite the oil deposits, has few schools and little electricity or running water. As one militant leader put it in early 2005, "I take that which belongs to me. It is not theft. The oil belongs to *our* people."[31]

Bolivia has faced a similar, although less violent, conflict over the allocation of natural gas riches. The election of Evo Morales as president in December 2005 represented triumph for the indigenous Aymara Indian population, who felt aggrieved at the lack of benefits for their people from natural gas exports. President Morales nationalized the oil and gas sector (which had been privatized only a decade earlier in 1996) in which foreign firms had invested. The change implied that foreign firms would pay more and the government would reap the benefit. One of the ironies in Bolivia was that the biggest single investor in Bolivian oil and gas was Petrobras—the Brazilian state-owned oil company, owned by a government that was leaning modestly to the left in 2006.[32] What is really at stake is not so much anti-Western sentiment but a struggle over which groups in society feel the benefit from the increased revenues in a society where the bulk of the population has felt little positive benefit in the past several decades.[33]

Similar problems emerged in Indonesia, where the Papuans, living on the Indonesian half of the island of New Guinea, engaged in violent demonstrations in 2006. These demonstrations were prompted by anger over the lack of economic benefits flowing to their local communities from large foreign-owned gold and copper mines, as well as over the environment degradation caused by the mines. This problem pits the impoverished local people against the U.S.-owned mining giant Freeport-McMoRan; its partner in Indonesia, the large Australian mining company Rio Tinto; and the Indonesian government and its military forces. The companies were accused of making paltry offers of payments to the local people, and the government was accused of being more interested in its own revenues because the companies together had been one of the largest taxpayers in Indonesia for many years.[34]

The international aspect of these disputes is understandable. Raw material deposits create economic rents for those extracting the resources. When global supply and demand conditions cause prices to rise, the rents can be very high. This may seem unfair, but the principle is exactly the same as the benefit that millions of homeowners in the United States get when supply and demand conditions drive up the price of real estate. In many parts of the world, Western firms drive hard bargains with host governments because the firms have the mining or drilling technology, the marketing capabilities, and the financing that local firms or governments lack. But host governments and local people then feel that they have been robbed, and many have nationalized the extractive industries in order to gain more of the profits for themselves—as Morales did in spring 2006 in Bolivia. The problem is that if the governments impose conditions that are too onerous, foreign firms will stay away. In 2006, many observers feared that the populist government of President Morales would make exactly this mistake, to the longer-term detriment of Bolivia because foreign firms would head elsewhere.[35]

Overall, possession of very large deposits of raw materials, and particularly oil and gas, can be more of a curse than a blessing for developing countries. They fail to diversify the economy in order to insulate society from the vagaries of commodity price fluctuations, and governments are too tempted to monopolize the profits for themselves rather than distribute them for the good of the broader public. Not all fail (and non-oil producers do not demonstrate the wide gyrations in GDP per capita shown in this section), but failure is an endemic problem. In the Middle East, this failure has had particularly unpleasant international consequences.

———————

THE problems of low-income countries may seem intractable. Poor people cannot afford to save, so they lack the financial resources for the investments necessary to create economic growth and development. Illiteracy keeps the workforce imprisoned in traditional technologies handed down within families. High fertility combined with dropping infant mortality creates high population growth rates that overwhelm the efforts to increase levels of affluence. However, the average picture that emerges from the data in this chapter is not quite so bleak. The growth rate of low-income countries has gone up since the mid-1990s. Savings and investment have been increasing over time as a share of GDP. Literacy is expanding and fertility continues to drop. Trade—bringing both better and cheaper goods from abroad and sending out those products in which the economy is capable of competing on global markets—has expanded steadily and is now at the global average. Foreign direct investment is expanding, bringing with it needed technology—including management technology. The very effort to attract foreign investment prods governments to create a legal and regulatory framework that is beneficial to both foreign firms and domestic firms. As a result, the picture is by no means as grim as is often assumed.

Nevertheless, the averages for low-income countries mask a wide variation in experience. Some poor countries have not experienced higher growth, and some have even experienced shrinking levels of income. Some of them have not benefited from an increase in trade or inward direct investment. Health issues remain severe, and some of the sub-Saharan African countries are experiencing a disastrous HIV/AIDS pandemic. With continued high birthrates and poor economic management, Africa and the Middle East have very high rates youth unemployment, providing fodder for radical movements.

Many of the poorest countries experience internal conflict. Although the civil wars and insurgencies in Africa may seem remote, Americans should not be sanguine that anger and frustration will not someday find an international outlet, as it has in the Middle East during the past several decades. Furthermore, the lack of health-care infrastructure implies that poor countries will continue to be the breeding grounds for new diseases that could create further internal problems for them or even spread to the United States and other advanced nations. Even if we are not moved by moral outrage at the plight of poor countries, the possibility of future terrorism or viral pandemics should provide a sufficient rationale to take the situation seriously.

One of the most troubling problems, however, is the curse of raw material abundance. Some of these countries are poor (Nigeria), but others appear on the surface to be fairly successful (Saudi Arabia). Countries such as Saudi Arabia have managed their wealth poorly, failing to develop a manufacturing or service sector capable of cushioning the economy from oil price fluctuations. Others, such as Nigeria, are simply kleptocracies, with a small ruling class siphoning off the wealth while the rest of society remains desperately poor. It is no wonder that these nations are seething masses of frustration, anger, and, sometimes, terrorist recruiting.

Not all poorly managed raw material exporters experience civil unrest or radical religious movements. But the experience of Bolivia and Venezuela, where new populist or socialist governments have been elected, should be fair warning that the raw material exporters of the developing world are frustrated with their situation. Rather than lamenting their political shift to the left, Americans need to understand the problems generated by the misallocation of export benefits and the need to support these countries as they seek a new approach, a subject that I explore in the next chapter.

The major conclusion to draw from this survey of unsuccessful economies is that the long-term solutions lie in a package of policies. Providing medicines and better health care without creating jobs does not work. Providing food aid does little to help if it is not combined with longer-term efforts to raise local food production or to provide nonagricultural jobs so societies can afford to buy food from abroad. Building roads and bridges when farmers do not have the financial resources, ability to read, or business skills to market their crops does not work. Reducing the import barriers to food exported from developing countries does little unless farmers in the developing world have the transportation infrastructure, education, and business know-how to sell their crops into export markets. Dumping foreign aid on corrupt regimes does not work. Developing and exporting raw materials may not work. But a combination of diplomacy, peace-making and peace-keeping efforts, technical assistance in the creation and operation of economic institutions (especially financial institutions), health assistance, educational assistance, and some infrastructure assistance can make a difference, as I advocate in the next chapter. The goal of U.S. foreign policy should be to provide a coordinated push that moves countries on to a self-sustaining path of economic growth.

CONCLUSION AND POLICY RECOMMENDATIONS

Americans live in a time of extraordinary opportunity. The economic world has changed in fundamental ways in the sixty-plus years since the end of the Second World War. We Americans are much more affluent, more interdependent with the rest of the world, and less likely to face a disastrous major war. Threats to peace and prosperity—both actual and potential—exist, but they are not insoluble. The fundamental solutions to these problems lie less in pursuing a muscular military posture and more in maintaining and improving economic performance and the global economic architecture.

Until the mid-twentieth century, great power rivalry occurred in a pre-industrial ideological mindset that viewed the control of territory both as necessary for prosperity and as a zero-sum game. The result was two devastating violent convulsions that left tens of millions dead. Even after these disasters, the deep ideological division over the appropriate political and economic nature of the state—capitalism versus communism—kept the world locked in a tense stand-off that could have exploded in an even more catastrophic war. This world is now thoroughly gone for the reasons discussed in chapters 1–2. Nuclear weapons certainly contributed to this outcome, making governments fearful of launching a conflict that would have been unbelievably destructive to themselves as well as their enemies. But other developments mattered as well. Imperialism was collapsing by the end of the Second World War, although the wars of liberation that were necessary in some cases dragged on as late as the 1960s. The Cold War complicated or postponed the positive benefits of the collapse of imperialism as the United States and the Soviet Union vied over the allegiance of the newly freed nations. But even this era has been over for almost two decades. The Soviet Union is now long gone. The world that is emerging in the aftermath of imperialism is knit together by rising flows of trade and investment and is governed loosely by a new set of international institutions, especially the Bretton Woods trio of the IMF, World Bank, and WTO. Although this network of interdependence and its governing institutions originally included only some of the Western-bloc nations, in the wake of the Cold War it has come to encompass most of the world.

Yet the international daily news facing Americans is an unending dismal stream of violence, threats, disasters, political upheaval, and terrorist attacks. Much of this is the normal human condition as imperfect people endeavor to cope with the stresses and strains of existence. After all, violence exists within U.S. society as well, including occasional homegrown terrorists. But some international threats and problems deserve to be taken seriously.

First, there remains at least a minor possibility of major war, with two of the most likely locations being the Korean peninsula and the Taiwan Straits. North Korea is hardly a great power, but it possesses workable nuclear weapons, and with or without nuclear devastation, the war would be a bloody one—not at all like the easy initial invasion of Iraq. The other possibility is that miscalculations by the Chinese government could lead to a decision to forcibly reunite Taiwan with the mainland, prompting a U.S. military response. China, too, is a nuclear power and an escalation of the conflict to nuclear exchanges is not inconceivable. Neither conflict is likely to occur, but neither can be entirely ruled out. Like World War I, either would be a profound tragedy, unnecessary and costly. Certainly both China and North Korea have aspects of their regimes that are unsavory, but China has been on a path of reform for almost three decades, and North Korea is a minor nation that is mainly a threat to its own people.

Second, the global economic system that has underwritten the success of modern-day capitalism is always subject to the possibility of crisis and failure, similar to the Great Depression of the 1930s. Faced with domestic economic collapse, governments would be tempted to abandon the successful regime of global trade and investment or even swerve to alternative economic and social models with the revolutionary zeal of the early twentieth century. After all, the communist struggle was inspired by the negative aspects of industrialization—squalid slums, low wages, sharp recessions, and the emergence of a new, overbearing, arrogant wealthy class. Another major global depression could inspire a new revolutionary ideology calling for the overthrow of governments and the creation of a new economic system.

Third, Americans are now subject to nonstate terrorist actors driven by religion and the anger over the uneven distribution of wealth in the world. At the moment, that threat is rooted mainly in radical Islamic groups in the Middle East. But the future could bring new disaffected groups in other parts of the world, especially in sub-Saharan Africa.

None of these problems is as threatening as the great armed conflicts of the twentieth century that cost tens of millions of lives and the destruction of cities across Europe and Asia. War with North Korea or China is a frightening enough prospect, but the economic changes described in chapter 5 have increased the opportunity costs of war for both countries. Americans, too, have an incentive to avoid the human and financial costs of these conflicts—do we really want to jeopardize our lives and prosperity over Taiwan or North Korea?

Meanwhile, market-based economies are spreading, and the Bretton Woods institutions continue to function reasonably well in maintaining a growing global economy. Economists and government officials understand the workings of market economies and their international interaction much better than in the 1930s. If a major depression were to occur, it would be more the result of bad political decisions than of a failure of economic understanding.

Finally, terrorism has so far been more of an irritant than a major threat to the nation, albeit it one that is difficult to address given its unconventional nature. Large-scale attacks, such as 9/11, are difficult to achieve if law enforcement agencies are vigilant and if cautionary measures are in place (such as airport security or the screening of arriving freight containers at ports).

Nevertheless, many in the foreign policy community believe that "everything changed" on September 11, 2001. Terrorism was a new and dangerous threat, including, at the extreme, the possibility of a nuclear attack. The U.S. government has responded to terrorism mainly through preemptive military action designed to snuff out international terrorists before they can cause more deadly, large-scale attacks. In 2006, U.S. military forces sat astride Afghanistan and Iraq, fighting insurgents and attempting to politically reshape these two nations (along with token forces from a number of other countries). To some extent, a targeted military response to decapitate the command structure of a specific large terrorist organization—Al Qaeda—was justified (although this goal remained unfinished five years after it began). This approach was also subject to terrible mistakes; the invasion of Iraq was based on false evidence of weapons of mass destruction and contributed nothing to combating terrorism.

This military approach also created considerable costs for the United States in four important ways. First, there is the obvious moral problem facing U.S. society concerning its presumed right to invade sovereign states in the absence of a direct threat. Second, forcibly remaking societies into stable democracies is very difficult because the military presence creates a highly artificial environment of both dependency (of those who choose to cooperate and who maintain the legitimacy of their political power mainly through U.S. military might) and violent opposition (by those outraged at the U.S. presence). Third, there are international costs for U.S. diplomacy. As Roger Cohen (a columnist for the *International Herald Tribune*) put it in 2004, the war on terrorism was "an obsession that the world doesn't share," with the result that the United States became isolated.[1] The Bush administration created a post in the State Department for public diplomacy, aimed at reversing this loss, but doing so requires a change in actual U.S. policy, not just a public relations campaign to change public opinion abroad. Fourth, military action represents a direct cost to the United States—in terms of both fiscal expenditure and loss of life. Even though George W. Bush was reelected in the midst of the Iraq occupation, the U.S. public was losing patience with these costs, as reflected in the Republican loss of both houses of Congress in the November 2006 elections. The $250 billion that the administration spent on Iraq through fiscal 2005 (and continued to spend at a rate of roughly $6 billion per month) was not a trivial sum and came at a time when the government was already running a large fiscal deficit that contributed to the record current-account deficit that most economists saw as increasingly problematic.[2] These are all issues that have been extensively thrashed out in public debates and need not be repeated here. But it is important to begin the discussion with the realization that the military-centered approach to global affairs adopted by the Bush administration has not been working very well.

What, then, is the alternative to this muscular military approach? If we view foreign policy as a three-legged stool with military, diplomatic, and economic legs, then, first, U.S. policy should adopt a much more cautious use of the military leg. Save the use of military power for those circumstances where no other approach to resolving international problems is possible (a hurdle that was certainly not cleared in the case of Iraq). Second, foreign policy should rely more on the diplomatic leg to avoid conflicts—especially in the principal flash points of North Korea and the Taiwan Straits. Diplomacy and negotiation are games that involve compromise—the other side must get something in order to be convinced to give something up. These games also involve the delicate process of lining up supporters to pressure the other side. Third, more emphasis should be put on a set of economic policies that provide long-term support for the goal of peace and prosperity, the third leg of the currently crooked stool—diplomacy and military still matter, but so does economics.

Others have made the case against the Bush administration's heavily military approach to solving world problems, the unilateralism of its diplomatic approach, and its dangerous unwillingness to offer carrots in delicate diplomatic situations such as that with North Korea. But whereas much ink has been spilled on those subjects, Americans remain woefully unaware of the importance of the economic side of foreign policy. Given the sources of threat—possible war in Asia, instability in the global economy, and terrorism—the long-term solutions lie in policies that reduce the probability and size of these threats. These solutions have a strong economic element and can be summarized as a set of policies to push in the direction of a world of winners without losers. Specifically, the following policies relate to the goal of peace and prosperity:

- *Policies that foster healthy growth in the U.S. economy and the expansion of economic engagement with the rest of the world.* Not only is growth a direct benefit to Americans, it has a major positive impact on the rest of the world because of the very large size of the U.S. economy and the deepening economic interconnections between the United States and the rest of the world. But some aspects of U.S. economic performance and structure need serious attention or the commitment to international openness could be in jeopardy.

- *Policies that maintain and reinforce the multilateral economic institutions aimed at promoting a growing global economy.* The IMF is the principal bulwark against international financial contagion of the sort that engulfed the world in 1929. The WTO has been a vehicle for fostering global economic growth through the expansion of trade as import barriers have fallen. Finally, the World Bank plays an important role in fostering economic development. Other organizations—the G-8 summits, the OECD, the IEA, and the like—also play a role in the loose governance of the global economy. (The UN is the key multilateral institution in the world of diplomacy, but its economic role is modest.) Criticism has swirled around all three Bretton Woods institutions for a number of years and needs to be addressed.

- *Policies to draw poor countries on to a path of successful economic growth (and to address the special problems of middle-income raw material exporters).* Such policies include a complex combination of diplomacy (to foster peace, internal political change, and receptivity to assistance), foreign aid, and the further opening of developed country markets to imports from poor countries.

All these policy areas are supposedly part of current U.S. policy, but have been relatively neglected in recent years. Furthermore, the U.S.

government has had a long-standing tendency to view economic policies in very narrow economic terms, disconnected from broader foreign policy goals. The connection of U.S. economic health, international financial stability, and the acceleration of growth of poor countries has rarely been viewed in broad strategic foreign policy terms in recent years.

During the Cold War, the situation was different. The growth of the U.S. economy and the openness of U.S. markets to the exports of our allies was viewed in strategic terms—designed to help these countries prosper and, therefore, remain allied to the United States. The IMF was designed as a mechanism to manage exchange rates among the allied powers and prevent a recurrence of the economic disaster of the 1930s. Foreign aid, both bilateral and through the World Bank, was a way of handing out favors to poor states in an effort to keep them from falling into the Soviet camp. U.S. policy aimed at winning hearts and minds in the unaligned parts of the world by confronting the Soviet Union with a prosperous bloc that would belie the propaganda claims of superiority of the Soviet system.

The end of the Cold War eliminated the strategic rationale for these economic policies. No longer locked in a struggle with the Soviet Union for the hearts and minds of people around the world, why should Americans care about foreign aid or use the IMF to bail out countries that cannot pay their international debts? But such policies are even *more* important now, for three critical reasons. First, with the end of the Cold War, participation in the IMF, WTO, and World Bank has increased as the former members of the Soviet sphere have joined, making them truly global institutions. Flawed though they may be, these global institutions provide an opportunity to manage economic issues on a truly global scale. Second, without the overlay of Cold War objectives, U.S. policy can actually concentrate on improving economic outcomes around the world rather than simply placating politically important allies. Third, these policies remain just as important strategically now as they were before because they hold one of the keys to obtaining peace and prosperity.

As the world's sole superpower, and with the emphasis on military solutions to global problems in recent years, the U.S. government has made the unfortunate presumption that it can act on its own as it sees fit; if the rest of the world disagrees with the U.S. definition of the problems and their solutions, tough. That may be true militarily—the United States possessed the military might to attack and occupy Iraq without any meaningful assistance from other countries. The debacle in Iraq has proven to be a humbling experience for those in Washington who subscribe to the view of the United States as a preeminent power that should act regardless of the opinion of other governments. But the concept of power is a much more nebulous one in the realm of economic institutions and policies. The U.S. government has the ability to follow foolish economic policies at home, but will the rest of the world choose to finance them? Politicians can choose to adopt protectionist policies, but how does the government then convince other countries to open their own markets? The U.S. government can press poor countries to adopt harsh reforms when they are in financial trouble, but why should they agree? Being the world's largest economy does not yield the kind of superpower status in global economic affairs that superficially appears to be the case for military power.

What does it take to exercise leadership in the economic world? One critically important element is cooperation. The U.S. government certainly has some amorphous power in the international economic arena. It is often U.S. officials who are the prime movers in international negotiations, doing much of the work in defining the agenda and cajoling other governments to go along. But Americans have no monopoly on either power or good ideas. And particularly in the WTO, reciprocal concessions are the rule. It is interesting, for example, to see the successful activism of small countries such as Australia in the WTO negotiating process. Therefore, the starting point for all the policies discussed here is to recognize that, although the U.S. government has some sort of ill-defined power in the global economic arena, success in achieving policy outcomes requires both diplomacy and flexibility—the U.S. government cannot force decisions on others and needs to listen when others object strongly. To the extent that the United States can and does exercise leadership, much depends on reputation rather than power; others do not listen when they lack respect for the United States. Joseph Nye's concept soft power is difficult to measure, but economic performance (including structural features such as health-care policy) has a bearing on the U.S. international reputation, in addition to diplomatic and military behavior. At the moment, that reputation is in tatters.

With that admonition about how international economic policy works, the following sections of this chapter lay out some key economic policy areas. Much of what follows consists of specific ideas and recommendations for institutional structures and policies. But the detailed content of these recommendations matters less than one overwhelming point. To put it in the vernacular of the day: this stuff really, really matters. In many ways, what the U.S. government and the American public need is to shake off their fascination with military might and their fear that economic issues are too technical (or just boring). In many ways, the ability of Americans to achieve continued peace and rising prosperity depends on handling economic issues successfully.

Domestic Economic Policy

Americans serve the international economic and foreign policy agenda of peace and prosperity best by maintaining a healthy, growing economy at home. Obviously, Americans benefit directly from their own economic performance. But the nation also gains in the sense of Joseph Nye's soft power if the rest of the world has (at least grudging) respect for U.S. economic success, making them more likely to accept U.S. leadership and policy positions in multilateral economic institutions. The sensibility of domestic macroeconomic policies and moderation of economic balance with the rest of the world also reduces the probability of international financial crisis. For the past dozen years, the United States has done well, generating robust economic and productivity growth. Nevertheless, there are several troubling issues confronting the U.S. economy, as discussed in chapter 3.

The first set of domestic issues concerns the structure of the U.S. market-based system, addressing the question of why many households do not feel better even if the economy is doing so well. The time has come to rethink the domestic system for two reasons. First, the vaunted U.S. economic flexibility needs to be underwritten by a better social safety net, otherwise discontented voters and the politicians they elect will undo that success—including openness to trade and investment. The open trade policies discussed later in this section depend on political support at home, and that support is eroding. As an economist, I can lecture you on why free trade and unfettered international investment are good for the United States, but domestic social policies need to ameliorate the costs to those who are displaced domestically or no one will believe the lecture. At the present time, political support at home for open trade and investment policies appears to be slipping. Second, the image of the United States depends on more than just the headline figures on economic growth. Many aspects of the economic system are rather repugnant to observers around the world. To underwrite the political support for open trade and investment, and improve soft power, the following domestic issues need urgent attention:

• *Develop a new national health policy*. Corporations bear the brunt of the cost of health care (for people under the age of 65), but this creates real problems for people who lose their jobs in the turmoil of global competition. Economic success certainly depends on an economic system in which the labor force is flexible, but the existing health-care system unduly disadvantages workers who lose their jobs, making this issue one more reason for those workers to oppose trade liberalization.

• *Expand portable 401(k) and 401(c) pension plans.* Similar to health care, a flexible labor market requires pension benefits that workers can take with them when they lose or change jobs. The past system of benefit-defined plans was designed in an earlier age specifically to get workers to stay with the firm. But benefit-defined plans assume that the corporation will continue to exist indefinitely, not only throughout the worker's career but through his or her retirement as well—a heroic assumption in today's world of enhanced global competition. The transition from benefit-defined to contribution-defined retirement plans has been underway for some time, but many companies offer no plan at all and workers still on benefit-defined plans continue to face the reduction or loss of their benefits.

• *Stop the widening gap between rich and poor.* Part of this widening gap may be due to the rising payoff to college education—although this view has been challenged.[3] The explosion in executive compensation has simply gotten out of hand. There is not much the government can do to stop the workings of the labor market for top executive talent, but government policy can address this issue through the tax system. For many decades, the income tax system was deliberately designed to be progressive—taxing the wealthy more and thereby moderating the gap in after-tax incomes for the sake of social policy. But the tax cuts in recent years have been skewed to favor the rich, allowing the gap to widen. The United States can still be the land of opportunity and individual success without allowing an increasing share of the national income to wind up in the hands of a very small elite. If not, the fabric of U.S. society will be undermined and the U.S. image abroad will be tarnished—reminiscent of the anger created by unbridled capitalism that inspired communism a century ago.

• *Assist displaced workers.* As the economy adjusts to greater openness, the downside for some individuals is loss of employment. Some firms and industries gain in a more open global environment; others lose. Economists accept these losses because the overall gain for the economy is positive. But economists rarely focus on how individuals manage the transition. If the jobs in the growing sectors are in different parts of the country or involve very different skills, workers losing their jobs can be badly disadvantaged for a long time. Beginning in 1962, the federal government provided something called Trade Adjustment Assistance (TAA), which gave workers who lost their jobs due to international competition extended unemployment benefits and financial assistance for retraining. This program was expanded a great deal in 1974, and at its peak in 1979 some 500,000 workers received benefits from it. However, TAA was scaled back drastically in the 1980s. The program was expanded once again and reorganized in 1994 and 2002, but the number of workers in it remains far below the level helped back in the 1970s—with annual new beneficiaries numbering fewer than 50,000 in recent years. By way of comparison, the United States spends far less on all forms of worker assistance (unemployment, TAA, and other programs) as a share of GDP than other advanced industrial countries—including Japan, which, unlike the European countries, is not known for generous labor benefits.[4] TAA needs further work in order to keep the political support for open trade and investment policies.

• *Pursue a more active energy policy.* Parts of chapters 2, 3, and 5 discuss aspects of energy supply, arguing that markets work quite well and that Americans should not view the energy situation as a crisis (and especially not one for which military power has any relevance). Nonetheless, a policy push to accelerate the shift away from fossil fuels as their prices rise over the next several decades would help reduce public anxiety. Environmental self-interest lies in the same direction; the faster reliance on hydrocarbon fuels falls, the less the long-term damage to global climate and air quality. Higher gasoline taxes, higher fuel-efficiency standards for automobiles and trucks, energy-efficiency standards for appliances, research support to develop renewable energy sources, and even rethinking nuclear power are all part of the package of energy policies that would reinforce existing market forces. Furthermore, other countries (such as China) are less likely to conserve or shift to other energy sources if they do not see the Americans acting in the same direction. Finally, this effort should involve a new U.S. initiative to convene other nations to forge a successor to the Kyoto Agreement that the Bush administration rejected.

The second set of issues has to do with macroeconomic imbalances. To recap the discussion in chapter 3, the U.S. economy generates a relatively low level of domestic savings (private, corporate, and government) to finance the investment necessary to build the capital equipment that helps provide economic growth. As a result, the United States runs a current-account deficit and borrows from the rest of the world to finance domestic investment. In the past several years, the size of that borrowing has expanded rapidly to 6 percent of GDP and may be poised to rise further, leading to questions of sustainability.

Chapter 3 acknowledges that economists disagree over the extent to which the current-account deficit is a problem. However, there are two issues that should be kept in mind. First, even if the current-account deficit and net capital inflow is sustainable at present levels, it does not behoove the United States to pursue macroeconomic policies that will enlarge the imbalance in the future. Even the optimists (including current Federal Reserve Chairman Ben Bernanke) agree with this conclusion. What can be done? After all, private-sector savings and investment are private-market-driven decisions. But government is an important com-ponent of the domestic savings/investment balance, and the rising gov-ernment deficit in the past several years has been the key element in the falling net savings of the economy and consequent increased reliance on foreign capital. With concerns rising about sustainability, proposing pol-icy changes to social security that would actually increase the government deficit (as the Bush administration attempted in 2005 with its proposal to create individual private social security accounts) is a peculiar choice.

Second, as a matter of global development, many economists believe that the flow of global capital should be from rich countries to poor coun-tries. As Joseph Stiglitz puts it, "the global financial system ought to chan-nel global savings to the poorest countries so they can use it to invest and grow; instead, it is channeling global savings to the richest country, so that its citizens, whose living standard is already beyond the wildest dreams of those in the developing world, can consume even more."[5] With rela-tively high savings and modest economic growth (and, therefore, modest needs for domestic investment), rich economies were long assumed to naturally have current-account surpluses and net capital outflows. After all, this was the pattern for Britain in the late nineteenth century, when it provided such capital investments around the world, and for the United States from the early twentieth century until the beginning of the 1980s. Successful developing countries, on the other hand, should be gener-ating high levels of economic growth, often outstripping their available domestic savings. Therefore, it is natural for these countries to have current-account deficits and net capital inflows. However, at the present, the largest capital flows are to the United States. Indeed, the developing world has, on average, had a current-account surplus in recent years. There are some perfectly logical reasons for this outcome, including high savings in other parts of the world, attractive rates of return on invest-ments in the United States, and the need of some developing countries to reduce high international debt levels (especially in East Asia after the 1997 financial crisis).[6] We need to ask if this is a desirable situation and whether some combination of policies would lead to a better outcome.

If the current-account deficit continues to grow as a percentage of GDP, as some predict, the probability of a wrenching global adjustment increases. Economists debate the nature of the correction and whether it will be mild or catastrophic. But clearly the larger the adjustment required, the greater the chance that it will be jarring—with a combination of a sharply falling dollar, steep recessions in the United States and other countries, falling political support at home for liberal trade and investment policies, and rising anti-U.S. attitudes abroad. At the extreme, a major crisis could undermine the existence of the IMF, the principal multilateral institution that deals with such situations and serves as part of the glue holding the world order in place.

In sum, the ability to maintain peace and prosperity in the world begins at home. The United States needs an economy better able to cope with the stresses of a globalized economy. The economic system needs to be both flexible—with industries and jobs in constant flux—and adept at dealing with the personal financial, social, and psychological stresses that accompany flexibility. Americans need an economy that not only provides rising affluence but also remains a positive example to the rest of the world, thereby enhancing international soft power. Americans also need an economy in better external balance to diminish the possibility of a jarring correction that might have very negative political spillovers. None of these steps have occurred since 2001.

Trade and Investment Policy

A central point raised in chapter 1 bears repeating: openness to trade is good for both economic efficiency and longer-term economic growth. Opening U.S. markets, therefore, is good for the United States, good for the rest of the world, and beneficial for broader U.S. foreign policy goals. As part of a strategy to promote U.S. growth, as well as to bring more poor countries on to a path of high economic growth, it is entirely appropriate to pursue a reduction of trade barriers around the world, as the U.S. government has done since the end of the Second World War. The role of the WTO in this process is considered later; for the moment, let us concentrate on the general approach of the U.S. government. Put simply, Americans should avoid protectionism at home, press for broad trade openness through the WTO, and downplay bilateral free trade areas.

The key issue in the opening years of the twenty-first century has been a new grand bargain between the developed and developing world. Embodied in the Doha Round of multilateral WTO negotiations, this bargain is supposed to include better access in the developed world for agricultural imports from poor countries in exchange for better access in poor countries for manufactured goods and services from developed countries. On agriculture, the sticking points include not just tariffs or quotas but the high level of subsidies that developed countries pay their farmers. All developed countries subsidize their farmers, and the United States is not the worst, although the amounts are high. The OECD estimates that government farm supports in 2004 were worth 20 percent of total farm income in the United States, 34 percent in the European Union, and an enormous 60 percent in Japan.[7] The Bush administration exacerbated this situation by implementing a major increase in U.S. farm subsidies in 2002.

The overall economic impact of opening agricultural markets in developed countries on the growth of poor countries should not be overestimated—the gains the poor countries would experience would be positive but not overwhelming. Nevertheless, progress on agricultural protectionism and subsidies would send a powerful political message to the developing world, a message that the rich countries are willing to rejigger the international trading system to help them. This would also meet the domestic need of governments in poor countries to demonstrate to their own publics that they have had success in dealing with the giant economies of the world. What a pity to hold such benefits hostage to the interests of a few large corporate farms growing a handful of crops such as cotton and sugar.

In addition, U.S. policy goals are far better served by dealing with trade on a global basis rather than through an expanding set of free trade areas. These narrow agreements create trade distortions and will result at some point in the future in the difficult process of unwinding them. In addition, these agreements can result in invidious comparisons among trade partners. It is unfortunate, for example, that one of the arguments used in spring 2005 to support passage of the Central American Free Trade Area (CAFTA) in Congress was that it would enable these countries to continue to export textiles to the United States in the face of intensified competition from China. It is not in the U.S. interest to promote one group of developing countries against another; the market, operating on a level playing field, should determine the winners and losers of competition in particular products. The CAFTA argument was based on the notion that Caribbean nations (unlike China) import their thread and fabric from the United States, but this hardly alters the calculation. Indeed if true, all CAFTA would do is provide an artificial boost to the U.S. textile industry, a labor-intensive industry in decline in all industrialized nations.[8]

Policy toward direct investment in the United States also faces challenges. The United States has been open to inward direct investment throughout its history, and chapter 3 shows how the size of investment has expanded in the past two decades. But even U.S. society periodically experiences a wave of angst about selling the country to the foreigners. In the 1970s, it was the Arabs (recycling their newfound wealth from oil earnings); in the 1980s, it was the Japanese (buying visible icons such as Rockefeller Center and Pebble Beach Golf Club, at inflated prices); and now it is the Arabs once again plus the Chinese in the two cases discussed in chapter 3 (the failed CNOOC attempt to purchase Unocal Oil and the failed DB World attempt to own a firm that operated port services in the United States). Both episodes involved an unseemly xenophobia. The Dubai case led to unsupported claims of national security danger because Dubai was the home of two of the 9/11 terrorists. The notion that a corporation (government-owned or not) should be considered suspect on these grounds was appalling, not to mention the fact that the firm would not have had control over any activities that could enable a terrorist group to slip a nuclear or chemical weapon in using a container, even if they were by some means able to penetrate the firm. Fanning the flames, the *Washington Post* published a front-page article on rising Arab investment in the United States, showing that it has gone up sharply in recent years (to $1.2 billion in 2004, and a somewhat lower $650 million in 2005). The article did admit that these amounts are actually very small; 1.2 percent of total direct investment inflows in 2004 and only 0.5 percent of the total stock of foreign-owned assets in the United States. But the headline and location of the article spoke louder than this comparative detail buried in the text.[9]

Such episodes of xenophobia work against U.S. economic and foreign policy interests in an interdependent world. Americans invest abroad as well—more than foreigners invest in the United States (if we look only at direct investment). How can Americans expect foreign governments to accept their investments when Americans make foreigner investors feel unwelcome in the United States? At the same time that some politicians expressed outrage over the attempted Chinese purchase of Unocal, for example, U.S. financial institutions were eager to purchase banks in China—investments that needed the approval of the Chinese government.[10]

The Dubai incident was one on which the official position of the Bush administration was entirely correct; it steadfastly stood behind its decision to clear the investment on national security grounds. But the administration showed little political savvy in its handling of the issue. Had the administration carefully consulted or communicated with Congress and local governments on an issue that it should have recognized would cause a negative reaction, it might have prevented the outcry, but it made no effort at advance consultation at all. Worse, the president defended the purchase on the grounds that the United Arab Emirates (of which Dubai is one) is an ally in the war on terror. Such strategic concerns have absolutely no relevance to what should be a pure business decision. The president should be ashamed to think that strategic friends deserve more favorable treatment than other countries in investing in the United States.

The administration's inept handling of this episode raised the possibility that the dissatisfaction with the administration might lead to using tightening national security as grounds for denying other investments. In the wake of the Dubai Ports fiasco, Congress began considering the revision of the Committee on Foreign Investments in the United States (CFIUS), a government organization attached to the Treasury Department that reviews foreign investments for national security conflicts. CFIUS enforces a section of the 1988 Trade Act popularly known as the Exon-Florio provision that allows the federal government to block a foreign acquisition if it is perceived as threatening national security. Few investments have been challenged, but possible changes might either loosen the definition of national security threats or transfer control of CFIUS from Treasury to another agency (with the Department of Defense mentioned as a possibility in 2006). Although a few acquisitions might involve genuine security problems, the very real danger in 2006 was that Congress might open the way for nationalism or xenophobia to block foreign investments in the United States. Such a change in the operation of CFIUS would be good neither for the U.S. economy nor for the effort to get other countries to be more open to foreign direct investment.[11]

Finally, as an adjunct to traditional trade and investment policy, the U.S. government also needs to reconsider its policy on student visas. For all the reasons discussed in Chapter 3, students should be encouraged to come from abroad. Although the administration claimed to have fixed the problems of delays and rejections of visa applications for students from countries not likely to harbor terrorists by 2006, I remain unconvinced. The visa process is cumbersome, unpleasant, and slow even for students and professors from developed countries such as Japan. This problem actually predates 9/11; the United States has seriously underfunded both the visa process abroad and the U.S. Citizenship and Immigration Service (USCIS) operations at home (with long lines and limited access to actual visa officers). Delays for even simple procedures are appallingly long, and mistakes are frequent. This is a national embarrassment. Indeed, it is surprising how many students come to the United States despite the delays and annoyances involved in obtaining a visa. The world of international education is growing more competitive, and students facing substantial visa hurdles will be more likely to choose to get their international experience elsewhere (in the European Union, Japan, or Australia, for example). Enhancing both the intellectual and soft power benefits of having international students, therefore, requires a further reform of visa processes.

The Low Profile of Economic Policy

Far too often U.S. security policy and economic policy proceed on completely separate tracks. In the 1980s, the only connections came occasionally when those concerned with security policy tried to moderate trade pressure on allies such as Japan, arguing that excessive trade tension might jeopardize the broader relationship. But the reverse—high-level officials arguing that some security or diplomatic policy might jeopardize broader economic interests—never happens. Nor do those working on economic issues cloak their initiatives in security terms very often. To his credit, Robert Zoellick, head of the Office of the United States Trade Representative in the first term of the Bush administration, did this in the wake of 9/11, calling for the start of the Doha Round on the grounds that the goals of the round would help poor countries prosper and thereby ameliorate the economic and social conditions that breed terrorism. Few, however, listened to Zoellick's call because the administration failed to pursue the round with any vigor. Zoellick (plus his successors in the Bush administration) and the staff at the Office of the United States Trade Representative (USTR) certainly worked hard on the Doha negotiations, but there appeared to be little input at critical times from the president or cabinet secretaries to nudge other governments toward compromise.

Perhaps the worst example of the lack of attention to economic issues comes from the handling of the occupation of Iraq. Those agencies that know the most about economic reconstruction—USAID and the economic bureaus of the State Department—were totally excluded from planning for postwar Iraq. In the occupation, U.S. soldiers are often responsible for local economic issues for which they have no training. It may be heartwarming, for example, to read of U.S. soldiers in Iraq donating school supplies raised on their own initiative from their home towns, but this is hardly an organized or effective way to go about rebuilding Iraq.[12] Similarly, the First Cavalry Division ran Operation Adam Smith, providing small business loans and teaching business skills—tasks entirely inappropriate for the military.[13] Would you like uniformed soldiers to be the ones advising you on how to run a business? At best, this is a ludicrous use of U.S. taxpayer money; at worst, it is a cruel joke.

Part of the problem is structural and involves the question of which departments or agencies participate in the foreign policy process. The National Security Council (NSC) is the principal cabinet-level coordinating body for U.S. foreign policy. The NSC is both an interagency committee and a stand-alone bureaucracy that formally includes economic participants. The statutory committee includes the president, vice president, secretary of State, and secretary of Defense. The national security advisor serves as the senior staff aid, and the secretary of the Treasury and head of the National Economic Council have been generally invited to attend.[14] However, anecdotal evidence suggests that neither the secretary of the Treasury nor the head of the NEC attend the meetings very often, nor do they intervene much in the decisions. The staff of the NSC has people who deal with economic issues at the level of the regional desks, but their input is subdued at best. Either the secretary of the Treasury and head of the NEC should be elevated to full statutory participation in the NSC or the NSC and NEC should be merged and the combined council given a clear mandate to consider economic issues in forming national security policy.

Part of the problem also comes from attitudes and career paths. In the State Department, for example, career foreign service officers proceed along largely separate career tracks—political/military, economic, consular, or administrative. The political/military affairs officers rarely serve tours in the economic parts of the State Department, and economic officers rarely serve in political/military posts. As I witnessed during several years in the U.S. Embassy in Tokyo, the result is an almost complete lack of interest in, and knowledge of, economic issues by the political officers, as well as the reverse, with economic officers often disinterested in political issues or the political implications of economic issues. Even at the level of political appointees, there is a broad separation in the U.S. government between those who know about and handle security policy and those who are tapped for economic posts. Occasionally, there are individuals who gain experience on both security and economic posts. Robert Zoellick, for example, served at Treasury, headed USTR, and went on to serve as deputy secretary of State. But the more common pattern is for security positions to be in the hands of those who have neither interest in nor experience with economic issues. Strobe Talbott, deputy secretary of State in the Clinton administration, and James Steinberg, deputy head of the NSC under the same administration, are typical examples of individuals working on security issues with little, if any, interest in economic issues. Primarily, what is needed is a change of attitude in which individuals who deal with security matters recognize that their issues have critically important economic components and those who deal with economic matters recognize that their issues have strategic implications beyond the narrow economic framework that they usually see.

Embracing Transition Economies

Through a combination of diplomacy and trade policy, it is in the U.S. foreign policy interest to embrace the principal transition economies—China, Russia, and India. They represent a large share of the world's population, they are nuclear powers. two of them are moving away from dysfunctional socialist economic systems, and they were on the other side of the divide during the Cold War (with India officially unaligned but leaning toward the Soviet Union). If these countries manage the transition to more market-oriented, internationally engaged, and economically successful trajectories, then the possibility of a return to the dangerous divides of the Cold War era will be substantially reduced. U.S. policy can help this outcome through the economic embrace of these countries.

The principal problem is with China. As discussed in chapter 5, China has had high growth, has proceeded quite far in transforming its economy away from socialism, has joined the WTO, has a high ratio of both exports and imports to GDP, and absorbs large amounts of foreign direct investment. China is now so heavily integrated into the global economy that the government must consider the negative impact of military aggression on the nation's growth and prosperity. Americans should be pleased that China has voluntarily become so thoroughly entwined with the global economy in the past two decades.

Yet China is a perennial topic of concern in Washington. The uproar over the failed CNOOC-Unocal investment has already been discussed. More broadly, consider the commentary of conservative critics in Washington. John Thacik, an analyst at the influential, conservative Heritage Foundation, berated the Bush administration for abandoning its initial antagonistic stance toward China, arguing that "Washington has gained little, if anything," from its post-9/11 embrace of China.[15] Recall also the earlier discussion in this book of John Mearsheimer, the University of Chicago professor who predicts that China will *necessarily* be a rival and threat to the United States. To give the conservative position credit, rising Chinese military expenditures certainly cause concern, as do belligerent statements about Taiwan. Whether China's economic rise will really result in a peaceful nation absorbed in providing for the prosperity of its people or one that uses its economic rise to build a stronger military force determined to invade Taiwan, therefore, remains in some doubt.

However, the surest way to drive China in the wrong direction is to frustrate the economic aspirations of the Chinese and to treat them as a de facto enemy. In spring 2005, the Bush administration exercised the safeguard clause in the agreement that admitted China into the WTO to re-impose quotas on textile imports from China for three more years.[16] Rhetoric by both the Bush administration and Congress about revaluing the Chinese currency also increased, as did expressions of concern over intellectual property rights violations. Intellectual property rights and currency rates are issues that deserve serious discussion, but the heated rhetoric that accompanied such discussions often painted China as a major threat to the United States. The reality is that inexpensive textile imports from China are beneficial not detrimental. Staples such as clothing are especially important to low-income people—so that rising imports of cheaper clothing from China work to the particular benefit of low-income families across America, one of the few breaks they have gotten in recent years. Currency revaluation is also desirable, but with the Chinese current-account surplus running at 4 percent of GDP in 2005, it is hardly a crisis. After all, Japan was also running a current-account surplus of 4 percent of GDP in 2005 (and with a much larger GDP, this is a much larger dollar amount) without incurring the wrath of the Bush administration. If the administration did not view Japan's surplus as a problem, why should it be concerned about China? More important, the Chinese current-account surplus is part of a global set of imbalances that includes the U.S. current-account deficit. The earlier section of this chapter emphasizes the need to reduce these imbalances, but browbeating the Chinese over their exchange rate while taking no macroeconomic measures at home is not a productive way to proceed.

Instead of painting China as a problem or threat, the U.S. government should be continuing to draw China into a closer economic embrace. This does not mean ignoring trade and investment issues but, rather, ensuring that they are dealt with in a reasonable manner. Often the tense bilateral negotiations to open up Japanese markets lasted for thirty years (and some problems to be negotiated remain today). Getting China to comply more fully with intellectual property right rules and other issues will be an equally protracted process.

Embracing China also implies accepting its investment in the United States. To return to the failed attempt to purchase Unocal, Americans should want the Chinese to buy into the global direct investment system by investing in the United States. Letting China play the same corporate acquisition games as everyone else in the global oil market (rather than seeing them as siphoning off "our" oil) would also allay the Chinese paranoia about energy supply. Expanding Chinese direct investment around the world will further embed the country in the global economic system, making it more of a true stakeholder.

Russia and India do not presently generate the kinds of rhetoric and policy concern in Washington that China does, but they are in somewhat similar positions. In 2004–2005 there was considerable foolish talk about the danger imposed by the shift of service-sector jobs to India, discussed in chapter 3.[17] Americans have nothing to fear from the economic rise of India, but the concern expressed over offshoring is worrisome. In this case, a gradual improvement in overall bilateral relations began in the late 1990s, reinforced by President Bush's trip to India in early 2006. Bilateral relations had been cool since the 1960s because of India's friendliness to the Soviet Union. India had also followed an import substitution policy for many years, behind stiff trade and investment barriers. The shift in Indian economic policy—opening up to more trade and investment while reducing bureaucratic interference in the economy—should be welcomed and encouraged.

Russia presents a more delicate situation. Russia had a particularly difficult transition away from socialism, with a 41 percent drop in GDP per capita from 1989 to 1996. Even with strong growth since 1996, income levels by 2003 were still below the 1989 levels.[18] Today, Russia has a potentially bright economic future, mainly as an oil and natural gas exporter. On the other hand, it could be subject to the very same dangers that some other middle-income oil and gas exporters have had if the profits are siphoned off by a small oligarchy (whether they be private corporations or the government itself). The decidedly antidemocratic tendencies of President Vladimir Putin are a concern in this context. But, as with China, the best way to nudge Russia in a direction that is both more successful economically and less threatening in security terms is to embrace Russia economically and work with it diplomatically. The more open the Russian economy becomes, and the more embedded U.S. and other foreign firms are in Russia, the greater the chance of influencing Russia to move in a more positive direction economically and politically. At times, embracing the Russians will involve sharp rebukes. The strong reaction of the European countries and the U.S. government to the brief Russian embargo of natural gas exports to Ukraine and Europe in 2006 was entirely appropriate. The Russian government needs to understand the consequences of foolish behavior in the global marketplace.

In recent years, these three countries plus Brazil have been lumped together as the BRICs. Brazil, however, is a bit different from the other countries. It is not a nuclear power; and it did not proceed as far down a socialist economic path in the past. But Brazil has the largest population and economy in Latin America, and some of the points about the others apply to Brazil as well. Brazil's President Luiz Inacio Lula da Silva is a populist, and anti-Americanism has been a staple of Brazilian rhetoric for many years. Coaxing Brazil out of its protectionism and encouraging the government to pursue better economic policies over the past several decades has been a delicate game, but one that needs to continue. As a large developing country with the respect of much of the rest of the developing world, Brazil's input is, for example, crucial for a successful outcome of the Doha Round.

All these points about the BRICs also apply to smaller developing countries. The unease over Bolivia's left-leaning President Morales in 2006 was, at the very least, premature. Americans need to recognize that the distribution of benefits from exporting raw materials is a serious and legitimate issue. To the extent possible, the U.S. government should be endorsing Bolivia's president and nudging him to modify the policies considered problematic (principally his rejection of U.S. policy toward growing coca).

U.S. Foreign Aid

The 1980s and 1990s were a time of "aid fatigue." The persistence of poverty in much of the developing world, and the perception that much aid had been motivated by the Cold War (as a reward or bribe to friendly governments) rather than by economic development goals, led to considerable skepticism and criticism of aid. Some burned-out foreign aid practitioners even came to the pessimistic conclusion that aid could not work because the causes of economic failure in parts of the world were too complex and the governments too weak or too corrupt.[19]

Writing off foreign aid as a failure is a mistake. Economists have learned a great deal about what works and what does not—and are still learning.[20] With the Cold War over, aid donors such as the United States can refocus on the difficult task of designing assistance that works rather than just rewarding friendly dictators. In approaching this task, however, there are two important points to keep in mind.

First, what matters is quality, not quantity. Economist Jeffrey Sachs claims that aid will work only if the advanced nations spend a lot more and calls for more than a doubling of global foreign aid.[21] This is a dubious proposition; there is no surer way to create waste, failure, and corruption than by suddenly throwing a lot more money at this problem. Indeed, Sachs's Columbia University colleague Jagdish Bhagwati objects on exactly these grounds—aid must, among other things, be mindful of the absorptive capacity of recipient countries.[22] What matters most is the quality of aid programs; they must be designed to meet the capabilities of the recipient governments and societies and be designed to actually nudge societies toward more successful economic growth and development. To be sure, this is a complex, difficult task, and further failed programs will certainly be numerous; but the attempt is worthwhile.

Second, in order to work, aid must involve a package approach, as noted at the end of the previous chapter. Too often foreign aid has been dominated by a single approach—such as emergency food or medical assistance—provided out of emotional humanitarian impulses without much thought to the longer-run issues of economic development. In this respect, Jeffrey Sachs is on stronger ground. His Earth Institute at Columbia University is running an experimental program in a rural part of Kenya that aims at dealing with the broadest possible range of problems—health, education, agricultural technology, and energy supply—that have been holding the region back.[23]

Foreign aid is a splintered business. Individual national governments provide aid, as do multilateral institutions (the World Bank and the regional development banks), not to mention the plethora of charitable nonprofit organizations outside government in a number of industrialized nations. My starting point for this chapter is U.S. foreign aid policy; later, in this chapter I consider the World Bank. In the U.S. government, foreign aid is handled by USAID, an independent agency loosely overseen by the State Department.

The Bush administration greatly expanded the foreign aid budget, although not enough to satisfy Jeffrey Sachs. From net disbursements of $10 billion in 2000, the level rose to $18 billion by 2004, or roughly a quarter of the total amount provided by the major donors (that is, the members of the OECD Development Assistance Committee).[24] In addition, the Bush administration established the Millennium Challenge Account (MCA), with grants to be disbursed by a quasi-private organization attached to USAID called the Millennium Challenge Corporation (MCC), as part of the U.S. response to the UN Millennium Development Goals. Under this program, the government established eligibility criteria—countries that meet the criteria for good governance become eligible for economic assistance from this new facility.[25] Finally, the administration has vastly increased resources to fight HIV/AIDS.

The expansion of the U.S. aid budget may seem to contradict the basic conclusion of this book that the government is overly focused on military might and focused too little on issues such as aid; however, there are problems with the U.S. aid program. First, the dirty secret in the increase of U.S. foreign aid spending is that much of the increase was for Iraq—lining the pockets of government contractors without much visible positive impact in that war-torn country. In fiscal 2004, bilateral aid to Iraq totaled a very large $18 billion, or a whopping 86 percent of the U.S. aid budget for that year. Admittedly, this figure may have been abnormally high because Iraq received only $4 billion in fiscal 2003 (18 percent of the total aid budget). But aberration or not, Iraq clearly accounted for a significant portion of the touted increase in the U.S. foreign aid effort.[26]

Second, the MCA was based on the same hard-nosed conservative principles advocated for the IMF in the Meltzer Report (discussed later in this chapter). As noted by the MCC, "countries will be selected to receive assistance based on their performance in governing justly, investing [in] their citizens, and encouraging economic freedom."[27] Although these criteria may well lead to aid that is more effective, because the recipient countries have already built the institutional infrastructure to use aid effectively and to grow successfully, it also means that the nations that need assistance the most will be excluded. The criteria are also sufficiently vague as to be subject to abuse by the administration in choosing which countries it believes govern justly or encourage economic freedom. This is especially a concern now, given the current fad of promoting democracy. In its first two years of operation, the amount of aid disbursed through the MCA was quite small—only $1.5 billion through 2005—although the goal was to increase the amount to $5 billion.

Third, the emphasis in the MCA on "economic freedom" raises worrisome questions of overemphasis on a conservative economic agenda that may not be appropriate for all developing countries, as previously noted. Although it is indeed important to foster private enterprise from the bottom up, enabling individuals to build commercial farms and small businesses as part of a market-based development strategy, development also needs the state to supply roads and other transportation infrastructure, water supply and sewage treatment, public health programs, and schools and education. No country, including the United States, the advanced countries of Western Europe, and Japan, developed solely through an emphasis on private enterprise.

So what should change?

- *Reduce strategic aid.* Aid policy should reduce the old emphasis on helping friends, to whom a sizable portion of the aid money continues to flow. Iraq may need help for years to come, but it is a clear example of throwing large sums of money at a problem stemming from a misguided invasion with dubious results.
- *Create a special interagency program on sub-Saharan Africa.* This region is the core of extreme poverty in the world, as explained in

chapter 6. Furthermore, it could easily become the locus of future prob-lems with terrorism. The United States needs an approach to Africa that coordinates peacekeeping and other efforts to prevent genocide, places continuous pressure on governments to reduce corruption, provides more aid through both the MCA and other accounts for countries that do not meet the requirements, and puts a greater focus on the package approach (described next). A 2006 Council on Foreign Relations task force report on Africa made a strong case for a larger, more coordinated approach for U.S. foreign aid to Africa, combining aid, trade policy, and diplomacy. The report suggests that either the NSC or the State Department could play the role of policy coordinator, but the point is that whichever agency ends up in charge, coordination is badly needed.[28]

• *Create a package approach.* Aid policy should include a stronger emphasis on tailoring a package of infrastructure projects, education, health, technical assistance to create the institutional architecture for a market economy, educational grants to study in the United States, and a more open trade policy. The scope of this package goes beyond the traditional focus of foreign aid policy.

• *Allow cautious debt relief.* Debt relief for very poor countries has been a burning topic. There may be little choice; some of these coun-tries are drowning under a burden of international debt that, realistically, they will never be able to repay. At the G-8 summit meeting in 2005, the leaders agreed to cancel $40 billion in debt for the eighteen most heavily indebted poor countries. These debts are in the form of loans owed to the World Bank, IMF, and the African Development Fund.[29] Although the amount may seem large, it represents only a portion of the international debts of poor countries. This is appropriate. On the one hand, a debt burden so high that it can never be repaid has both economic and politi-cal consequences. Recall that the onerous reparations imposed on Ger-many at the end of World War I left the nation in economic distress and contributed to the negative politics that brought the Nazis to power. On the other hand, extensive debt relief raises moral hazard problems. Even the concessional lending of the World Bank should go to care-fully selected projects with a high probability of repayment. A belief that periodic debt relief will be granted by the donors lessens the diligence of both the lenders and borrowers to pick projects carefully.

• *Create and lead stronger donor committees.* For some aid recipients, donor countries have banded together to form a coordinating committee to share information, reduce overlap, and avoid working at cross-purposes. This approach should be expanded. Committees should include repre-sentatives from the IMF, World Bank, UN, regional development banks, other bilateral donors, and major nongovernmental organization (NGO) donors. This is an area in which the United States should be able to use its leadership to convene and guide—but also listen to others.

U.S. foreign aid policy is finally emerging from almost two decades of fatigue. Aid policy needs to proceed carefully; simply throwing more money at economic development will fail as surely as it did in the 1960s and 1970s. But this is a time of great opportunity and provides a chance to focus on the debilitating problems of sub-Saharan Africa before they fester and develop a new, unpleasant security dimension.

Dealing with the International Monetary Fund

The IMF is the principal multilateral institution for dealing with international financial stability; it monitors the economic situation in its member countries and deals with crises when they occur, as discussed in chapter 1. This is an essential job. In a world that is increasingly integrated economically, a catastrophic crisis in one part of the global economic system is quickly transmitted around the world, as occurred in 1997–1998 with an initial financial crisis in Thailand that eventually involved Indonesia, Malaysia (although to a lesser degree), Korea, Argentina, and Russia (although for different reasons), with implications for the United States and other developed nations. However, the IMF is an imperfect institution and has been subject to a number of criticisms.[30] Some of these are highly technical, but the broad criticisms include the following:

• *Opaqueness and governance.* The IMF makes its decisions in a nontransparent process run by nonelected officials. At the extreme, developing countries see this as imposing the will of rich nations on poor ones. In addition, many countries around the world view the power balance at the IMF as heavily skewed toward the rich developed nations, and toward the United States in particular (a view enhanced by the physical location of the IMF headquarters in Washington, D.C.).

• *Bad decisions and misguided conditionality.* When the IMF provides emergency loans to developing countries in crisis, it imposes conditions designed to rectify the problems that caused the crisis—a stick to accompany the carrot of the loans to pay their international creditors. But the macroeconomists who run the IMF do not understand local conditions, in this view, and in using rigid economic models, they impose the wrong macroeconomic policy conditionality in times of crisis.[31]

• *Misguided capital liberalization.* Over the past two decades, the IMF has mistakenly pushed developing countries to liberalize their capital accounts (an accusation hotly denied by the IMF itself). Exaggerated or not, it is clear that the U.S. government from the mid-1980s to the present has favored the liberalization of access to financial markets (including capital account liberalization, so U.S. financial institutions can move money in and out of countries) and pushed the IMF in this general direction.[32]

• *Indulgent lending and moral hazard.* The IMF tends to step in when a crisis occurs, regardless of the nature of the problem. The IMF has even resorted to ad hoc bailout measures beyond its own formal rules. This indulgent bailout policy leads to moral hazard—developing countries borrow internationally with little regard to the feasibility of repaying, and industrialized country commercial financial institutions willingly lend regardless of the risk, with both sides confident that the IMF will bail them out should a crisis occur. As George Shultz (secretary of State in the Ronald Reagan administration), William Simon (secretary of the Treasury in the Richard Nixon and Gerald Ford administrations), and Walter Wriston (chairman of Citi Corporation) put it, "The promise of an IMF bailout insulates financiers and politicians from the consequences of bad economic and financial practices and encourages investments that would not otherwise have been made."[33] In their view, what the world needs is not bailouts but a global system of bankruptcy rules and enforcement similar to what the United States has domestically. Such a system would place more of the cost of cleaning up problems on the commercial creditors.

Some of these points have merit, but in general the criticisms of the IMF go too far and some reforms have already occurred. There is no real evidence, for example, that the moral hazard problem caused excessive lending to Asian countries; the notion that the IMF would ride to the rescue does little to explain the excessive commercial lending, whereas the generally poor credit-risk analysis by Japanese banks (at home and abroad) that were the largest lenders to Southeast Asia in the mid-1990s explains a lot. Furthermore, commercial lenders in all the crisis cases in the 1990s took serious financial hits, making it difficult to believe that they walked away from these crises feeling that they had been insulated. The Shultz, Simon, and Wriston paper, for example, was a partisan political attack on the Clinton administration in the wake of the 1997 Asian financial crisis. The correctness of macroeconomic policy advice continues to be debated, but at least we can say that the IMF has shown flexibility in altering its position when new information becomes available (as was the case in the opening months of the Asian financial crisis).

As previously noted, a key concept in the conservative critique is based on a belief that the international financial system should be like the domestic one. At home, the United States has rules for financial markets and their oversight, and investors accept the consequences of risk. When firms fail, bankruptcy laws administered by courts sort out the consequences for the investors. Although imperfect, the domestic system works reasonably well most of the time. Short of the extreme recommendations to simply abolish the IMF and let international finance operate as it does at home, the Meltzer Report (an independent commission authorized by Congress and headed by Alan Meltzer, an economist at Carnegie Mellon University, that made its recommendations in 2000 on reform of both the IMF and the World Bank) proposed setting clear and rather stringent preconditions for eligibility for emergency IMF loans. These conditions would presumably create a powerful reason for governments to pursue better policies, so that they would qualify for help. In principle, this idea seems attractive. The problem, however, lies in the fact that national boundaries matter; international financial rules are not likely to become a clone of the domestic situation. Furthermore, eligibility rules could well increase the possibility of international crisis if problems occur in the countries not eligible for IMF loans. Put in other words, eligibility rules would refocus IMF lending to countries that are the least likely to get into trouble, further sharpening the divide between successful developing countries and the losers.

In addition, there is a moral and political issue. Leaving crises to the market or limiting eligibility for IMF loans implies telling poor countries facing international financial crises that they must simply face the consequences. The large 12 percent drop in GDP per capita in one year in Indonesia, for example, pushed millions of people back into abject poverty, at least temporarily. The conservative agenda would lead to more draconian contractions in poor countries. This is not an outcome that the rich countries should be willing to make on either moral or self-interested foreign policy grounds. Even though the Asian financial crisis ended fairly quickly—with help from the IMF—the political repercussions of the anger over the presumed failures of the U.S. government and the IMF in addressing the problem as it emerged in the summer and fall of 1997 still reverberate throughout the region. To relate such developments to the broader theme of this book, the establishment of hard-nosed preconditions that Alan Meltzer advocates is likely to increase that sort of anger in those parts of the world where terrorism exists or could erupt in the future.

What are the alternatives?

• *Promote some further transparency.* To maintain its legitimacy, the IMF needs to shed more of its reputation for secrecy, although progress has already occurred in this direction. We can add that simply changing demeanor matters as well; IMF officials have an unsavory reputation for arrogance not justified by their imperfect understanding of the problems.

• *Alter and broaden the power base.* The IMF (and the World Bank) operates under a gentleman's agreement on the nationality of the top position (the IMF for the Europeans and the World Bank for the Americans). The time has come to stop this old-boy practice and open up the leadership more broadly. Similarly, developing countries have complained that the voting power of the members remains skewed toward the United States and Europe. Developing countries need to feel that they have more of a stake in decisions, or else they will feel increasingly antagonistic toward the IMF. By 2006, an alteration of voting rights at the IMF was at least under discussion—an alteration that would increase the power of rising Asian economies largely at the expense of European countries. However, the Europeans have traditionally balked at such changes, so accomplishing this goal remains difficult.[34]

• *Keep conditionality.* The IMF has already reduced the extent of conditionality to what it regards as a reduced set of essential elements. The new conditionality guidelines, adopted in 2002, emphasized "national ownership of policies, parsimony in conditions, tailoring of policies to member circumstances, coordination with other multilateral institutions, and clarity in the specification of conditions."[35] These points address the kind of complaints directed at the IMF in the 1990s, although what will matter is how the IMF interprets and implements its own guidelines in a future crisis. But the most important point is that the basic concept of conditionality in IMF lending remains valid. The conditionality in the case of the Asian financial crisis might have been misguided at first, but the condition of lending only if the recipient government agrees to address the underlying problems that caused the crisis remains a legitimate one.

• *Approach capital liberalization more cautiously.* The IMF needs to continue the soul searching taking place since 1997 on the question of capital account liberalization. For a developing country to open its borders to international capital flows while trying to maintain a pegged exchange rate is dangerous, as is opening up when the domestic financial sector is still weak.

• *Clarify the responsibilities of the IMF and the World Bank.* A longstanding issue has been the increasing overlap between the IMF and the World Bank, with the IMF moving into long-term structural lending to developing countries, which is properly the function of the World Bank. The IMF should stick to the macroeconomic and financial-sector problems leading to financial crises and leave the question of the promotion of economic development to the World Bank.

In a world with one government, the conservatives would be right—the IMF would be largely unnecessary because financial markets would be governed by one set of clear global rules about the consequences for lenders and borrowers when the borrowers are unable to repay. But, even in this case, the moderate conservatives would be right that the IMF still has a role in helping countries that perform well but face short-term liquidity crises (that is, face a situation in which they are financially sound but face an unexpected short-term problem meeting international financial obligations to lenders). But the world is not so neat and tidy; our world has many sovereign nations. The bailouts of Mexico in 1995 and the East Asian countries in 1997 actually worked well—sharper crises were averted and the countries involved returned to strong growth paths rather quickly. Not only were the economic problems dampened, but more serious political damage was averted—despite the fondness that Asians still have for criticizing both the IMF and the U.S. government for the initial responses to the crisis. Therefore, these modest reforms of the IMF should suffice to reinforce its legitimacy and cope with future crises.

The World Bank

Like the IMF, the World Bank has been criticized from the left as an opaque organization dominated by the United States, out of touch with developing countries, and promoting the destruction of the environment and local cultures through large infrastructure projects.[36] From the right, the bank has been criticized as supporting corrupt governments and socialism because in many developing countries large infrastructure projects (dams, electric power plants, and the like) have been under the jurisdiction of government organizations. Martin Wolf, a former World Bank official in the 1970s, has written a particularly scathing criticism, accusing the Bank of having followed a "Stalinist vision of development," complete with demands for recipient countries to establish five-year economic plans and a rigid view that just increasing the stock of capital would produce economic growth.[37] That criticism in the 1980s led to a strong focus on privatization as a condition for Bank loans in the 1990s. More recently, the 2000 Meltzer Report criticized the Bank for lending too much money to middle-income countries and too little to the poorest countries that need the money the most.[38]

There is no doubt that many World Bank projects in the past have been ill-conceived, so criticisms from both the left and the right were deserved. However, many of these issues have been addressed over the past decade.[39] Furthermore, the criticism from the left is largely about the issue of development itself; economic growth and industrialization are most certainly disruptive processes, uprooting premodern patterns of society in all countries. The antiglobalization, pro-environmental activists who criticize the World Bank are actually in the position of supporting a continuation of grinding poverty. Development is a choice that the bulk of humankind has clearly chosen to make, so the complaints of the left about the disruption of traditional lifestyles of poor premodern societies do not necessarily reflect the aspirations of poor societies.[40] To be sure, the Bank did too little to prevent environmental degradation in the past, but its attitude and policies have changed.

Complaints about supporting corruption and inefficient socialist states may also have been justified—up to a point. Looking back from 2006, the emphasis in the past on lending to governments to create state-owned enterprises was obviously flawed. But, putting this in the context of the times (the 1950s–1970s), it is well to recall that many developed countries were doing the same—Britain, France, and Japan, among them. The developed world has now shifted away from that model (as discussed in chapter 1) but state ownership of some basic industries such as electric power was believed, at the time, to be a legitimate approach. In the developed countries, there was also pessimism about whether it was possible to develop a viable private sector in poor countries, given the low levels of education, lack of business experience, and lack of local financial institutions to put money in the hands of entrepreneurs. Government bureaucracies were simply the best educated, and often the only, organizations with which to work. What the World Bank (and bilateral aid donors) failed to appreciate was the extent to which this socialist approach would simply foster inefficiency, corruption, and the financial aggrandizement of the small ruling cliques in poor countries. Martin Wolf's contempt for what the Bank was doing was justified, but the policies were an understandable part of the times.

On the other hand, privatization is not the solution to all problems and needs to be carefully tailored nation by nation. Certainly private enterprise can be more efficient than state enterprises and may be a useful pressure point in dealing with corrupt political regimes. But in corrupt states, what is the guarantee that private enterprises will be any better, especially if ownership is handed over to the cronies of the ruling elite? In addition, some states still may not have the human capital needed to hand electric power companies or other large operations over to the private sector. Finally, some forms of infrastructure are still provided only by governments throughout the world, including roads, water supply, sewers, education, and, in virtually every country except the United States, health care. These aspects of infrastructure are crucially important to development—microfinance projects for farmers to market their vegetables in the city have little chance of success without decent roads or an education that enables the farmer to run a successful commercial business.

What about social and environmental concerns? Some groups want the World Bank to end loans for dams, mines, and oil and gas drilling. These projects can cause environmental damage; in addition, mining and drilling often feed the ruling kleptocracies. An independent review commission of the World Bank recommended to the Bank that it phase out oil and mining projects. The Bank's management rejected the proposal, but did agree to introduce new safeguards concerning how revenues from such projects are used.[41] We can easily question why the World Bank should support projects in an industry in which there are many large international firms that have the commercial financing and technology available to do all the oil and gas drilling that any developing country needs. Furthermore, such private-sector firms are certainly superior to the probably corrupt and inefficient state-run mining and drilling companies that the Bank might support. However, commercial oil companies or mining companies generally have little interest in the overall development of the countries in which they operate; if corruption is the name of the game, they have little problem in accepting the situation. The World Bank, on the other hand, can make a difference if it is serious about its new safeguards on how such projects are run and how their revenues are distributed.

The Meltzer Report observation that much of World Bank lending goes to sufficiently successful developing countries that already have access to global private-sector capital markets is correct. But Sebastian Mallaby, an outside observer, and the Bank itself have argued quite convincingly that these loans (made at commercial interest rates) provide profits to the Bank that it can use to subsidize loans to poor countries. Furthermore, some of the countries that do have access to global capital markets still need the kind of loan that comes from the World Bank because they need the conditionality and technical assistance that come with such loans to build more robust financial markets and non-financial private sectors. The Meltzer Report advocates ending loans and concentrating on grants to those countries unable to raise money in international capital markets. The problem with grants, however, is that they require constant replenishment of World Bank funds by its donor members. It is difficult to believe that the major donors, subject to the political whims of democratic government, would consistently earmark substantial parts of their own foreign aid programs for the World Bank every year.[42]

Overall, the World Bank needs relatively little reform. Its professional staff has decades of experience—from many past mistakes—and is learning about what works and does not work in economic development. The Bank has undergone considerable reform in the past decade. The present focus on loans and technical assistance prioritized to build institutional capacity in developing countries to run successful market economies is appropriate, along with some physical infrastructure projects to enable economic activity. Issues that remain to be addressed, however, include the following:[43]

• *Promote greater transparency and improved governance*. This is the same issue as for the IMF. The presidency should not be restricted to Americans and the balance of power on the board needs to be recalculated to give developing countries a greater voice.

• *Expand independent outside review*. The Bank has begun a system of independent reviews, but this should be expanded to provide an impartial analysis of what works and what does not. For example, the Poverty Action Lab, a group of economists at the Massachusetts Institute of Technology, has been conducting what economists call randomized evaluations to answer the question of which projects and approaches work and which do not. The kind of rigorous testing of results that this group pioneered is just beginning to be adopted by the World Bank and should be expanded.[44]

• *Strengthen safeguards on projects*. The commitment to providing safeguards on the uses of the revenues from mining and drilling projects is laudable. But the critical nature of the problems endemic to raw material–exporting nations indicates that these policies need a higher priority and careful monitoring.

• *Clarify the boundary with the IMF*. This is mainly a matter of moving the IMF out of areas that should be the responsibility of the World Bank, but there remain fuzzy areas concerning the financial sector: Should the World Bank or the IMF work with developing countries to strengthen their financial sectors? One institution or the other should have lead responsibility.

• *Expand grant-based work with the poorest countries*. Rather than accepting the Meltzer Report proposals to simply shut down commercial lending and focus entirely on grants, the lending operations should actually be expanded to provide the funds to run an expanded grant program for poor countries. These countries need technical assistance—training, institution building, and policy advice—that comes from grant aid.

These modest proposals should strengthen the World Bank, enabling it to continue to perform a useful service. It is understandable that some who have toiled in the field of economic development for many years have become cynical and pessimistic. But this is a time of opportunity in which to actually make some progress, learning from the mistakes of the past.

IF nothing else, readers of this book should come away with an appreciation of how extraordinary and extensive the transformation of the global economy has been since the end of the Second World War in 1945. The world today is much more interdependent, and governments oversee this system through a set of multilateral institutions that did not even exist until after the war. The liberal theory of international relations argues that these ties make the world more peaceful—a conclusion that is largely correct. But the global economic system requires constant attention and care. Even with the positive changes that have occurred, the world still has many spots where the magic of growth and interdependence have yet to take hold. And the institutions that loosely govern the global economic system are imperfect and are struggling with the difficulty of divergent economic interests in the post–Cold War era.

The economic developments, issues, and policies that form the subject matter of this book are part of a multidimensional U.S. foreign policy, which I describe as a three-legged stool. This stool has been rather tilted in recent years. The United States is certainly the military superpower of the world, but it has used this power excessively and in very questionable circumstances, such as the invasion of Iraq. The diplomatic leg has been somewhat damaged—with too much unilateralism in the first term of the Bush administration and an excessive emphasis on spreading democracy in the second. The international U.S. reputation, and its soft power, has taken a major hit. Finally, the economic leg has been underappreciated and insufficiently nurtured. Future peace and prosperity depends on fixing the stool.

We Americans live in a time of extraordinary possibilities, and if we can seize hold of the opportunities, we can shape a better and more peaceful world. The goal of a world of winners without losers captures the essence of what should guide our policy approach. Even if such an outcome is not possible in a literal sense, it represents the direction in which the world needs to move. If we fail, the world we live in could easily unravel, with more tension, terrorism, and an increased chance of major conflict. The choice should be obvious.

NOTES

Introduction

1. Norman Angell, *The Great Illusion* (New York: G.P. Putnam's Sons, 1910).

2. Thomas Friedman, *The World Is Flat: A Brief History of the Twenty-First Century* (New York: Farrar, Straus, and Giroux, 2005) is a typical example of the exaggerated accounts of the new trade in services.

3. For a review of the shift away from government intervention in the economy, see Daniel Yergin and Joseph Stanislaw, *The Commanding Heights: The Battle between Government and the Marketplace That Is Remaking the Modern World* (New York: Simon and Schuster, 1999).

4. For an extensive review of the realist and liberal approaches to international relations, see Joshua S. Goldstein, *International Relations* (New York: Longman, 2003), 71–125.

5. Robert O. Keohane and Joseph S. Nye, *Power and Interdependence: World Politics in Transition* (Boston: Little, Brown, 1977).

6. See Richard Rosecrance, *The Rise of the Trading State: Commerce and Conquest in the Modern World* (New York: Basic Books, 1986), and *The Rise of the Virtual State: Wealth and Power in the Coming Century* (New York: Basic Books, 1999).

7. Thomas L. Friedman, *The Lexus and the Olive Tree* (New York: Anchor Books, 2000), 83–92.

8. Thomas L. Friedman, *The World Is Flat: A Brief History of the Twenty-First Century* (New York: Farrar, Straus, and Giroux, 2005).

9. Robert Gilpin, *The Challenge of Global Capitalism: The World Economy in the 21st Century* (Princeton: Princeton University Press, 2000), 13–14.

10. Henry Kissinger, *Diplomacy* (New York: Simon and Schuster, 1994).

11. For a relatively recent statement of Waltz's position, see "Globalization and Governance," *PS Online*, December 1999, available at http://mtholyoke.edu/acad/intel/walglob.htm (September 15, 2004).

12. Niall Ferguson, "Sinking Globalization," *Foreign Affairs* 84, no. 2 (March/April 2005): 64–77.

13. For a classic exposition on these economic factors in creating power, see Hans J. Morgenthau and Kenneth W. Thompson, *Politics among Nations: The Struggle for Power and Peace*, 6th ed. (New York: Alfred A. Knopf, 1985), 127–41. This is an updated version of Morgenthau's original book that defined the realist position, published in 1948.

14. For a clear statement of John Mearsheimer's views on China, see "John Mearsheimer Interview: Conversations with History; Institute of International Studies, UC Berkeley," available at http://globetrotter.berkeley.edu/people2/Mearsheimer/mearsheimer-con6.html. His book laying out his overall neo-realist view is *The Tragedy of Great Power Politics* (New York: W. W. Norton, 2001).

15. Thomas P. M. Barnett, *The Pentagon's New Map* (New York: G.P. Putnam's Sons, 2003), especially 9–58, 295–335.

1. The World Transformed

1. Hernando de Soto, *The Mystery of Capital: Why Capitalism Triumphs in the West and Fails Everywhere Else* (New York: Basic Books, 2000).

2. Rondo Cameron and Larry Neal, *A Concise Economic History of the World from Paleolithic Times to the Present*, 4th ed. (Oxford: Oxford University Press, 2003), 168–69, 209.

3. Harold Underwood Faulkner, *American Economic History* (Harper Brothers, 1954), 268–70.

4. Douglas C. North and Robert Paul Thomas, *The Rise of the Western World: A New Economic History* (Cambridge, UK: Cambridge University Press, 1973), 54, 76.

5. Ron Chernow, *Alexander Hamilton* (New York: Penguin Press, 2004), 344–61.

6. William Shakespeare, *Hamlet*, act 1, scene 3. The complete quotation is available at http://infoplease.com/askeds/said-neither-borrower-lender-be.html (April 26, 2007).

7. Chernow, *Hamilton*, 297–309.

8. Bureau of the Census, U.S. Department of Commerce, *Historical Statistics of the United States: Colonial Times to 1970* (Washington, D.C.: U.S. Government Printing Office, 1975), 208–9.

9. J. S. Holliday, *The World Rushed In: The California Gold Rush Experience—An Eyewitness Account of a Nation Heading West* (New York: Simon and Schuster, 1981).

10. "Life Expectancy by Age, 1850–2001," *Infoplease*, available at http://print.infoplease.com/ipa/A0005140.html (December 13, 2004).

11. James C. Riley, *Rising Life Expectancy: A Global History* (Cambridge, UK: Cambridge University Press, 2001), 1.

12. For an excellent history of the Homestead Strike in 1892 and the longer history of labor relations at the Carnegie Steel Works, see the popular history Les Standiford, *Meet You in Hell: Andrew Carnegie, Henry Clay Frick, and the Bitter Partnership That Transformed America* (New York: Crown Publishers, 2005).

13. Max Eastman, ed., *Capital, the Communist Manifesto, and Other Writings by Karl Marx* (New York: Modern Library, 1959), 355.

14. See Daniel Yergin and Joseph Stanislaw, *The Commanding Heights: The Battle for the World Economy* (New York: Simon and Schuster, 2002).

15. Peter Grier, "Rich-Poor Gap Gaining Attention," *The Christian Science Monitor*, June 14, 2005, available at http://www.csmonitor.com/2005/0614/p01s03-usec.htm (February 28, 2006).

16. Examples include William E. Odom and Robert Dujarric, *America's Inadvertent Empire* (New Haven: Yale University Press, 2004); Jim Garrison, *America as Empire: Global Leader or Rogue Power?* (San Francisco: Berrett-Koehler, 2004); Niall Ferguson, *Colossus: The Price of America's Empire* (New York: Penguin Books, 2004).

17. A. G. Kenwood and A. L. Lougheed, *The Growth of the International Economy 1820–2000*, 4th ed. (New York: Routledge, 1999), 26–34.

18. The World Trade Organization, "The 128 Countries That Had Signed GATT by 1994," available at http://www.wto.org/wto/english/thewto_e/gattmem_e.htm (February 4,

2005); "Understanding the WTO: The Organization: Members and Observers," available at http://www.wto.org/wto/english/thewto_e/whatis_e/tif_e/org6_e.htm (February 4, 2005).

19. Angus Maddison, *The World Economy: Historical Statistics* (Paris: OECD, 2003).

20. For a brief summary of IMF functions, see International Monetary Fund, "The IMF at a Glance," available at http://www.imf.org/external/np/exr/facts/glance.htm (March 11, 2006).

21. Davesh Kapur, John P. Lewis, and Richard Webb, *The World Bank: Its First Half-Century, Volume 1: History* (Washington, D.C.: Brookings Institution, 1997), 9.

22. OPEC Statistics: Transportation, "Table 66: Freight Costs in the Spot Market, 1980–2000," available at http://www.ieicenter.com/Statistics/Opec.asp (December 2, 2004).

23. Daniel Y. Coulter, "Globalization of Maritime Commerce: The Rise of Hub Ports," in Sam J. Tangredi, *Globalization and Maritime Power* (Washington, D.C.: Institute for National Strategic Studies, National Defense University, 2002).

24. Stewart Taggart, "The 20-Ton Packet," *Wired News*, no. 7.10, October 1999, available at http://www.wired.com/wired/archive/7.10/ports_pr.html (December 21, 2004).

25. For a discussion of this and other aspects of the transportation revolution since the 1950s, see "Delivering the Goods," *The Economist*, November 13, 1997, available at http://www.economist.com/PrinterFriendly.cfm?Story_10=352733 (December 6, 2004).

26. Pan-Am website, http://www.panamair.org/History/earlydays.htm.

27. Kenneth L. Calkins, "Boeing's Flying Boat: A Great Adventure in Aviation and a Unique Chapter in Air Transportation History," *Columbia Magazine* 17, no. 2 (2003), available at http://www.wshs.org/wshs/columbia/articles/0203-a3.htm (February 1, 2006). The current dollar value is calculated from U.S. Bureau of Labor Statistics Calculator, available at http://data.bls.gov/cgi-bin/cpicalc.pl (February 1, 2006).

28. United Airlines, from San Francisco to Hong Kong, 14.5 hours, $551 per ticket; Cheaptickets.com (February 1, 2006)).

29. Radhakrishna Hiremane, "From Moore's Law to Intel Innovation—Prediction to Reality," *Technology@Intel Magazine*, available at http://www.intel.com/technology/magazine/silicon/moores-law-0405.htm (February 1, 2006).

30. "One World?" *The Economist*, October 16, 1997, available at http://www.economist.com/PrinterFriendly.cfm?Story_ID=103256 (December 6, 2004).

31. Thomas Friedman, *The World Is Flat: A Brief History of the Twenty-First Century* (New York: Farrar, Strauss, and Giroux, 2005).

32. John Kenneth Galbraith, *The Affluent Society* (Boston: Houghton Mifflin, 1958).

33. On the question of the connection between trade and economic growth, see Jeffrey A. Frankel and David Romer, "Does Trade Cause Growth," *American Economic Review* 89, no. 3 (1999): 379–99; Gary Burtless, Robert Z. Lawrence, Robert E. Litan, and Robert J. Shapin, *Globaphobia: Confronting Fears about Open Trade* (Washington, D.C.: Brookings Institution, 1998); Martin Wolf, *Why Globalization Works* (New Haven: Yale University Press, 2005).

34. Services trade data are from World Bank, *World Development Indicators 2005* (CD-ROM) (Washington, D.C.: World Bank, 2005).

35. World Bank, *World Development Indicators 2003* (CD-ROM) (Washington, D.C.: World Bank, 2003).

36. International Monetary Fund, *International Financial Statistics* (CD-ROM) (Washington, D.C.: IMF, September 2005).

2. Economic Change and International Relations

1. Gregg Easterbrook, "The End of War? Explaining 15 years of Diminishing Violence," *The New Republic* 232, no. 20 (May 30, 2005): 18–21.

2. Norman Angell, *The Great Illusion: A Study of the Relation of Military Power in Nations to Their Economic and Social Advantage* (New York: G.P. Putnam's Sons, 1910).

3. Robert O. Keohane and Joseph S. Nye, Jr., *Power and Interdependence: World Politics in Transition* (Boston: Little, Brown, 1977).

4. Kenneth N. Waltz, "Globalization and Governance," *PS Online*, December 1999, available at http://www.mtholyoke.edu/acad/intrel/walglob.htm (September 15, 2004).

5. Kenneth N. Waltz, *Man, the State, and War: A Theoretical Analysis* (New York: Columbia University Press, 2001). Note that this book was originally published in 1954; the 2001 edition is a reprint, not a revision of the original.

6. Ibid., 16.

7. David Howarth, *1066: The Year of Conquest* (New York: Barnes and Noble, 1977).

8. Norman Cantor, *In the Wake of the Plague: The Black Death and the World It Made* (New York: Harper Perennial, 2002), provides a useful analysis of the nature of late medieval society and the blurry line between government and personal wealth.

9. Waltz, *Man, the State, and War*, 159.

10. John B. Judis, *The Folly of Empire* (New York: Scribner, 2004), 42.

11. For a history of the struggle between England and Holland over Indonesian nutmeg, see Giles Milton, *Nathaniel's Nutmeg: Or the True and Incredible Adventures of the Spice Trader Who Changed the Course of History* (New York: Penguin, 2000).

12. On the Nicaragua and the Dominican Republic episodes, see Judis, *Folly of Empire*, 42.

13. I. M. Destler, *American Trade Politics*, 4th ed. (Washington, D.C.: Institute for International Economics, 2005), especially 233–52.

14. John W. Dower, *War without Mercy: Race and Power in the Pacific War* (New York: Pantheon Books, 1986) details the propaganda views of the Pacific War period.

15. Data from World Bank, *World Development Indicators 2005* (CD-ROM) (Washington, D.C.: World Bank, 2005). Per capita GDP declined in 1989, 1990, 1991, and 1993 (with a temporary upturn in 1992).

16. On the treatment of the Bonus Army, see Paul Dickson and Thomas B. Allen, *The Bonus Army: An American Epic* (New York: Walker and Company, 2005).

17. Jared Diamond, *Guns, Germs, and Steel: The Fates of Human Societies*, new ed. (New York: W. W. Norton, 2005).

18. "Who Are OPEC Member Countries," available at http://www.opec.org/library/FAQs/aboutOPEC/q3.htm (February 13, 2006).

19. Neil Buckley, George Parker, and Sarah Laitner, "Russia Insists It Is Reliable Gas Supplier," *Financial Times*, March 14, 2006, p. 5.

20. Stefan Wagstyl, "Cheney Hits at Putin over Energy 'Blackmail.'" *Financial Times*, May 5, 2006, p. 1.

21. Kerin Hope, Theoror Troev, and Isabel Gorst, "Go-Ahead for €-900m Pipeline to East Pressure on Bosporus," *Financial Times*, April 12, 2005, p. 4.

22. International Energy Agency, *Key World Energy Statistics 2004* (Paris: IEA, 2004), 6, 10.

23. National Security Council, White House, *The National Security Strategy of the United States* (Washington, D.C.: National Security Council, March 2006), 41.

24. International Energy Agency, *Key World Energy Statistics 2004*, 11.

25. James Brooke, "Drawing the Line on Energy: China and Japan Wrangle Over Oil and Gas Projects in Disputed Waters, *New York Times*, March 29, 2005, p. C1.

26. For a thorough discussion of the East China Sea problem, see Selig S. Harrison, *Seabed Petroleum in Northeast Asia: Conflict or Cooperation* (Washington, D.C.: Woodrow Wilson International Center for Scholars, 2005).

27. "China and Japan: So Hard to Be Friends," *The Economist*, March 26, 2005, p. 24.

28. Sam J. Tangredi, ed., *Globalization and Maritime Power* (Washington, D.C.: National Defense University Press, 2002), 159.

29. For an inflammatory article on the expansion of terrorists into high-seas piracy, see Gal Luft and Anne Korin, "Terrorism Goes to Sea," *Foreign Affairs* 83, no. 6 (November/December 2004): 61–71. They make a valid case about the existence of incidents of piracy involving terrorist groups but provide little convincing evidence that this is evolving into a major global threat.

30. Jonathan H. Noer and David Gregory, *Chokepoints: Maritime Economic Concerns in Southeast Asia* (Washington, D.C.: National Defense University Press, 1996), 2.

31. Ibid., 42.

32. "OPEC Statistics: Transportation," available at http://www.ieicenter.com/Statistics/Opec.asp (February 28, 2006).

3. The United States

1. U.S. Department of Commerce, *Statistical Abstract of the United States: 2006* (Washington, D.C.: U.S. Government Printing Office, 2006), 443, 832.

2. U.S. Department of Commerce, services data available at http://www.bea.gov/di/1004serv/tabB.xls (February 14, 2006).

3. Thomas Friedman, *The World Is Flat: A Brief History of the Twenty-First Century* (New York: Farrar, Straus, and Giroux, 2005).

4. Martin Neil Baily and Robert Z. Lawrence, "Don't Blame Trade for US Job Losses," *McKinsey Quarterly*, available at http://www.mckinseyquarterly.com/article_print.aspx?L2=7&L3=10&ar=1559 (March 1, 2006).

5. Diana Farell, Martha A. Laboissière, and Jaeson Rosenfeld, "Sizing the Emerging Labor Market," *McKinsey Quarterly*, August 3, 2005, available at http://www.mckinsey quarterly.com (August 3, 2005).

6. "Edmunds.com Looks Back at 2005 and Forecasts 2006 Automotive Trends," available at http://www.edmunds.com/help/about/press/108914/article.html (February 14, 2006).

7. "U.S.-Japan Economic Partnership for Growth: U.S.-Japan Investment Initiative 2005 Report," available at http://www.state.gov/p/eap/rls/rpt/49017.htm (February 14, 2006).

8. Dale McFeatters, "When Survival Is Job One," Scripps Howard Editorial, January 24, 2006 (via Nexus).

9. Balance of payments data are from Bureau of Economic Analysis, U.S. Department of Commerce, available at http://www.bea.gov/bea/international/bp_web/simple.cfm?anon=71&table_id=1&area_id=3 (May 10, 2005); GDP data are from Bureau of Economic Analysis, U.S. Department of Commerce, available at http://www.bea.doc.gov/bea/dn/nipaweb/TableView.asp#Mid (May 10, 2005).
The denominator in this statistical series is GDP (because these other financial flows include purchases of government debt, so private fixed-capital formation is not an appropriate denominator). These financial flows tend to be quite volatile, influenced by constantly changing relative interest rates between home and abroad, so the numbers mentioned are based on three-year moving averages in order to smooth out the volatility.

10. "Fulbright Program Overview," available at http//:www.iie.org/FulbrightTemplate.cfm?Section=Fulbright Program Overview (February 15, 2006).

11. Alan Finder, "In Reversal, Graduate School Applications from Foreigners Rise," *New York Times*, March 23, 2006, p. A20.

12. National Science Foundation, Science and Engineering Indicators 2004, available at http://www.nsf.gov/statistics/seind04/c2/c2s3.htm#c2s3l4a. (May 8, 2005).

13. Institute for International Education, "Leading Places of Origin," *Open Doors 2004*, available at http://opendoors.iienetwork.org/?p=49933 (May 9, 2005).

14. Institute for International Education, "Leading Destinations of U.S. Study Abroad Students, 2001/02 & 2002/03," *Open Doors 2004*, available at http://opendoors.iienetwork. org/?p=49942 (May 9, 2005).

15. Energy Information Agency, U.S. Department of Energy, "Table 1.1 Energy Overview, 1949–2003," *Annual Energy Review*, available at http://www.eia.doe.gov/emeu/ aer/overview.html (May 10, 2005).

16. These growth rates are calculated from GDP data from the U.S. Department of Commerce, Bureau of Economic Analysis, and from population data from the U.S. Department of Commerce Census Bureau (2005 estimated population) and U.S. Department of Commerce, *Statistical Abstract of the United States: 2006*, 8.

17. United Nations Development Program, *UNDP Human Development Report 2005* (New York: United Nations Development Program, 2005), 270.

18. On soft power, see Joseph S. Nye, Jr., *The Paradox of American Power: Why the World's Only Superpower Can't Go It Alone* (Oxford: Oxford University Press, 2002), 8–12.

19. For a survey of these explanations, see Menzie D. Chinn, "Council Special Report: Getting Serious about the Twin Deficits," CSR no. 10 (New York: Council on Foreign Relations, September 2005); Edwin M. Truman, "Postponing Global Adjustment: An Analysis of the Pending Adjustment of Global Imbalances," Working Paper Series no. WP 05-6, Peterson Institute for International Economics, Washington, D.C., July 2005; Noriel Roubini, "Global Imbalances: A Contemporary Rashomon Tale with Five Interpretations," available at http//:www.roubiniglobal.com (August 10, 2005).

20. Ben Bernanke, "The Global Savings Glut and the U.S. Current Account Deficit," The Federal Reserve Board: Remarks by Governor Ben S. Bernanke at the Sandridge Lecture, Virginia Association of Economics, Richmond, Vir., March 10, 2005, available at http://www.federalreserve.gov/boarddocs/speeches/2005/200503102 (May 26, 2005).

21. Richard N. Cooper, "Living with Global Imbalances: A Contrarian View," *Policy Briefs in International Economics*, no. PB05–3, Peterson Institute for International Economics, Washington, D.C., November 2005.

22. Among the critics are Chinn, "Council Special Report"; Truman, "Postponing Global Adjustment"; Roubini, "Global Imbalances."

23. Catherine L. Mann, "The U.S. Current Account, New Economy Services, and Implications for Sustainability," *Review of International Economics* 12, no. 2 (2004) available at http://www.iie.com/publications/author_bio.cfm?author_id=47 (May 9, 2006).

24. Truman, "Postponing Global Adjustment."

4. The European Union

1. Joseph V. O'Brien, "World War II: Combatants and Casualties (1937–45)," available at http://web.jjay.cuny.edu/~jobrien/reference/ob62.html (April 6, 2006).

2. John Gillingham, *European Integration 1950–2003: Superstate or New Market Economy?* (Cambridge, UK: Cambridge University Press, 2003), 3–33.

3. "Schuman Plan Declaration, 9 May 1950," available at http://europa.eu.int/abc/ symbols/9-may/decl_en.htm (April 6, 2006).

4. Jacques Pelkmans, "The Significance of EC-92," *Annals of the American Academy of Political and Social Science* 531 (1994): 96.

5. Eurostat, "Air Passenger Transport by Reporting Country," available at http://epp. eurostat.ced.eu.int (May 3, 2006).

6. Concerning the frenzy of acquisitions in the telecommunications industry at the end of the 1990s, see "France Telecom Confirms US$37bn Acquisition of Orange," *Mobile Tech News*, May 30, 2000, available at http://www.mobiletechnews.com/info/2000/05/30/095248. html (April 14, 2006); "Vodafone," *Wikipedia*, available at http://en.wikipedia.org/wiki/ Vodaphone (April 19, 2006). On the lack of progress on power deregulation, see George

Parker, Sarah Laitner, and Thomas Catan, "Lights Out? How Europe Is Trying to Fix a Power Failure," *Financial Times*, April 5, 2006, p. 11.

7. European Union, "Europa—The EU at a Glance—Europe in 12 Lessons—Economic and Monetary Union—and the Euro," available at http://europa.eu.int/abc/12lessons/index7_en.htm (April 6, 2006).

8. Eurostat, "Air Passenger Transport by Reporting Country."

9. NATO, "Welcome to NATO," available at http://www.nato.int/welcome/home.htm (April 6, 2006).

10. Brian Hanson, "What Happened to Fortress Europe?: External Trade Policy Liberalization in the European Union," *Industrial Organization* 52, no. 1 (1998): 55–85.

11. Barry Eichengreen, "European Monetary Unification," *Journal of Economic Literature* 31, no. 3 (1993): 1321.

12. Maurice Obstfeld, Alberto Alesina, and Richard N. Cooper, "Europe's Gamble," *Brookings Papers on Economic Activity* no. 2 (1997): 241–317; Martin Feldstein, "The Political Economy of the European Economic and Monetary Union: Political Sources of an Economic Liability," *Journal of Economic Perspectives* 11. no. 4 (1997): 23–42.

13. C. Fred Bergsten, "The Dollar and the Euro," *Foreign Affairs* 76, no. 4 (July/August 1997).

14. For a positive view of the EMS, see Desmond Dinan, "The European Community: To Maastricht and Beyond," *Annals of the American Academy of Political and Social Science* 531 (January 1994): 15.

15. To put this in more technical terms, the standard deviation of inflation rates, expressed as a percentage of the average inflation level, peaked at 67 percent of the average in 1978 and thereafter fell to 36 percent by 2004 (roughly the same degree of variance as back in 1970 before the inflationary burst and varying national responses to it occurred).

16. For one analysis of problems and how to fix them, see Martin Neil Baily and Jacob Funk Kirkegaard, *Transforming the European Economy* (Stockholm: Institute for International Economics, 2004).

17. Chris Smyth and George Parker, "Ministers Seek to Liven up Ecofin Meetings with Bit of Controversy," *Financial Times*, April 7, 2006, p. 3.

18. Mark Landle4r and Paul Meller, "Unity in the European Market, Except When It Comes to Takeovers," *New York Times*, March 14, 2006, p. C1.

19. Anne-Sylvanie Chassang, Keith Johnson, and Gabriel Kahn, "France Moves to Block Italian Suitor for Suez," *Wall Street Journal*, February 27, 2006, p. A3.

20. "EU Hopeful Croatia Hails Accession of Bulgaria, Romania," *EU Business*, January 2, 2007, available at http://www.eubusiness.com/news_live/1167753602.1/view (January 9, 2007).

21. George Parker, "Romania Set for Green Light on Entry to the EU," *Financial Times*, April 6, 2006, p. 1.

22. Charles A. Kupchan, "Europe's Constitutional Crisis: Lessons Learned," *Handelsblatt*, June 23, 2005, available at http://www.cfr.org/publications/8205/europes_constitutionsal_crisis.html (April 20, 2006).

23. "The Tattered Constitution," *Deutche Welle*, May 30, 2005, available at http://www.dw-world.de/dw/article/0,1564,15999,00.html (April 20, 2006).

5. East Asia

1. On Japan's prewar economic development, see Takafusa Nakamura, *Economic Growth in Prewar Japan* (New Haven: Yale University Press, 1983). On the origins of the Pacific war, see James Crowley, *Japan's Quest for Autonomy: National Security and Foreign Policy 1930–1938* (Princeton: Princeton University Press, 1966); Herbert Feis,

The Road to Pearl Harbor: The Coming of the War between the United States and Japan (Princeton: Princeton University Press, 1950).

2. For one expression of doubt and concern on Japan's future in the late 1940s, see Edwin Reischauer, *Japan and America Today* (Stanford: Stanford University Press, 1953), especially p. 14.

3. For a review of this period of rapid growth, see Hugh Patrick and Henry Rosovsky, eds., *Asia's New Giant* (Washington, D.C.: Brookings Institution, 1975). See also John W. Dower, *Embracing Defeat: Japan in the Wake of World War II* (New York: W. W. Norton, 1999) for a general history of conditions and attitudes in Japan during the occupation years.

4. For further information on Japan's energy policies, see Shigeko N. Fukai, "Japan's Energy Policy," *Current History* 87 (April 1988): 169–84.

5. Robert M. Orr, Jr., "Balancing Act: Japanese Foreign Aid Policy in the Middle East," in *Japan and the Middle East*, edited by Edward J. Lincoln, 29–39 (Washington, D.C.: Middle East Institute, 1990).

6. See Ron Morse, "Japan and OPEC in the Global Energy Market," in *Japan and the Middle East*, edited by Edward J. Lincoln, 9–16 (Washington, D.C.: Middle East Institute, 1990).

7. For a discussion of U.S.-Japanese trade relations, see Edward J. Lincoln, *Unequal Trade* (Brookings Institution, 1990); *Troubled Times: U.S.-Japan Trade Relations in the 1990s* (Washington, D.C.: Brookings Institution, 1999).

8. Clyde V. Prestowitz, Jr., *Trading Places: How We Allowed Japan to Take the Lead* (New York: Basic Books, 1988), 295.

9. Nicholas R. Lardy, *Integrating China into the Global Economy* (Washington, D.C.: Brookings Institution, 2002), 11.

10. World Bank, *World Development Indicators 2005* (CD-ROM) (Washington, D.C.: World Bank, 2005). Lardy notes that even in this time period we need to be cautious about the accuracy of national income data for China and that these World Bank data are somewhat lower than the official Chinese government numbers; Lardy, *Integrating China into the Global Economy*, 11–13.

11. On the weaknesses of Chinese firms, see George Gilboy "The Myth behind China's Miracle," *Foreign Affairs* 83, no. 4 (2004): 33–48.

12. Lardy, *Integrating China into the Global Economy*, especially 63–105.

13. World Bank, *World Development Indicators 2005.*

14. "Top 15 Investors in China," *Invest in China*, available at http://www.fdi.gov.cn/common/info.jsp?id=ABC00000000000027430 (February 28, 2006).

15. Lardy, *Integrating China into the Global Economy*, 7.

16. Gilboy, "Myth behind China's Miracle," 39.

17. Bruce Einhorn, "Why Taiwan Matters," *Business Week* (May 16, 2005), pp. 76–81.

18. Quoted in Edmund L. Andrews "Capital Nearly Speechless on Big China Bid," *New York Times*, June 24, 2005, p. C1.

19. Naotaka Matsukata, "China's Counterfeit Commitment to Patents," *Financial Times*, August 5, 2004, p. 17.

20. See David Shambaugh, "China Engages Asia: Reshaping the Regional Order" (paper presented to the NDU/AEI seminar on Japan, March 2005, Washington, D.C.).

21. All these data are from the World Bank, but there are inconsistencies among different data series; the GDP growth rate for the Philippines and the per capita GDP growth rates cited here imply a population growth rate of 5.4 percent, which is incorrect.

22. Treasury Malaysia, "Foreign Direct Investment in Approved Projects by Country and Industry," available at http://www.treasury.gov.my/view.php?dbIndex=0&website_id=1&id=792 (February 28, 2006).

23. For proposals calling for a "grand bargain" with North Korea, see Mitchell B. Reiss, "Rising Stakes in North Korea, *Policy Forum Online*, 05-63A, August 2, 2005, available at http://www.nautilis.org/fora/security/0563Reiss.html (May 4, 2006); Michael O'Hanlon and Mike Mochizuki, "Toward a Grand Bargain with North Korea," *Washington Quarterly* 24, no. 4 (2003): 7–18.

6. Areas of Poverty

1. For a brief overview of the establishment of the Millennium Development Goals, see United Nations, "The Millennium Development Goals and the United Nations Role," available at http://www.un.org/millenniumgoals/background.html (March 10, 2006).

2. The countries in the low-income category are Afghanistan, Angola, Bangladesh, Benin, Bhutan, Burkina Faso, Burundi, Cambodia, Cameroon, Central African Republic, Chad, Comoros, Democratic Republic of Congo, Republic of the Congo, Côte d'Ivoire, Equatorial Guinea, Eritrea, Ethiopia, Gambia, Ghana, Guinea, Guinea-Bissau, Haiti, India, Kenya, Democratic People's Republic of Korea (North Korea), Kyrgyz Republic, Laos, Lesotho, Liberia, Madagascar, Malawi, Mali, Mauritania, Moldova, Mongolia, Mozambique, Myanmar, Nepal, Nicaragua, Niger, Nigeria, Pakistan, Papua New Guinea, São Tome, Senegal, Sierra Leone, Solomon Islands, Somalia, Sudan, Tajikistan, East Timor, Togo, Uganda, Uzbekistan, Vietnam, Yemen, Zambia, and Zimbabwe. The per capita GDP for these countries measured in purchasing power parity terms in 2000 ranged from $460 to $3,200. World Bank, *World Development Indicators 2005* ROM) (Washington, D.C.: World Bank, 2005). The countries in the least-developed group are taken by the World Bank from a UN classification and include fifty countries (with a few that are not in the World Bank list): Afghanistan, Angola, Bangladesh, Benin, Bhutan, Burkina Faso, Burundi, Cambodia, Cape Verde, Central African Republic, Chad, Comoros, Democratic Republic of the Congo, Djibouti, Equatorial Guinea, Eritrea, Ethiopia, Gambia, Guinea, Guinea-Bissau, Haiti, Kiribati, Laos, Lesotho, Liberia, Madagascar, Malawi, Maldives, Mali, Mauritania, Mozambique, Myanmar, Nepal, Niger, Rwanda, Samoa, Sao Tome, Senegal, Sierra Leone, Solomon Islands, Somalia, Sudan, Tanzania, Timor-Leste, Togo, Tuvalu, Uganda, Vanuatu, Yemen, and Zambia. The United Nations Framework Convention on Climate Change (UNFCCC), "List of Least Developed Countries," available at http://unfccc.int/files/cooperation_and_support/ldc/application/pdf/ldcbyregion.pdf (March 3, 2006).

3. World Bank, World Development Indicators 2005.

4. Ibid.

5. World Bank, *Global Monitoring Report 2005* (Washington, D.C.: World Bank, 2005), 69–71.

6. World Bank, *World Development Indicators 2005.*

7. United Nations, *The Millennium Development Goals Report 2005* (New York: United Nations, 2005), 6.

8. Central Intelligence Agency, "Mozambique," *CIA Factbook*, available at http://www.cia.gov/cia/publications/factbook/geos/mz.html (March 2, 2006).

9. On the kidnappings and killings see "Royal Dutch Shell PLC: At Least Eight People Killed in Nigeria Oil-Pipeline Attack," *Wall Street Journal*, December 21, 2005, p. 1.

10. Princeton N. Lyman and J. Stephen Morrison, "The Terrorist Threat in Africa," *Foreign Affairs* 84, no. 1 (2004): 75–76.

11. Details on the Democratic Republic of the Congo are based on Central Intelligence Agency, "Congo, Democratic Republic of the," *CIA Factbook*, available at http://www.cia.gov/cia/publications/factbook/geos/cg.html (March 3, 2006).

12. Transparency International, "Corruption Surveys and Indices," available at http://www.transparency.org/surveys/index.html#cpi (July 7, 2005).

13. Central Intelligence Agency, "Rank Order—HIV/AIDS—Adult Prevalence Rate," *CIA Factbook,* available at http://www.cia.gov/cia/publications/factbook/rankorder/2155 rank.html (March 3, 2006).

14. AVERT, "AIDS Orphans, the Facts," available at http://www.avert.org/aidsorphans.htm (March 6, 2006).

15. Based on population from World Bank, *World Development Indicators 2005.* The population ages 0–14 in sub-Saharan Africa in 2003 was 308 million, which puts the ratio of orphans to the total at 3.9 percent.

16. BBC News, "Deadly Bird Flu Found in Africa," available at http://news.bbc.co.uk/2/hi/africa/4692916.stm (March 6, 2006).

17. Anthony Lake and Christine Todd Whitman (chairs), and Princeton N. Lyman and J. Stephen Morrison (project directors), *More Than Humanitarianism: A Strategic U.S. Approach toward Africa,* Council on Foreign Relations Independent Task Force Report no. 56 (New York: Council on Foreign Relations, 2006).

18. International Labour Office, *Global Employment for Youth* (Paris: ILO, August 2004), 1, 7.

19. Jeffrey D. Sachs and Andrew M. Warner, "Natural Resource Abundance and Economic Growth," NBER Working Paper no. 5398, National Bureau of Economic Research, Cambridge, Mass., December 1995.

20. Bhagwati, Jagdish, "Immiserizing Growth: A Geometrical Note," *Review of Economic Studies* 25 (June 1958): 201–205; Harry G. Johnson, "Economic Expansion and International Trade," *Manchester School* 23 (1955): 95–112.

21. World Bank, *World Development Indicators 2005.*

22. Ibid. Saudi manufacturing in 2003 was 10 percent of GDP, services were 40 percent, and the primary sector (agriculture, fisheries, forestry, and mining) was 50 percent. Of the various pieces of the primary sector, agriculture was under 5 percent (and the World Bank does not provide data on the others). Construction is typically 5–10 percent of GDP. This implies that mining is somewhere in the range of 35–40 percent of GDP.

23. Data on the composition of GDP in Norway are from World Bank, *World Development Indicators 2005.*

24. "Tackling the Oil Curse," *The Economist,* September 25, 2004, pp. 16–17.

25. "Economic Boom Deflects Pressure for Saudi Reform," *Financial Times,* March 24, 2006, p. 8.

26. World Bank, *World Development Indicators 2005.*

27. Peter Eigen, "Africa: Oil Profits Fuel Corruption in Government, Business," *Global Information Network,* October 3, 2005, p. 1.

28. Central Intelligence Agency, "Nigeria," *CIA Factbook,* available at http://www.cia.gov/cia/publications/factbook/geos/ni.html (March 7, 2006).

29. Lydia Polgreen, "Armed Group Shuts Down Part of Nigeria's Oil Output," *New York Times,* February 25, 2006, p. A5.

30. "International: A Spectre of Turmoil and Conflict: Nigeria," *The Economist,* February 25, 2006, p. 62.

31. Craig Timberg, "In Fight over Oil-Rich Delta, Firepower Grows Sophisticated," *Washington Post,* March 6, 2006, p. A10 (emphasis added).

32. Paulo Prada, "Bolivia Nationalizes the Oil and Gas Sector," *New York Times,* May 2, 2005, p. A5.

33. Daphne Eviatar, "An Election Run on Gas: Can Bolivia's New President Deliver on His Promise to Nationalize Natural Resources and Legalize Coca?" *Fortune,* January 23, 2006, p. 24.

34. Jane Perlez, "The Papuans Say, This Land and Its Ores Are Ours," *New York Times,* April 5, 2006, p. A4.

35. See for example, Jorge G. Castañeda, "Latin America's Left Turn," *Foreign Affairs* (May/June 2006): 28–43.

Conclusion and Policy Recommendations

1. Roger Cohen, "The War on Terror: An Obsession the World Doesn't Share," *New York Times*, December 5, 2004, p. 4.1.

2. Dollar expenditures in Iraq are from Amy Belasco, "The Cost of Iraq, Afghanistan, and Enhanced Base Security since 9/11," *CRS Report for Congress* (Congressional Research Service, October 7, 2005), 1.

3. Paul Krugman, "Graduates versus Oligarchs," *New York Times*, February 27, 2006, p. A19.

4. On TAA, see Lori Kletzer and Howard F. Rosen, "Easing the Adjustment Burden on U.S. Workers," in *The United States and the World Economy: Foreign Economic Policy for the Next Decade*, edited by C. Fred Bergsten (Washington, D.C.: Institute for International Economics, 2005), 79–113; this chapter is available at http://www.iie.com/publications/chapters_preview/3802/10iie3802.pdf. See also Howard F. Rosen, "Reforming Trade Adjustment Assistance: Keeping a 40-Year Promise" (paper presented at the conference on Trade Policy in 2002, February 26, 2002, Institute for International Economics), available at http://www.iie.com/publications/papers/paper.cfm?ResearchID=450 (January 10, 2007).

5. Joseph Stiglitz, "Dealing with Debt: How to Reform the Global Financial System," *Harvard International Review* 25, no. 1 (spring 2003): 57.

6. See, for example, Ben S. Bernanke, "The Global Savings Glut and the U.S. Current Account Deficit," Sandridge Lecture, Virginia Association of Economics, Richmond, Virginia, March 10, 2005, available at www.federalreserve.gov/boarddocs/speeches/2005/200503102...(May 26, 2005).

7. "Farm Support's Deep Roots," *The Economist*, June 21, 2005, p. 1.

8. See Robert Portman, "Why Fear CAFTA?" (Op-Ed) *Wall Street Journal*, May 10, 2005, available at http://www.ustr.gov/Document_Library/Op-eds/2005/Why_Fear_CAFTA.html (March 9, 2006).

9. Paul Blustein, "Mideast Investment Up in U.S.," *Washington Post*, March 7, 2006, p. 1. The article itself is factual and not inflammatory, but the headline and its placement as a leading (above the fold) story on page 1 are not neutral at all.

10. Brian Bremner, "China: The Year of Citi?" *Businessweek* (January 23, 2006), p. 44.

11. On the existing organization and operation of CFIUS, see United States Department of the Treasury, "Committee on Foreign Investments in the United States (CFIUS)," available at http://www.ustreas.gov/offices/international-affairs/exon-florio/ (April 14, 2006); on proposed changes to CFIUS in 2006, see Christopher Nelson, "Treasury Tries to Get Ahead on CFIUS," *Nelson Report* (March 14, 2006).

12. Lisa Foderado, "Today's Assignment: Helping Iraqis Learn; Airman Inspires School to Honor Flag Day with Gift to Children Affected by War," *New York Times*, June 15, 2005, p. A20.

13. Richard w. Stevenson, "Bush Says Patience Is Needed as Nations Build a Democracy," *New York Times*, May 15, 2005, p. A12.

14. "The National Security Council," available at http//:www.whitehouse.gov/nsc/ (September 9, 2004).

15. John J. Tkacik, Jr., "Time for Washington to Take a Realistic Look at China Policy," *Backgrounder* (published by the Heritage Foundation), no. 1717, December 22, 2003.

16. U. S. Department of State, "U.S., China Sign Comprehensive Bilateral Textile Agreement," November 8, 2005, available at http://usinfo.state.gov/xarchives/. (May 9, 2006).

17. As an example of hyperbole about India, see Thomas Friedman, *The World Is Flat: A Brief History of the Twenty-First Century* (New York: Farrar, Straus, and Giroux, 2005).

18. Data from the World Bank, *World Development Indicators 2005* (CD-ROM) (Washington, D.C.: World Bank, 2005).

19. Thomas Dichter, "Time to Stop Fooling Ourselves about Foreign Aid: A Practitioners View," Cato Institute Foreign Policy Briefing no. 86, Washington, D.C., September 12, 2005; William Easterly, *The Elusive Quest for Growth: Economists' Adventures and Misadventures in the Tropics* (Cambridge, Mass.: MIT Press, 2002).

20. For a readable assessment of development issues, how to understand them, and how to deal with them, see Jeffrey D. Sachs, *The End of Poverty: Economic Possibilities for Our Time* (New York: Penguin Press, 2005).

21. "How to Save the World," *The Economist*, October 28, 2004, p. 102.

22. Jagdish Bhagwati, "A Chance to Lift the Aid Curse," *Wall Street Journal*, March 22, 2005, p. A14.

23. Marc Lacey, "Kenyan Village Serves as Test Case in Fight on Poverty," *New York Times*, April 4, 2005, p. A3.

24. Organisation for Economic Cooperation and Development, *Net ODA from DAC countries from 1950 to 2003*, available at http://www.oecd.org/document/11/0,2340,en_2649_34447_1894347_1_1_1,00.html (June 15, 2005).

25. Millennium Challenge Corporation, "The Millennium Challenge Account," available at http://www.mcc.gov/about_us/overview/index.shtml (June 16, 2005).

26. Kurt Tarnoff and Larry Nowels, "Foreign Aid: An Introductory Overview of U.S. Programs and Policy," CRS Report to Congress no. 98-916, Congressional Research Service, Washington, D.C., April 15, 2004), available at http://fpc.state.gov/documents/organization/31987.pdf (January 10, 2007).

27. Millennium Challenge Corporation, "Millennium Challenge Corporation."

28. Anthony Lake and Christine Todd Whitman (chairs), and Princeton N. Lyman and J. Stephen Morrison (project directors), *More than Humanitarianism: A Strategic U.S. Approach toward Africa*, Council on Foreign Relations Independent Task Force Report no. 56 (New York: Council on Foreign Relations, 2006).

29. International Monetary Fund, "The Multilateral Debt Relief Initiative (MDRI)," available at http://www.imf.org/external/np/exr/facts/mdri.htm (May 7, 2006).

30. On the criticism of the IMF and plans for its reform, see Anna J. Schwartz, "Time to Terminate the ESF and the IMF," Cato Foreign Policy Briefing no. 48, Washington, D.C., August 26, 1998; Charles W. Calomiris, "How to Invent a New IMF," Hoover Institution Public Policy Inquiry: International Monetary Reform Proposals, Stanford University, May 1999; Allan H. Meltzer (chairman), *Report of the International Financial Institution Advisory Commission* (Washington, D.C.: U.S. Congress, March 2000), available at http://www.houses.gov/jec/imf/ifiac.htm (May 5, 2006); Martin Feldstein, "Refocusing the IMF," *Foreign Affairs* 76, no. 2 (March/April 1998): 20–34; Peter B. Kenen, "Appraising the IMF's Performance," *Finance and Development* 41, no. 1 (March 2004): 41–45; Alan S. Blinder, "Eight Steps to a New Financial Order," *Foreign Affairs* 78, no. 5 (September–October 1999): 50–64; Nouriel Roubini, "60 Years of the Bretton Woods Institutions: Strategic Review and Reform Agenda," speech to the G-20 deputy finance ministers and central bank governors, Chongqing, China, March 14, 2005, available at http://www.roubiniglobal.com; Morris Goldstein, "An Evaluation of Proposals to Reform the International Financial Architecture" (paper for the NBER Conference on Management of Currency Crises, March 28–31), 2001, Monterey, California; Christian Weller, "Meltzer Report Misses the Mark," Economic Policy Institute Issue Brief no. 141, Washington, D.C., April 13, 2000; Kenneth Rogoff, "The Sisters at 60," *The Economist*, July 22, 2004, p. 66; Stanley Fischer, "In Defense of the IMF: Specialized Tools for a Specialized Task," *Foreign Affairs* 77, no. 4 (July/August 1998): 103–107.

31. For a pointed criticism of the IMF, see Joseph E. Stiglitz, *Globalization and Its Discontents* (New York: W. W. Norton, 2002), especially 89–132.

32. Ibid., see, for example, 12–16. This was vigorously rebutted by Kenneth Rogoff (director of research at the IMF), "An Open Letter," available at http://imf.org/external/np/vc/2002/070202.htm (May 4, 2006); Thomas C. Dawson (director of the External Relations Department of the IMF), "Stiglitz, the IMF and Globalization" (speech to the MIT Club of Washington), available at http://www.imf.org/external/np/speeches/2002/061302.htm (May 4, 2006).

33. George P. Shultz, William E. Simon, and Walter B. Wriston, "Who Needs the IMF?" Hoover Institution Public Policy Inquiry: International Monetary Fund, Stanford University, February 3, 1998, available at http://www.imfsite.org/abolish/heedshultz.html (March 8, 2006).

34. Krishna Guha and Chris Giles, "IMF Wants More Say for Rising Economies," *Financial Times*, April 6, 2006, p. 1.

35. International Monetary Fund, "IMF Executive Board Discusses Review of the Conditionality Guidelines," available at http://www.imf.org/external/np/sec/pn/2005/pn0552.htm (May 26, 2005).

36. There are numerous liberal NGOs and individuals actively engaged in criticizing the World Bank. See, for example, Charles Mutasa, "A Critical Appraisal of the World Bank Policies in Developing Countries—Presentations—People's Health Assembly—December 2000," *People's Health Movement,* available at http://www.;phmovement.org/pha2000/presenations/mutasa/html (March 9, 2006); Shalmali Guttal, "Disclosure, or Deception? Multilateral Institutions and Access to Information," *Global Policy Forum,* March 2002, available at http://www.globalpolicy.org/socedcon/bwi-wto/wbank/2002/03access.htm (March 9, 2006); "Democratizing the World Bank and IMF: Statement of the IFI Democracy Coalition," *IFI Democracy Coalition,* February 7, 2005, available at http://www.new-rules.org/docs/ifidemocracycoalitionstatement.htm (March 9, 2006); "World Bank Official Review Advises: Respect Human Rights, Pull Out of Coal and Oil Financing," *Oxfam America* December 2, 2003, available at http://www.oxfamamerica.org/newsandpublica tions/press_releases/archive2003/art6600.html (March 9, 2006); Emil Salim, "World Bank Must Reform on Extractive Industries," Mines and Communities Charter, available at http://www.minesandcommunities.org/charter/eirpress8.htm (March 9, 2006).

37. Martin Wolf, "Martin Wolf vs. the World Bank," *Globalist,* Friday June 25, 2004, available at http://www.theglobalist.com/DBWeb/StoryId.aspz?StoryId=3981 (September 9, 2004).

38. Allan H. Meltzer (chairman), *Report of the International Financial Institution Advisory Commission* (Washington, D.C.: U.S. Congress, March 2000), available at http://www.houses.gov/jec/imf/ifiac.htm (May 5, 2006).

39. See Sebastian Mallaby, *The World's Banker: A Story of Failed States, Financial Crises, and the Wealth and Poverty of Nations* (New York: Penguin Press, 2004).

40. This is a point that Sebastian Mallaby makes with devastating effect as he dismisses many of the claims and demands of radical environmental groups claiming to represent the real interests of people in developing countries. Ibid., 7–9.

41. Andrew Balls, "World Bank Rejects Call to End Mining and Oil Projects," *Financial Times,* June 21, 2004, p. 1.

42. Mallaby, *The World's Banker.*

43. This list draws in part on an excellent set of proposals by Nancy Birdsall and Devish Kapur, *The Hardest Job in the World: Five Crucial Tasks for the New President of the World Bank* (Washington, D.C.: Center for Global Development, June 1, 2005).

44. Celia Dugger, "World Bank Challenged: Are the Poor Really Helped," *New York Times,* July 28, 2004, p. A4.

INDEX

Note: Page numbers followed by an *f* indicate figures; those with a *t* indicate tables.